TRANSACTIONS

of the

American Philosophical Society

Held at Philadelphia for Promoting Useful Knowledge

VOLUME 83, Part 5

Johannes Klenkok:
A Friar's Life, c. 1310–1374

Christopher Ocker
Assistant Professor of History,
San Francisco Theological Seminary

THE AMERICAN PHILOSOPHICAL SOCIETY

Independence Square, Philadelphia

Library of Congress Catalog
Card Number-93.71200
International Standard Book Number 0-87169-835-8
US ISSN 0065-9746

TABLE OF CONTENTS

ABBREVIATIONS

AA   *Analecta Augustiniana*

BF   *Bullarium Franciscanum*

BGPTM   Beiträge zur Geschichte der Philosophie und Theologie des Mittelalters

BRO   A.B. Emden, *A Biographical Register of the University of Oxford to 1500*

CICan   *Corpus Iuris Canonici*

CICiv   *Corpus Iuris Civilis*

CSEL   *Corpus Scriptorum Ecclesiasticorum Latinorum*

CUP   *Chartularium Universitatis Parisiensis*

DDC   *Dictionnaire de droit canonique*

HDR   Handbuch zur deutschen Rechtsgeschichte

PL   Migne, J.-P. ed. *Patrologiae Cursus Completus, Series Latina*

RB   Stegmüller, Friedrich. *Repertorium Biblicum*

SLdr   *Sachsenspiegel Landrecht*

TRE   *Theologische Realenzyklopädie*

UB   *Urkundenbuch*

ZRG,KA   *Zeitschrift der Savigny-Stiftung für Rechtsgeschichte, kanonistische Abteilung*

add   *addit/addunt*
corr   *corrigit/corrigunt*
del   *delet/delent*
leg   *lege*
ms   *manuscriptus*
om   *omittit/omittunt*
trans   *transponit*

The following abbreviations refer to the four manuscripts of Johannes Klenkok's *Exposicio litteralis in quattuor libris Sentenciarum:*

E1   Erfurt, Wissenschaftliche Allgemeinbibliothek, Amplon. Q. 118, ff. 86r-107v, 119r-135v (books I, II).

E2   Erfurt, Wissenschaftliche Allgemeinbibliothek, Amplon. F. 117, ff. 1-166.

K   Klosterneuburg, Stiftsbibliothek, Ms. 304, ff. 68r-195r.

S   Siena, Biblioteca Comunale, G.V.16., ff. 1r-105v (books I, III, IV, and the *redactio lectoris* of book II).

PREFACE

This is an account of the life and circumstances of a little known Augustinian friar with an interesting career, Johannes Klenkok. I attempt to reconstruct his biography more accurately than has been achieved up to now, but in so doing I consider as much as possible the organizations and habits that this individual shared with those among his contemporaries of a similar station in life, namely, mendicant friars. The sources led me to pay particular attention to the character of education within the mendicant orders and to Johannes Klenkok's campaign against the *Sachsenspiegel*, the first written code of traditional German laws.

When quotations from manuscripts require textual notes, they are added immediately after the quotation. The manuscripts used in this study employ very inconsistent punctuation, and therefore, I have tried to punctuate in a way that suits the syntax. The reader may wish to bear in mind that most manuscripts used in this study are records of oral presentation, some of it made in the less exacting environment of convent schools, rather than in the university, and the language is sometimes very inelegant.

Much of this was written as part of a larger project in which I accumulated many debts, and I shall try to separate those that pertain to these pages from those that pertain to the whole. Professor Karlfried Froehlich of Princeton Theological Seminary supervised the research when it was part of my doctoral dissertation. I benefited from his intuition, meticulous review, and numerous corrections. Professor Jane Dempsey Douglass of the same school also offered suggestions, corrections, and encouragement, for which I am grateful. Nevertheless, I bear full responsibility for these pages and for any errors that here may appear.

I wish to thank the following libraries for their generous assistance in acquiring books and articles, for providing microfilms, and for permission to use their manuscript collections: Augustinus-Institut, Würzburg; Bayerische Staatsbibliothek, Eichstätt; Herzog-August Bibliothek, Wolfenbüttel; Stadtbibliothek, Mainz; Speer Library, Princeton Theological Seminary; Wissenschaftliche Allgemeinbibliothek, Erfurt. I owe special thanks to

Frau Riess of the library of the Institut für Europäische Geschichte for tireless assistance in acquiring interlibrary loans. The Deutscher Akademischer Austauschdienst supported initial research in Klenkok's writings with a research grant in 1988, when I also enjoyed the hospitality of the Augustinus-Institut in Würzburg and the generous advice of its director, Dr. Adolar Zumkeller, and of Professor Dr. Willigis Eckermann. The late Professor Dr. Peter Manns received me as a research fellow of the Institut für Europäische Geschichte in Mainz, where I enjoyed three years of research and where I also benefited from the advice of Professor Dr. Rolf Decot. Professor William Courtenay has made helpful and provocative suggestions. Most recently, I have been encouraged by the interest and criticism of colleagues at San Francisco Theological Seminary and the Graduate Theological Union, among whom I wish to mention Professor Robert Coote and Dr. Mary P. Coote. My wife, Varda Koch Ocker, has tolerated an average friar of fourteenth-century Germany with the grace of a historian, and she has provided much helpful criticism.

INTRODUCTION

We know late medieval friars according to two stereotypes. One is the bad friar, who is known by his moral failings, like the pugnacious *lymytour* of Chaucer's *Summoner's Tale*, licensed by the bishop to preach and beg but seething with greedy threats and exploitation. He cuts a pretty loathsome figure whose true character and destiny, revealed in a scatological vision "ye han ofte tyme herd telle," has to do with a home in Satan's body and the custom torments of eternal judgement.[1] The other stereotype is the mendicant theologian, who is known by intellectual accomplishment, which is evidence of a trained mind and which will be judged according to intellectual canons. For a great mendicant thinker, like the Franciscan William Ockham, being a Friar Minor might seem to imply no more than a creative affinity with other minds.[2] One stereotype is really a literary cliché and polemical. The other is really a mental system and doubtlessly owned by individuals. Neither is a true image of a friar's life.

---

[1] *The Complete Works of Geoffrey Chaucer* (New York: Houghton Mifflin, 1933), pp. 112-20. The vision will be found in the summoner's prologue.

[2] For Ockham, Marilyn McCord Adams, *William Ockham*, vol. 26/1-2 of *Publications in Medieval Studies* (Notre Dame, Indiana: University of Notre Dame Press, 1987). Lineages of intellectual affinity existed not only among the Franciscans but also among the other three major mendicant orders (Dominicans, Augustinian Hermits, and Carmelites). For the emergence of schools of thought, an excellent introduction is William J. Courtenay, *Schools and Scholars in Fourteenth-Century England* (Princeton: Princeton University Press, 1987), pp. 171-92. For Franciscans, Dominicans, and Augustinians, consider Franz Ehrle, *Der Sentenzenkommentar Peters von Candia des Pisaner Papstes Alexanders V.*, vol. 9 of *Franziskanische Studien* (Münster in Westfalen: Aschendorf, 1925), esp. pp. 252-67, and C. Ocker, "Scholastic Traditions and Their Cultural Contexts in the Later Fourteenth Century: An Augustinian Friar at Oxford, Erfurt, Magdeburg, and Prague," *Proceedings of the Patristic, Medieval, and Renaissance Conference*, 12/13(1987-1988):209-20. For Dominicans, William Hinnebusch, *The History of the Dominican Order*, 2 vols. (New York: Alba House, 1973), 2:149-90. For Augustinians, Adolar Zumkeller, "Die Augustinerschule des Mittelalters: Vertreter und philosophisch-theologische Lehre," *Analecta Augustiniana*, 27(1964):167-262, and C. Ocker, "Augustinianism in Fourteenth-Century Theology," *Augustinian Studies*, 18(1987): 81-106, esp. 82-86. For Carmelites, B. Xiberta, *De Scriptoribus Scholasticis Saeculi XIV. ex Ordine Carelitanorum* (Louvain: Revue d'histoire ecclésiastique, 1931).

The literary type of the bad friar reflects something public and real. One can be critical and appreciate the connection of the figure to social reality.[3] To live as a priest, monk, or friar carried a set of variable obligations and dependent relationships within structured communities—towns, dioceses, and religious orders—which were suffering many of the tensions afflicting late medieval Europe. Clerical parties developed a fabulous variety of theological and exegetical arguments for the social organization that preserved the privileges and the roles of their respective groups, and they reviled their enemies, many of whom belonged to their own estate. Some of the most complex and vivid abuse was exchanged between friars and their clerical and monastic opponents. The vituperations of priests, monks, and nuns[4] inspired their neighbors. Anyone concerned with the travails of Christianity could sully favored enemies, be it in Latin or in a vernacular. The literary type of the bad friar reflects these bigotries of late medieval religion, but it is remote and tendentious evidence of a friar's life.

The image of the friar as intellectual also presents a slanted view of the historical character. Thought is evidence of a private mind; an intellectual tradition, evidence of private minds that agree, whether they communicate or not. They can agree because of the sheer strength of the ideas that they share, which is what one expects of philosophers.[5] That is how intellectual historians know theologians of the fourteenth century, as intrepid imaginations, catalysts of philosophical progress, even harbingers of Luther, Copernicus, and Galileo, and in each case a private genius connected to one's peers through inexorable legacies and shared syllogisms.[6] "But with all our gratitude for these endur-

---

[3]But for arguments against the validity of the charges brought against friars, see Arnold Williams, "Chaucer and the Friars," *Speculum*, 28(1953):499-513. Contrast Carolly Erickson, "The Fourteenth-century Franciscans and Their Critics," *Franciscan Studies*, 35(1975): 107-35, 36(1976):108-47.

[4]Kathryn Kerby-Fulton, "Hildegard of Bingen and Anti-Mendicant Propaganda," *Traditio*, 43(1987):386-99.

[5]But contrast such expectation with the observations of A. Seiffert, "Studium als soziales System," *Schulen und Studium im sozialen Wandel des hohen und späten Mittelalters*, ed. J. Fried, vol. 30 of *Vorträge und Forschungen* (Sigmaringen: Jan Thorbecke, 1986), p. 609.

[6]The most historically precise view of new developments in the fourteenth century is rendered by Courtenay, *Schools*, who notes the centrality of the university of Oxford in the first quarter of the century and who avoids exaggerated estimations of historic achievements. John E. Murdoch brought attention to the importance of theological texts as evidence of scientific advance. See Murdoch "From Social into Intellectual Factors: An Aspect of the Unitary Character of Late Medieval Learning," in *The Cultural Context of Medieval Learning*, ed. John E. Murdoch and Edith Dudley Sylla, vol. 26 of *Boston Studies in the Philosophy of Science* (Boston: D. Reidel Company, 1975), pp. 271-348. See also idem, "Mathesis in philosophiam scholasticam introducta. The Rise and Development of the Appli-

ing gifts, we cannot forget the conditions which attended them."[7] Geniuses tend to be few. Moreover, the rarified science of theology was bound to the social and political interests of larger groups of people. That is why much brainpower was spent on evangelical poverty and papal authority in the fourteenth century, to name a most obvious example: both pertained to the constitution of religious communities and the foundations of their legitimacy, at the heart of the conflicts among clergy.[8] In fact one might argue that at least since John Duns Scotus, speculative finesse also had a lot to do with moral casuistry, penitential savoir-faire, penance being a lucrative field in which friars excelled. It had to do with the success of mendicant priests, most of them being prosaic themselves.

We can overcome our dislike of mediocrity and our fascination with scandal to consider the exceptional average. Neither an uncommon genius nor a religious criminal is likely to represent the typical strains of life in a civilization. The average will be found on the periphery of philosophical accomplishment, where, too, satire may be a distracting parody of life.

---

cation of Mathematics in Fourteenth-Century Philosophy and Theology," in *Arts libéraux et philosophie au moyen âge. Actes du quatrième congrès international de philosophie médiévale, Université de Montréal, 27 août-2 septembre 1967* (Montréal: Institut d'Étudès Médiévales, 1969), pp. 215-65. For nominalism and the Copernican revolution, Heiko Oberman, "Reformation and Revolution: Copernicus' Discovery in an Era of Change," *Cultural Context of Medieval Learning*, pp. 397-435, and reprinted in Oberman, *The Dawn of the Reformation* (Edinburgh: T. and T. Clark, 1986), pp. 179-203. For broad conclusions, consider idem, *Contra vanam curiositatem*, vol. 113 of *Theologische Studien* (Zürich: Theologischer Verlag, 1974). For nominalism and Luther, idem, "*Facientibus quod in se est Deus non denegat gratiam: Robert Holcot O.P. and the Beginnings of Luther's Theology*," *Harvard Theological Review*, 55(1962):317-42, reprinted in *Dawn*, pp. 84-103. See also A.C. Crombie, *Augustine to Galileo*, 2 vols., 2nd ed. enl. (London: Heinemann, 1959), pp. 117-20.

[7]This proviso of John Dewey's 1929 Gifford Lectures—applied to the legacy of Plato and Aristotle—pointed to the division in ancient philosophy of the higher and truer realms of mental reality from the "inferior world of changing things with which experience and practical matters are concerned." The division also may have existed in philosophies of the late Middle Ages, but they do not reflect the place of intellectual activity in late medieval culture as a whole. John Dewey, *The Quest for Certainty. A Study of the Relation of Knowledge and Action* (New York: Perigee Books, 1980), p. 16. I might note that there are pragmatic ways to conceive of medieval thought. Consider David B. Burrell, "Creation, Will and Knowledge in Aquinas and Duns Scotus," in *Pragmatik. Handbuch pragmatischen Denkens*, ed. Herbert Stachowiak, vol. 1, *Pragmatisches Denken von den Ursprüngen bis zum 18. Jahrhundert* (Hamburg: Felix Meiner, 1986), pp. 248-79.

[8]The vernacular image of the bad friar, so prominent in English literature of the fourteenth century, originated in the 1250s, in the polemic of a prominent subdeacon, Guillaume de Saint-Amour, against the Dominicans and Franciscans of the University of Paris. Penn R. Szittya, *The Antifraternal Tradition in Medieval Literature* (Princeton: Princeton University Press, 1986). The repugnance that other clergy felt toward the friars was cultivated in conflicts over privileges. P. Hugolin Lippens, "Le droit nouveau des mendiants en conflit avec le droit coutumier du clergé séculier du Concile de Vienne à celui de Trente," *Archivum Franciscanum Historicum*, 47(1954):241-92.

To dwell on a friar who was not a genius is to resurrect some-one from an oblivion, by any other standards, deserved. Oblivion was the typical fate of friars who, like the Augustinian Hermit, Johannes Klenkok (c. 1310-1374), enjoyed fairly successful ca-reers, but whose names were almost completely forgotten within a couple of generations of death, until antiquarians and histori-ans connected the names with the vestiges. Klenkok's lack of in-terest in autobiography, typical of most medieval theologians, leaves us with disparate evidence: commentaries that celebrate their plain orthodoxy, some versions of a contentious pamphlet, the record of one disputation, a couple of documents and entries in registers, and one letter written on someone else's behalf. Yet such poverty reveals an intentionally constructed character.

Surreptitious revelations occur in the sources from the begin-nings of friars' lives. The beginnings are obscure. The obscurity tells the most important feature of their identity within the cul-ture of late medieval Europe: the public image of the individual was predominantly painted with the colors of a religious order. A mendicant community was a group of men (women's houses present special problems) in their walls in a corner of town, liv-ing the customs of a stringently ordered and purposeful society. The community was tightly fixed to a network of houses and chapels in the vaguely circumscribed territory that was politically and economically dependent upon the city, and also bound to convents of an ethnic and geographic region and to convents of the entire world. Seldom is there certain knowledge of birth, families, or novitiate. The houses often waited until their friars had died to scribble their names in a register for the first time— for the anniversary masses said for the souls of the dead. The provincial chapters recorded them when they were chosen to go to a general school and again when they were reassigned as pro-fessors in their own schools; fewer friars were recorded here and in the registers of universities as masters normally lecturing for the one- or two-year stint allowed members of the mendicant orders. Even these few destined to leadership have piecemeal biographies.

The poverty of the sources makes most friars whose lives are known appear to have been more a succession of offices than peo-ple, or more intellects than personalities. This is in large part due to the success of their cultural program and their own roles in car-rying it out. They appear to be elite, above the ordinary conven-tual—and presumably, far above the men and women of the streets, shops, markets, and fields—mystifying themselves with the secret language of scholasticism, blissfully or chronically aloof from the world of everyone else. This is misleading, for their interaction with all friars and with broad groups of people forced them to adapt even the most rarified theology to public roles and practical interests, as a closer look at the course of their lives and their writings can show.

Johannes Klenkok is the average case of a moderately successful friar. The main features of his life are an unknown date of birth, an education easiest to chronicle at its higher stages, teaching and leadership offices in the order, a papal appointment, and death.[9] The lack of information about the details of his life is not merely the product of accident but, as I have suggested, the result of a self-imposed, holy oblivion, in which the individual is

---

[9]This outline is true of the vast majority of fourteenth-century friars with moderately successful careers. Comparative evidence will be noted throughout this study. For preliminary comparisons, one may consider prosopographical data for two German Augustinians and one Italian Augustinian, who approached the pinnacles of their orders but not of the church. *Thomas of Strasbourg*: born late thirteenth century at Hagenau; novitiate, dates and place unknown; provincial school, presumably Strasbourg, dates unknown; c. 1316, studied at the general school in Padua; subsequently lector at the general school in Strasbourg and, at least part of the time, diocesan inquisitor; Pentecost, 1332, *definitor* of his province at the general chapter of Venice; 1335-1337, bachelor of the *Sentences* at Paris; 1337-1339, presumably master at Paris; 1343, elected prior provincial of the Rheinland-Schwaben province of his order; 1345-1357, general prior of his order; died early 1357. Adalbero Kunzelmann, *Geschichte der deutschen Augustiner-Eremiten*, 4 vols., vol. 26 of *Cassiciacum* (Würzburg: Augustinus-Verlag, 1969-1979), 2:196-201; R. Schwarz, "Thomas von Strassburg," RGG 6:864-65. *Hermann of Schildesche*: born 8 September, sometime before 1300, to a Johannes and a Gertrud; novitiate at Herford, dates unknown; conventual at Osnabrück, attended a provincial school and a general school, but dates and locations unknown; 1320, named *lector principalis* of the general school at Magdeburg and *definitor* at the provincial chapter; c. 1324-1326, *lector* at the general school in Erfurt; 1324, vicar of the minister general of the order at the chapter of the province of France and chosen by the general chapter of the order to pursue the course of a bachelor of the Bible at Paris, only to receive a papal privilege to begin at the more advanced bachelor of the *Sentences* in 1326 but not to begin for some years; 1328-1329, *lector* of the Herford convent; Pentecost, 1329, provincial *definitor* at the general chapter of Paris; c. 1330-1332, bachelor of the *Sentences* at Paris; before 1334, promoted to master at Paris; after 1334-1338, provincial prior of the Saxon-Thuringian province; summer 1338, delegate of German bishops trying to mediate a settlement between Ludwig of Bavaria and the papal curia; c. 1340-1357, general vicar, penitentiary major, and cathedral lecturer of the diocese of Würzburg; died 8 July 1357. Adolar Zumkeller, *Schrifttum und Lehre des Hermann von Schildesche O.E.S.A. (+1357)*, vol. 15 of *Cassiciacum*, (Würzburg: Augustinus-Verlag, 1959), pp. 1-3. *Gregory of Rimini*: born c. 1300, novitiate and attendance at a provincial school, dates and place(s) unknown; 1323-1338, *lector* at the general school in Bologna; 1338, delegate of the province of Romagna to the general chapter of his order; c. 1338-1342, *lector* at the general school in Padua; 1341, presumably chosen by the general chapter to become a bachelor at the University of Paris; 1342-1343, heard lectures at Paris; 1344, read the *Sentences* as bachelor or published them; 1343-1344, *magister studentium* of the general school of his order at Paris; 1345, promoted master by the University's faculty of theology and remained master for a year; 1347, returned to the general school in Padua; 1351-1357, lectured at the general school in Rimini; 1357-1358, prior general; died November, 1358. Venicio Marcolino, "Einleitung," *Gregorii Ariminensis O.E.S.A. lectura super primum et secundum Sententiarum*, ed. D. Trapp and V. Marcolino, 6 vols., vols. 6-12 of *Spätmittelalter und Reformation, Texte und Untersuchungen* (Berlin: Walter de Gruyter, 1981-1987), pp. xi-xxi.

forfeited to a constructed social identity, the religious vocation of an Augustinian friar. This forces an impersonal biography, which is a distinct advantage, insofar as it portrays the individual as a participant in a structured environment. It forces more consideration of the partisanship of opinion and the circumstances of activity. Klenkok's memory exists as a middling public figure, not as a personality, both in his early life and education and in his brief, thirteen-year career.

I. ICH WERE EIN SASSE GEBOREN

Johannes was born to a family called Klenkok in the county of Hoya, just south of the archbishopric of Bremen in Lower Saxony. His father, Heinrich, was castellan in Thedinghausen, an administrative outpost of the archbishop intensely disputed by Hoya's counts.[1] In 1290, Heinrich and his wife, Margaretha, appeared in a document—Heinrich as castellan of the archbishop of Bremen.[2] Sometime during the next decades the allegiance of the clan changed. A document of 1343 specifically names five Klenkok brothers as subjects of the count of Hoya; the transaction suggests that two remaining Klenkoks, one of whom was Johannes, were also subject to the count's jurisdiction.[3] This information complements the most reliable evidence for the place of Johannes' birth. Once in a passing comment, Johannes revealed that he was born in the castle of the count of Hoya.[4] This could only have occurred after 1290, after the Klenkoks had become subjects of the archbishop of Bremen's enemy. The change of allegiance must have occurred before August 1314, when count Otto of Hoya controlled Thedinghausen and formed a confederation against the archbishop of Bremen; at that point, knight Heinrich Klenkok was no

---

[1]Kurt Brünig, ed., *Niedersachsen und Bremen*, vol. 2 of *Handbuch der historischen Stätten Deutschlands* (Stuttgart: Alfred Kröner, 1986), pp. 450-51. Theodor Müller, *Das Amt Thedinghausen. Seine Geschichte und seine Entwicklung* (Thedinghausen: Gutenberg-Werkstätte, 1928), pp. 18-48. For literature on the knight's estate in Germany, see Heinrich Mitteis, Heinz Liberich, *Deutsche Rechtsgeschichte. Ein Studienbuch*, 18th expanded ed. (Munich: C.H. Beck, 1988), pp. 210-11, 215-17, 220.

[2]G. Gustav Homeyer, *Johannes Klenkok wider den Sachsenspiegel* (Berlin: Königliche Akademie der Wissenschaften, 1855), p. 382. Christian Ludwig Scheidt, *Bibliotheca historica Goettingensis*, part 1 (Göttingen and Hannover: Polwiz und Barmeier, 1758), pp. 110-11 no. 1.

[3]Scheidt, *Bibliotheca*, p. 113 no. 4.

[4]*Postilla super Actus Apostolorum*, Eichstätt, Bayerische Staatsbibliothek, Ms. 204, f. 168ra-168rb, where Klenkok comments abruptly on the four squads of soldiers (*quattuor quaterniones*) who guarded the apostle Peter when he was imprisoned by Herod and on the chains from which an angel miraculously released him (Ac. 12.4, 6):

quaternionibus. Glossa:[a] quaternio sub se habet milites quatuor, sicud centurio, centum. *cathenis.* Cathene dicit magister,[b] et ita est adhuc Rome monstrantur, ymo membrum unum unius cathenarum illarum et in castro unde sum natus, uidelicet in Hoya, ibi apportatum per istorum comitum patruum[c] uidelicet Cherardum comitem eiusdem castri.

a. *Biblia sacra cum glossis, interlineari et ordinaria, Nicolai Lyrani postilla et moralitatibus, Burgensis additionibus et Thoringi replicis* (Lyon: Anthoine Vincent, 1545), 6:186va, hereafter cited *Glossa cum Lyra*. b. Petrus Comestor, *Hist. in Ac.*, lxiii, PL 198:1687. c. *sic.* Klenkok then turns to another term of the passage, *custodes* in Ac. 12.6.

longer at the disputed castle, but it is impossible to determine when he vacated. The *terminus post quem* of Johannes' birth is sometime between 1290 and 1314. It allows the hypothetical estimate of Johannes Klenkok's biographers—that he was born around 1300—although he may have been born as late as 1320.[5]

Johannes probably never lived in the well-fortified castle of Thedinghausen, the Wasserburg, for the fact that he was born in the castle of Hoya implies that his father and his family were living among that count's retinue.[6] Later in life, he remembered the

---

[5]D. R. Ehmck, W. von Bippen, eds., *Bremisches Urkundenbuch* (Bremen: C. E. Müller, 1873-1902), 2:144-48, 150-55; no. 141-43, 146, esp. no. 146 (p. 153). See also Müller, *Amt*, p. 20, and the *Historia archiepiscoporum Bremensium*, lines 181-316, in Johann Martin Lappenberg, ed., *Geschichtsquellen des Erzstifts und der Stadt Bremen* (Aalen: Scientia Verlag, 1967 reprint of the Bremen edition of 1841), pp. 32-38. Count Otto of Hoya formed a confederation of several counts with the city of Bremen against her archbishop 19 August 1314. A settlement with the archbishop was signed 6 December 1314. It included the return of Thedinghausen to the archbishop, who repurchased it from lord Johann Cluvere, apparently vassal of the count of Hoya, who had obtained it for 50 Mark silver.

A letter to cardinal Pierre of Vergne of 1372, where Johannes called himself "annis senex," has suggested to his biographers that he was born at the turn of the century. Homeyer, *Johannes*, p. 395. Böhlau, "Lebensgeschichte," p. 542. Trapp, "Notes," p. 358. The context of the passage stresses the relative difference in age between Johannes and Pierre, in which Johannes disavowed any natural claim to seniority according to age and ascribed seniority to Pierre according to his greater virtue. Pierre may have been very young in 1372, and Johannes much younger than 70 years and still the cardinal's senior. Pierre was bachelor of laws (attested 1387, CUP 3:510; he studied at Montpellier; Bernard Guillemain, *La cour pontificale d'Avignon* [1309-1376] [Paris: Éditions E. de Boccard, 1962] p. 218), presumably having attained the degree before coming to office in 1371. He would remain in office a fairly long term of 32 years (Guillemain, *Cour*, pp. 212-13), dying in 1414. Cardinals as young as 19 years had been known in Avignon, although they were uncommon (ibid., pp. 208-11). As shall be seen, Klenkok became subdeacon in 1343. The minimum age was 14 (Willibald Plöchl, *Geschichte des Kirchenrechts*, 4 vols. [Munich: Herold, 1953-1966], 2:253-54), but Klenkok believed the age to be 18 (IV *Sent.*, d. 25, E2 f. 59vb, K f. 178r-178v, S f. 91va), which likely reflects what he experienced. He might, therefore, have been as young as 18 in 1343, but he was probably a few years older, because another document shows that he was old enough to travel but probably younger than 12 in 1325 (note 10). Thus, he could have been born as late as about 1320. Klenkok's view of the age of eligibility for ordination reflects a notable bias toward senescence. Contrast Boniface VIII, who allowed the reception of lower orders as early as the seventh year, with the possession of benefices (Klenkok, in IV *Sent.*, d. 25, limited benefices to those at least 25 years of age). Klaus Arnold, *Kind und Gesellschaft im Mittelalter und Renaissance. Beiträge und Texte zur Geschichte der Kindheit*, series B, vol. 2 of *Sammlung Zebra* (Paderborn: Schöningh; Munich: Lurz, 1980), pp. 21-22. Klenkok himself once defined the ages of life: 0-7 years, infancy; 8-12 years, childhood (*puer*); 13-25 years, adolescence; 26-36, youth (*iuuenis*); 37-50, adulthood (*uir*); 50-80, old age (*senex*). *Postilla super Actus*, Eichstätt, Ms. 204, f. 132ra.

[6]Gottfried Kiesow, et al., *Bremen. Niedersachsen*, Georg Dehio, ed., *Handbuch der deutschen Kunstdenkmäler* (Darmstadt: Wissenschaftliche Buchgesellschaft, 1977), pp. 905-06. The archbishop of Bremen had built the Wasserburg to fend off the encroachment of the counts of Hoya; it had been completed only in 1285. In 1338, Heinrich of Neu-Bruchhausen appears to have controlled Thedinghausen by election of the council of Bremen. *Brem. UB*, 2:429. This shows that the archbishop of Bremen, after reacquiring the castle in 1314, pawned it to the city of Bremen relatively soon. Before 1346, the Oldenburg count, Gerhardt I of Neu-Bruchhausen, acquired houses in Thedinghausen owned by the archbishop who pawned them, which his son, Gerhardt II later sold to the count of Hoya. The castle Wasserburg fell into the archbishop's hands again, only to be pawned to the city of Bremen again in 1377 (after which the archbishop would not regain the castle for

castle and once mentioned to his students, a little pompously, that Count Gerhard kept there, "in the castle where I was born," a precious relic—a piece of one of the two chains that bound Peter the apostle to two soldiers in Herod's prison (note 4). This rare flush of pride, flaunting a decent social background, suggests that he grew up in the castle and considered it a privilege. The self-disclosure corrects his biographers, who believed that he was born in Bücken, a town south of Hoya.[7] It also reveals an enduring consciousness of his family's class.

Heinrich was an officer of a territorial administration, a German castellan. He represents those people of the fourteenth century who were assuming the functions occupied earlier by the malleable knightly class of Germany, the *ministeriales*, whose traditional social position was steadily eroding to become a mere title of knighthood.[8] Such officers proved themselves more useful to lords than the old ministerials who through the years had accumulated interests of their own and the autonomy to carry them out. While ministerials entrenched themselves as lower nobility and the ruling elites of German towns, bailiffs, judges, and castellans moved securely into the ministerial class.[9] But by the time

---

nearly two centuries; the castle was destroyed in the 17th century). Kiesow, op. cit., and Georg Sello, *Die territoriale Entwicklung des Herzogtums Oldenburg* (Osnabrück: H. Th. Wenner, 1975 reprint of the edition of Göttingen, 1917), pp. 219-20. The castle of Hoya was occupied until 1503 and later became the site of an *Amtsgericht*. Curt Tillmann, *Lexikon der deutschen Burgen und Schlösser*, 4 vols. (Stuttgart: Anton Hiersemann, 1958-1961), 1:436. For the role of castles in consolidating princely administration, Benjamin Arnold, *Princes and Territories in Medieval Germany* (Cambridge: Cambridge University Press, 1991), p. 180, provides an excellent summary.

[7] A Low Saxon manuscript of the *Sachsenspiegel* written in 1417 and containing the *articuli reprobati* (to be discussed in the next chapter) includes a biographical note on Klenkok making two spurious claims: that Johannes was born in Bücken and that Johannes was doctor of both laws (which claim shall be discussed in due course). These allegations have misled Klenkok's biographers, who have not examined the *Postilla super Actus Apostolorum*. Homeyer, *Johannes*, pp. 382, 427. Hans Böhlau, "Zur Lebensgeschichte des Augustinermönches Johannes Klenkok, Bekämpfers des Sachsenspiegels," *Historische Vierteljahrschrift*, 29(1934):541-75, here 542 (but not claiming that Klenkok was doctor of laws). Damasus Trapp, "Notes on John Klenkok (d. 1374)," *Augustinianum*, 4(1964):358-404, here 358. Bücken is located in the same county and near the city of Hoya. It was the site of an ancient collegial church and apparently home of the noble family, von Hodenberg, before the establishment of the counts of Hoya in the thirteenth century. Brünig, *Niedersachsen und Bremen*, pp. 81-82. In addition to Klenkok's own statement of his birthplace, there appears to be no evidence of a knight's residence in Bücken.

[8] Carlo Guido Mor, "Das Rittertum," trans. from Italian by Ilse Kraski, in *Das Rittertum im Mittelalter*, ed. Arno Borst, v. 349, *Wege der Forschung* (Darmstadt: Wissenschaftliche Buchgesellschaft, 1976), pp. 247-65, here 249-50. For knighthood as a social class, Johanna Maria van Winter, "Die mittelalterliche Ritterschaft als 'classe sociale,' " trans. from Dutch by Heinz Wolters, *Rittertum im Mittelalter*, pp. 370-91. For officers replacing ministerials, Karl Bosl, *Europa im Aufbruch* (Munich: C.H. Beck, 1980), p. 255. For the prestige of the *ministeriales*, Benjamin Arnold, *German Knighthood. 1050-1300* (Oxford: Clarendon Press, 1985), pp. 69-75.

[9] Bosl, *Europa*, pp. 236, 255.

Klenkok made his passing admission, the status of his family was no longer so relevant as it had been when he was a boy: St. Peter's chains mattered more.

Nothing is heard of Johannes until 1324, when he appeared with his brothers Tideric and Ortgise before Count Otto of Oldenburg, but Johannes played no role in the transaction, and this implies that he was still beneath the age of legal majority (twelve years).[10] Tideric must have been the eldest of the boys, for he maintained a prominent role in family affairs. By 1328, he had obtained the title of knight of Thedinghausen.[11] It may be that father Heinrich had died by then, which would explain Tideric's prominence, but his wife must have lived until 1342, the year in which a short spate of legal transactions over family property began, giving additional implications about Johannes' background.

Two groups of Klenkoks claimed to be heirs in 1342: Tideric and Johannes (Ortigse must have already died) formed one party, and five other brothers formed another—Rudolf, Hartbert, Alard, Herbord, and Conrad. Both parties commanded property. The party of five transacted a donation with the Benedictine nunnery, Heiligenrode, which the family had long supported (Klenkok women may have lived there).[12] Tideric redeemed property in Veine that his father had pawned, and he, together with his son and his brother Johannes as witness, sold it.[13] But it seems that both parties wished to command the entire inheritance of Hein-

---

[10]Scheidt, *Biblioteca*, p. 114 no. 5. Although the *Sachsenspiegel* did not prescribe an age of legal majority, its stipulations for those who had come of age were usually interpreted to apply to anyone over 12 years. Karl August Eckhardt, ed., *Sachsenspiegel*, 2 vols. (Göttingen: Musterschmidt Verlag, 1955-1956), 2:81, cf. 1:104, n. 79-79 [sic]. Friedrich Ebel, *Magdeburger Recht*, vol. 2, *Die Rechtsmitteilungen und Rechtssprüche für Breslau*, part 1, *Die Quellen von 1261 bis 1452*, vol. 89/II/1 of *Mitteldeutsche Forschungen* (Cologne: Böhlau, 1989), p. 46 no. 60 (a case of 1352-1363). Klaus Arnold noted a contrasting age of majority in the Golden Bull of Charles IV of 18 years. K. Arnold, *Kind und Gesellschaft*, p. 25. Alexander Gal, ed., *Die Summa legum brevis levis et utilis des sogenannten Doctor Raymundus von Wiener-Neustadt* (Weimar: Hermann Böhlaus Nachfolger, 1926), pp. 156f. provides a more differentiated view of attainment of majority (with full majority reached only in the twenty-fifth year). The presence of a young boy at a transaction of family business is not surprising, since distinctions of maturity beyond infancy were blurred at best. Consider James A. Schultz, "Medieval Adolescence: The Claims of History and the Silence of German Narrative," *Speculum*, 66(1991):519-39, and Shulamith Shahar, *The Fourth Estate. A History of Women in the Middle Ages*, trans. by Chaya Galai (New York: Routledge, 1990 reprint of the edition of 1983), pp. 140-41.

[11]In a document according to which he and Ortgise helped execute the terms of another knight's inheritance settlement, Albert Plump, over property in Verden. Scheidt, *Bibliotecha*, p. 117 no. 7.

[12]21 December 1342. Ibid., p. 116 no. 8. See also ibid., pp. 110-11 no. 1 and pp. 116-17 no. 9.

[13]28 October 1342. Ibid., pp. 111-12 no. 2. Homeyer mistakenly identified Tideric's son Conrad as a brother of Tideric and Johannes. Homeyer, *Johannes*, p. 383.

rich, for the five brothers brought a suit against Tideric and Johannes for the property, which was decided by Count Gerhard of Hoya 13 November 1343. The five brothers based their suit on the *Sachsenspiegel*, which maintained the predilection of traditional Germanic law to prevent the alienation of family property by granting inheritance rights to the extended family.[14] The five brothers must have been cousins of Tideric and Johannes. Count Gerhard decided in favor of Heinrich's two sons by granting them full rights to the unknown property in question. The affair may have spawned Johannes' conviction that the *Sachsenspiegel*'s provisions for the transfer of family property were grotesquely unjust.

But as had been usual for boys reaching puberty, Johannes was now leaving his family.[15] Inadvertently, the documents show that Johannes had become a subdeacon in 1343.[16] That this should be known from a transaction of family business, the sale of property in Veine, shows that the transition to the clergy and a new place in society had not yet required the abolition of family ties.[17] Although Hoya belonged to the diocese of Bremen, Johannes may have been ordained in the cathedral of Osnabrück (in the province of Cologne), for he once referred familiarly to the Osnabrück custom of keeping alms in safe storage to protect against mice (which is also why they should be quickly distributed to the poor, their proper owner), a custom Klenkok may have witnessed as a new cleric.[18] A secure ecclesiastical career required family money

---

[14]Scheidt, *Biblioteca*, p. 113 no. 4. Hans Josef Kullmann, "Klenkok und die 'articuli reprobati' des Sachsenspiegels" (Ph.D. dissertation, Frankfurt am Main, Johann-Wolfgang-Goethe Universität, 1959), pp. 87ff., for the *Sachsenspiegel*, and for Klenkok's later attack on these principles.

[15]Bosl, *Europa*, p. 256. Shahar, *Estate*, pp. 138-39.

[16]Scheidt, *Biblioteca*, pp. 111-12 no. 2, lists Johannes without title; ibid., p. 113 no. 4 (dated 13 November 1343), Johannes is called *clericus*. Therefore, he received the first of the lower clerical grades between 28 October 1342 and 13 November 1343. Ordinations usually took place on Good Friday and Holy Saturday. Plöchl, *Geschichte*, 2:266. Accordingly, Johannes probably received the first grade in the spring of 1343.

[17]Johanna Maria van Winter very provocatively suggests that, in medieval Gelders and neighboring areas, only two groups represent genuine social classes—knights and clergy. "Ritterschaft als 'classe social,'" p. 390. To enter a clerical grade was not only to move, at least technically, from the household of the count to the household of a bishop, but to relinquish one pervasive social identity for another.

[18]But he probably did not manage alms himself. *Postilla*, Eichstätt 204, f. 133vb:

Sic in diocesi osnabrugense consuete[a] fuerunt elemosine certe, ne glires illas nocerent. Sed elemosinis neglectis minimis temporibus glires diruerunt.[b] Debent ergo prelati frangere panes, quoniam omnia bona ecclesie bona pauperum sunt, quia minus utiliter consummere peius est quam aliena rapere.

a. *leg* consueto. b. *ms* redierunt.

For the subdeacon's work, R. Naz, "Sous-diaconat," DDC 7:1074-78.

to patronize benefices that would support the priest or, better, well placed ecclesiastical friends to acquire desirable offices on one's behalf. We may assume that the Klenkoks were estranged in the province of Bremen, and what little we know of Tideric and Johannes finds them selling and never buying. Three years later, when Johannes confirmed one of Tideric's liquidations of estate property in Verden, Johannes was an Augustinian friar.[19] His religious vocation immediately improved his chances for a reasonably successful academic and ecclesiastical career. It also marked a move to another sphere of his world, from subjection to a bishop to the realm of a universal religious order, the mendicant order of Augustinian Hermits.

The two Augustinian convents closest to the city of his birth were in Herford, about one hundred kilometers to the south, and in Osnabrück, about one hundred kilometers to the south-south-west. If Johannes had first become a cleric of the diocese of Osnabrück, he may likely have converted in the same town and not in Herford as has been suggested.[20] The fact that he is mentioned in a family property transaction of 1346 suggests that he was then still a novice, not yet having broken his legal claim to the family estate, and since a mendicant novitiate would be as brief as a year, he had probably entered the order very recently.[21] Little is known of the cloister of Osnabrück: it was founded in 1287; it had been attacked by a coalition of the cathedral chapter, the chapter of the church of St. Johannes, and the city of Osnabrück in a

---

[19]The document is dated the fourth Tuesday after Easter ("tertia feria post dominicam Jubilate"; *Jubilate* is the third Sunday after Easter, and *feria tertia* is Tuesday) 1346. Scheidt, *Biblioteca*, pp. 112-13 no. 3.

[20]In the early sixteenth century, the Augustinian friar, Johannes Schiphower, offered a biographical note on Johannes Klenkok. His source was the writings of Gander of Meppen, a student of Klenkok. Before quoting Gander, Schiphower says Klenkok was "de conventu Hervordiensi," which has been taken to refer to Herford, although "Hervordia" was the Latin rendering of both Herford and Erfurt. Because Gander, in the quotation that follows, ascribed Klenkok to Erfurt, it is most probable that Schiphower's text presents an alternative spelling of the same city, and does not intend the city of Herford (the phonetic basis of spelling allowed such inconsistency). Schiphower more likely associated Klenkok with Erfurt, where he spent almost a decade as professor. W. Eckermann, "Eine unveröffentlichte historische Quelle zur Litteraturgeschichte der westfälischen Augustiner des Spätmittelalters," AA 34(1971):185-235, here 210-12. Graesse, Benedict, Plechl, *Orbis Latinus*, 3 vols. (Braunschweig: Klinkhardt und Biermann, 1972), 2:235. Bütow noted the lack of documentary evidence for Klenkok in Herford, but also the lack of evidence contradicting a time there; op. cit., p. 543 n. 8. Contrast Homeyer, *Johannes*, pp. 382, 387-88. Bütow, "Lebensgeschichte," p. 543. Trapp, "Notes," p. 358.

[21]Jacques Hourlier, *L'Age classique (1140-1378). Les religieux*, vol. 10 of *Histoire du droit et des institutions de l'Église en occident* (Paris: Éditions du Cerf, 1974), p. 177, for papal legislation requiring at least a one-year novitiate, which implies that the friars, like other religious orders, were inclined to cut the novitiate short (other orders were allowed to do so).

property dispute of 1294 (the first of many to occur in the early fourteenth century); a provincial chapter was held there in 1331.[22] If Johannes did profess his vows in this town, he probably did not stay long, for he would be quickly hustled into the order's schools. Before becoming a subdeacon, he had attained the minimum requirement to begin studies as an Augustinian: enough literacy to read the divine office. A friar would now ordinarily attend a grammar school, although some slipped, even incompetent, into more advanced schools.[23] The standard for graduating grammar school was painless—knowledge of grammar and the ability to speak clearly.[24] Johannes may well have known that much Latin as a subdeacon and could, therefore, immediately begin studying dialectics (and probably a melange of other subjects) in a *studium provinciale*.[25] Although there is evidence of a low-level school at Osnabrück as early as 1328, it may not have operated for more than a few years at a time, until the early fifteenth century.[26] At least eleven other cloisters of the Saxon-Thuringian

---

[22]Kunzelmann, *Geschichte*, 1:73-75, 5:123-24, with references. Kaspar Elm, "Termineien und Hospize der westfälischen Augustiner-Eremiten-Klöster Osnabrück, Herford und Lippstadt," *Jahrbuch für Westfälische Kirchengeschichte*, 70(1977):11-49, here 14.

[23]A general chapter of 1312 forbade tonsuring converts before they had attained minimal literacy. Eclecko Ypma, *La formation des professeurs des Éremites de Saint-Augustin de 1256 à 1354* (Paris: Centre d'Études des Augustins, 1956), p. 148 (pp. 147-59 conveniently collects constitutional documents pertaining to education in the order that were previously edited in volumes 2 to 4 of *Analecta Augustiniana*). A general chapter of 1332 required that all clerics, as soon as they could read Latin and sing the divine office, be sent to grammar school. Ibid., p. 149. The general chapter of 1338 complained that students were reaching the *studia generalia* with insufficient knowledge of grammar and logic. Ibid., p. 149. For the movement of students, in general, consider Hans-Joachim Schmidt, *Bettelorden in Trier. Wirksamkeit und Umfeld im hohen und späten Mittelalter* (Trier: Trierer historische Forschungen, 1986), pp. 315-18; Kaspar Elm, "Mendikantenstudium, Laienbildung und Klerikerschulung im spätmittelalterlichen Westfalen," *Studien zum städtischen Bildungswesen des späten Mittelalters und der frühen Neuzeit*, ed. B. Moeller et al., (Göttingen: Vandenhoeck und Ruprecht, 1983), pp. 586-617.

[24]General chapter of 1332, Ypma, *La formation*, p. 149. The prerequisite grammar was undoubtedly the elementary Latin students acquired by studying texts like Donatus' *Ars minor* (for which, see Jo Ann Hoeppner Moran, *The Growth of English Schooling, 1340-1548* [Princeton: Princeton University Press, 1985], p. 27 and the literature listed in n. 14, there). The grammar school itself probably taught the speculative grammar common in schools of the liberal arts associated with non-mendicant foundations (the best studied German examples were in Erfurt, where linguistic theory was strongly influenced by English developments; Jan Pinborg, *Entwicklung*, and idem, "The Fourteenth-Century Schools of Erfurt, Repertorium Erfordiense," *Cahiers de l'Institut du moyen âge grec et latin*, 1[1982]: 171-92).

[25]This would have been about 1346. Johannes became master at Oxford a mere 13 years later, as will be seen, which is chronologically possible but probably precludes any time in a grammar school. For the curriculum, note 3, page 17.

[26]The earliest reference to an Augustinian lecturer in Osnabrück is from 1328. Kunzelmann, *Geschichte*, 5:317. Another reference of 1337 may suggest that a lecturer was still teaching there nine years later. Ibid., 5:325. Because he apparently worked alone, the school must have been a grammar school, a school of logic, or a provincial school. More frequent references are known from the early fifteenth century. N. Teewen, A. de Meijer,

province had lecturers at one time or another in the fourteenth century; of these, the cloisters of Würzburg and Gotha almost certainly housed *studia provicialia*.[27] The remaining cloisters may have housed provincial schools, schools of grammar, or schools of logic (if they existed apart from provincial schools in this region).[28] Provincial chapters or provincial priors on behalf of their chapters assigned the students.[29] Extant records are ex-

---

"Documents pour servir à l'histoire médiévale de la province augustinienne de Cologne," *Augustiniana* 9(1959):202-20, 339-56, 431-77; 10(1960):115-77, 297-327, 424-61; 11(1961):181-224, 383-413, 602-44, here 10:116, 117, no. 216, 218. See also Kunzelmann, op. cit., 4:30, 209. In 1434, the *studium generale* of Magdeburg was transferred to Osnabrück (because of the former cloister's resistance to reform) for three years (the move allegedly reduced the population of the Magdeburg cloister from 30 priests to 3); the school was restored to Magdeburg in 1438. The mention of a lecturer from Osnabrück in 1452 may suggest that a school, perhaps a *studium provinciale*, continued to operate there. Kunzelmann, *Geschichte*, 5:114, 115 n. 625, 116, 354. It should be noted that some schools, which frequently consisted of a single teacher, especially at a more elementary level of education, were traveling or occasional, in order to spread the burden of financing students among several convents or to accommodate a small number of students. There exists a plan of 1415 for a school to rotate among eight Pomeranian convents of the Augustinian Order. Jerzy Kłoczowski, "Panorama geografico, cronologico e statistico sulla distribuzione degli 'studia' degli ordini mendicanti: Europa centro-orientale," *Le scuole degli ordini mendicanti (secoli xiii-xiv)*, vol. 17 of *Convegni del Centro di Studia sulla spiritualità medioevale* (Rimini: Maggioli Editore, 1978), pp. 127-49, here 134. This probably occurred more frequently; the Dominicans, in any event, adapted a system of rotating schools of natural science and of philosophy. William Hinnebusch, *The History of the Dominican Order*, 2 vols. (New York: Alba House, 1966, 1973), 2:19. Consider also a Franciscan lecturer's account of his movements between Halberstadt, Magdeburg, and Erfurt, quoted in Ferdinand Doelle, "Das Partikularstudium der sächsischen Provinz im Mittelalter," *Franziskanische Studien*, 14(1927):244-51, here 247-48, and the movement of Latin teachers outside the mendicant orders, Moran, *Growth*, p. 112.

[27]Würzburg lecturers are known for the years 1349, 1358, 1359, 1373, 1374, and 1383. Adolar Zumkeller, *Urkunden und Regesten zur Geschichte der Augustinerklöster Würzburg und Münnerstadt*, 2 vols. (Würzburg: Schöningh, 1966, 1967), 1:95, 123, 128, 131, 160f., 187f. Gotha lecturers are mentioned for 1342, 1349, 1350, 1355, 1392, and 1395. Kunzelman, *Geschichte*, 5:153-54. Well known theologians lectured in each of these schools, Hermann of Schildesche in Würzburg and Heinrich of Friemar the Elder in Gotha.

[28]The cities (with years of references to lecturers) are Münnerstadt (1356, 1380-1385, 1394; Zumkeller, *Urkunden*, 2:599, 614-17, 623), Neustadt (1381-1383, 1387; Kunzelmann, *Geschichte*, 5:164), Eschwege (1343, 1384; ibid., 5:149 n. 806, 173), Helmstedt (1320; A. Overmann, *Urkundenbuch der Erfurter Stifter und Klöster*, 3 vols. [Magdeburg, 1926-1934], 1:1116; Zumkeller, *Urkunden*, 1:52; Kunzelmann, *Geschichte*, 5:184 [an entry in Gregory of Rimini's register mentions a convent library in 1358; Gregorius de Arimino, *Registrum generalatus, 1357-1358*, ed. A. de Meijer (Rome: Institutum Historicum Augustinianum, 1976), p. 307 no. 565]), Lippstadt (1368; Kunzelmann, *Geschichte*, 4:26f. n. 98; 5:189), Herford (1328, 1329, 1332, 1337; ibid., 5:197), Quedlinburg (1316; ibid., 5:218), Friedeberg (1379f.; ibid., 5:232-33; Hans Bütow, "Johannes Merkelin, Augustinerlesemeister zu Friedeberg/Neumarkt, Leben und Schriften," *Jahrbuch für Brandenburgische Kirchengeschichte*, 29[1934]:3-35, here 12-13). For provincial schools teaching logic, consider the general chapter of 1338. Ypma, *La formation*, p. 149. Provinces appear to have been free to establish as many grammar schools as they wished; consider the Italian provincial chapter of 1297, ibid., p. 147. A general chapter of 1315 required two grammar schools per province, which probably represents the minimum and not a rigidly fixed number. Ibid., p. 148.

[29]For an example of the provincial chapter delegating the task to the provincial prior, consider the Italian provincial chapter of 1326; ibid., pp. 147, 148.

tremely rare.[30] Since neither he nor any contemporary has told us, it is impossible to know where Johannes began to study philosophy and theology.

[30]A fragment used in the binding of a codex of the Windesheim Ratsbibliothek (Hs. 40) from the first half of the fourteenth century contains the request of an Augustinian prior named Hermann that two conventuals, Heinrich Gostenhofer and Hermann Stein (Hermannus de Lapide) be granted admission to a *studium provinciale*. A. Zumkeller, *Manuskripte von Werken der Autoren des Augustiner-Eremitenordens in mitteleuropäischen Bibliotheken*, vol. 20 of *Cassiciacum* (Würzburg: Augustinus-Verlag, 1966), p. 178 no. 372. Some acts of only six chapters of the Saxon-Thuringian province of the Augustinian Order are known from a fifteenth-century copy preserved in the Bayerische Staatsbibliothek (Clm 8491; Zumkeller, *Manuskripte*, p. 515 no. 1461); the chapters were held at Gotha (1368, for which see p. 43, below), Sangerhausen (1370), Herford (1379), Langensalza (1384), Friedeberg/Neumarkt (1401), and Quedlinburg (1410). These were included in a quire (ff. 161r-174v) that contains copies of some miscellaneous documents and forms of absolution, together with excerpts from the Augustinian constitution (f. 162r-v), plenty of free space to write in additions (particularly on ff. 163r-164v), and the excerpts of provincial acts (ff. 165r-166r). The acts contain nothing of student appointments to schools. Contrast Dominican acts. Dominican school assignments are better known from the extant acts of provincial chapters. Heinrich Finke, "Zur Geschichte der deutschen Dominikaner im 13. und 14. Jahrhundert," *Römische Quartalschrift*, 8(1894):367-92; B. M. Reichert, "Zur Geschichte der deutschen Dominikaner am Ausgange des 14. Jahrhunderts," ibid., 14(1900):79-101, 15 (1901):124-52; idem, "Akten der Provinzialkapitel der Dominkanerordensprovinz Teutonia aus den Jahren 1398, 1400, 1401, 1402," ibid., 11(1897):287-331; Vladimir Koudelka, "Zur Geschichte der böhmischen Dominikanerprovinz im Mittelalter," *Archivum Fratrum Praedicatorum*, 25(1955):75-99, 27(1957):39-119; Thomas Kaeppeli, Kapitelsakten der Dominikanerprovinz Teutonia (1349, 1407)," ibid., 22(1952):186-95, 26(1956):314-19; Berthold Altaner, "Aus den Akten des Rottweiler Provinzialkapitels der Dominikaner vom Jahre 1396," *Zeitschrift für Kirchengeschichte*, 48(1929):1-15; Fritz Bünger, "Ein Dominkaner Provinzialkapitel in Luckau (1400)," ibid., 34(1913):74-88.

II. FIDEI CATHOLICE NULLATENUS REPUGNANTES

Although the lives of friars studying in the *studia provincialia* are hidden in an inauspicious silence, these were intended to be the most numerous and widespread mendicant schools, and they were the principal vehicle for infusing the intellectual stock of an order's identity into the minds of as many as possible. The schools were also used to impart the skills that made friars such effective preachers and confessors.[1] The teachers were trained in the order's "general schools," where friars of an order from all of Christendom studied with two (sometimes three) professors trained in a university. The system provided for the widest possible dissemination of scholastic theology among the friars,

---

[1]The chapter title is taken from the lengthiest educational legislation of the Augustinian friars in the fourteenth century, issued by the general chapter of 1345 at Paris under the general, Thomas of Strasbourg. The chapter forbade, by papal mandate, adherence to or teaching of any doctrines in philosophy or theology that contradict the canonical scriptures, "canonical" doctors, or the works approved by the Roman church. AA 4(1911/12):257-58. This preceded the papal bull issued the day after the revocation of errors by Nicolas of Autrecourt at the curia and sent by Clement VI to the scholars and masters of Paris against those whose speculative philosophy departed from the text of the Bible and the expositions of the saints and doctors, abandoning the good, old philosophy and using vain philosophy in its stead. CUP 2:587-90 no. 1125 (20 May 1346). The Augustinian general chapter of 1348 at Pavia, also under Thomas of Strasbourg, forbade students from hearing lectures on Ockham's logic. Ibid., p. 276. Each province was to have one lecturer to treat the entire "new and old" logic over a three-year period, according to the general chapter of 1338. Chapter 36 of Thomas of Strasbourg's additions to the constitution called for as many provincial schools as possible. Ypma, *La formation*, pp. 149-50. The Dominicans were the creators of the mendicant system of education, which encompassed all friars at its lowest levels and at each successive stage, a more select group. Originally intending to supply all convents with theological lecturers, the Dominicans created provincial schools because of the insufficient number of teachers. The Franciscans appear to have used centralized schools in the custodies from the beginnings of their educational system, although much remains to be learned about them. Augustinians and Carmelites adapted the Dominican system. C. Douais, *Essai sur l'organisation des études dans l'ordre des frères prêcheurs au treizième et au quatorzième siècles* (Paris: Alphonse Picard, 1884). Ypma, *La formation*. Doelle, "Partikularstudium." William J. Courtenay, "The Franciscan *Studia* in Southern Germany in the Fourteenth Century," *Gesellschaftsgeschichte. Festschrift für Karl Bosl zum 80. Geburtstag*, ed. Ferdinand Seibt, 2 vols., (Munich: R. Oldenbourg, 1988), pp. 81-90 (Prof. Courtenay kindly provided me with a pre-publication copy of the essay, for which I am grateful). Dieter Berg, *Armut und Wissenschaft. Beiträge zur Geschichte des Studienwesens der Bettelorden im 13. Jahrhundert*, vol. 15 of *Bochumer historische Studien* (Düsseldorf: Schwann, 1977), pp. 57-144. F. B. Lickteig, *The German Carmelites at the Medieval Universities* (Rome: Institutum Carmelitanum, 1981), pp. 39-76. Prof. Courtenay has recently called attention to mendicant schools outside the universities, particularly the *studia generalia*, and the need to give them greater consideration, *Schools and Scholars in Fourteenth-Century England* (Princeton: Princeton University Press, 1988), p. 166.

which was entirely consistent with the character of much scholastic thought, all of which was formulated by clerical groups with practical interests.[2] The general chapter of the Augustinian Order only stipulated that lecturers give a three-year sequence covering the *Prior Analytics* and the *Posterior Analytics* of Aristotle, but the writings of lecturers betray a potpourri that included philosophy, Bible, theology, and canon law.[3] Secular clergy might

---

[2]Arno Seifert has called this a commitment to "theoretical praxis." "Studium," pp. 608-19. Klaus Wriedt has stressed the role of clergy in education and its consequences, "Bürgertum und Studium in Norddeutschland während des Spätmittelalters," ibid., pp. 487-525. Contrast H. Grundmann, *Vom Ursprung der Universität im Mittelalter*, 2nd ed. (Darmstadt: Wissenschaftliche Buchgesellschaft, 1960), stressing the role of a purer desire for knowledge, and J. Le Goff, *Les intellectuels au moyen âge* (Paris: Seuil, 1957, 1985), pp. 147-49, unconvincingly associating the increase of speculation with the rise of aristocratic control of colleges, and Isnard Frank, "Die Spannung zwischen Ordensleben und wissenschaftlicher Arbeit im frühen Dominikanerorden," *Archiv für Kulturgeschichte*, 49(1967):164-207, and idem, *Die Bettelordensstudia im Gefüge des spätmittelalterlichen Universitätswesens*, vol. 83 of *Institut für Europäische Geschichte Mainz, Vorträge* (Stuttgart: Franz Steiner Verlag, 1988), arguing that mendicant educational systems tended to uproot the orders from original penitential and pastoral aims and led first to the development of academic traditions peculiar to the individual orders and, with the increasing incorporation of mendicant general schools in new universities, their demise. Cf. Jacques Verger, "*Studia* et universités," in *Le scuole*, pp. 175-203, here 175f., for the friars' adaptation of the university model to their own schools.

[3]The legislation of general chapters regarding provincial schools (as well as that regarding general schools) was preoccupied with matters pertaining to admission to higher schools. General chapters of 1324, 1338, and 1341, and chapter 38 of the *additiones* of Thomas of Strasbourg prescribe the philosophical curriculum. Ypma, *La formation*, pp. 148-50, 153. The writings of lecturers show that the curriculum was, however, more diverse. For example, Hermann of Schildesche, after teaching in the general schools of Magdeburg and Erfurt, returned to the provincial school of Herford in the late 1320s, where he certainly worked on his *Introductorium iuris* and where he might have brought it to completion and where he perhaps wrote his *Tractatus contra haereticos negantes immunitatem et iurisdictionem sanctae ecclesiae*. A. Zumkeller, *Schriftum und Lehre*, pp. 2-3, 89-91; consider also pp. 134-35. Hermann Stein, lector in Nürnberg (died after 1368), wrote a *Tractatus de quadraginta mansionibus filiorum Israel in deserto* in 1365 and, according to Jordan of Quedlinburg, many incomplete works. Zumkeller, *Manuskripte*, pp. 51-52 no. 86. Idem, *Schriftum*, pp. 132-34. Peter of Monte Robiano (died after 1326) wrote the *Historia beati Nicolai de Tolentino* as lector in 1326. Zumkeller, *Manuskripte*, p. 335 no. 703. Johann Salm (died after 1341), wrote a commentary *In Canticum canticorum*. Ibid., p. 274 no. 605. Johann of Schäffolsheim, lector in Strasbourg, wrote pseudonymous mystical letters in the mid-fourteenth century. Ibid., pp. 265-66 no. 581-83. A lector named Thomas authored mystical sayings sometime in the fourteenth century. Ibid., pp. 380-81 no. 815-16. Theoderich of Himmelpforten, lector sometime in the fourteenth or fifteenth century, wrote a *Hortulus virginitatis*. Ibid., pp. 374-76 no. 807. A lector named Nicolaus wrote a commentary on the fourth book of the *Sentences* (actually questions on the fourth book). Ibid., p. 335 no. 703. Konrad Zenn (died 1460), lector in Nürnberg, wrote a *Tractatus de quotidiana communione laicorum*, two works on the monastic life, and a *Nota contra eos qui tenent extraordinaria sanctorum festa*. Ibid., pp. 105-06 no. 223-26. Johann Ertzem, prior (and presumably lector) in Freiburg im Breisgau, wrote treatises on the books of Esther and Ruth in 1464. Ibid., pp. 233-34 no. 487. More could be deduced from lectors' scribal activity (see ibid., pp. 56, 96, 216-17, 241, 244, 252, 254, 264, 320, 352; no. 98, 200, 454, 500, 512, 513, 540, 546, 578, 657, 763) and books in their possession (ibid., pp. 168, 175, 215, 267, 275, 330; no. 345, 362, 445, 584, 609, 688; most of these examples, however, are from the fifteenth century). Consider also the Dominican lecturer at Ulm, Johann Müntzinger, and his commentaries on the *Vater unser* and the Pauline epistles (A. Lang, "Johann Müntzinger, ein schwäbischer Theologe und Schulmeister am Ende des 14. Jahrhunderts," *Geisteswelt des Mittelalters*, 3 vols.,

attend some of these schools (as well as some *studia generalia*).[4] A bishop could put a mendicant lecturer to work on his clergy; a city council might push for the acquisition of a good convent lecturer.[5] Good schools grace the town.[6] Although provincial schools seem always to have remained small, about three to twelve students, education maintained its own prestige, and the application of scholastic finesse to the sources and problems of spirituality and a public ministry would confirm the students' sense of the importance of their religious roles in public life.[7] Johannes probably spent the normal three years in such a school.

Supplement vol. 3 of BGPTM [Münster: Aschendorf, 1935], 2:1200-30) and the late thirteenth-century *Tabula utriusque iuris* of the Franciscan lector, Johannes of Erfurt (Bertrand Kurtscheid, "Die Tabula utriusque iuris des Johannes von Erfurt," *Franziskanische Studien*, 1[1914]:269-90; Norbert Brieskorn, *Die Summa confessorum des Johannes von Erfurt*, series 2, vol. 245 of *Europäische Hochschulschriften* [Frankfurt am Main: Peter D. Lang, 1980], 1:15-18). Heinrich of Friemar's exceedingly popular *Tractatus decem preceptorium* experienced later redactions that may be the work of convent lectors. Bertrand-Georges Guyot, "Quelques aspects de la typologie des commentaires sur le *Credo* et le *Décalogue*," *Les genres littéraires dans les sources théologiques et philosophiques médiévales. Définition, critique et exploitation* (Louvain-la-Neuve: Institut d'Études Médiévales de l'Université Catholique de Louvain, 1982), pp. 239-48, here 246. The revision of texts is also known for other, not strictly theological, literature, for example, a revision of Nicolaus of Eymerich's *Directorium inquisitoris* (1376) by a cantor and inquisitor of Cracow named Peter from the early fifteenth century. Wilhelm Wattenbach, "Über das Handbuch eines Inquisitors in der Kirchenbibliothek St. Nicolai in Greifswald," vol. 4 of *Abhandlungen der königlichen Akademie der Wissenschaften zu Berlin, philosophisch-historische Abhandlungen* (Berlin: Königliche Akademie der Wissenschaften, 1889), pp. 1-28, here 4. The Dominicans more closely modeled their provincial schools of theology after the university and normally staffed them with a teacher to lecture and perform disputations, a lecturer of the *Sentences*, and a master of students. See the acts mentioned in note 30, page 15, above.

[4]Verger, "*Studia*," p. 190. Doelle, "Partikularstudium," p. 247. Elm, "Mendikantenstudium," pp. 602-05. A. Murray, "Archbishop and Mendicants in Thirteenth-Century Pisa," *Stellung und Wirksamkeit*, p. 67. Dieter Berg, *Armut und Wissenschaft*, p. 113. Kurtscheid, "Tabula," p. 270. Cf. Schmidt, *Bettelorden*, pp. 319-20, who found no evidence of this in Trier.

[5]Zumkeller, *Schriftum*, p. 3. A. Herzig, "Die Beziehung der Minoriten zum Bürgertum im Mittelalter. Zur Kirchenpolitik der Städte im Zeitalter des Feudalismus." *Die alte Stadt*, 6(1979):46.

[6]Hartmut Kugler, *Die Vorstellung der Stadt in der Literatur des deutschen Mittelalters* (Munich and Zürich: Artemis Verlag, 1986), pp. 157-60. Johannes of Hildesheim, Epp. 38, 50. Hendricks, ed., "A Register of Letters and Papers of John of Hildesheim, O.Carm (d. 1375)," *Carmelus* 4(1957), pp. 207-08, 225-28. Consider also Nicholaus of Bibra's indictment of mendicant students, *Carmen satiricum*, edited by Theobald Fischer, vol. 1 of *Geschichtsquellen der Provinz Sachsen und angrenzender Gebiete* (Halle: Waisenhaus, 1870), pp. 91-92 (which points, if with their infamy, to their prominence).

[7]The most complete data on school size exist for the Dominicans. See the acts referred to in n. 30, page 15, above, which often include the names of all the students studying in a convent. The data lends a first impression of remarkable inconsistency in enrollment, much like university matriculations. The latter have been subjected to painstaking statistical analysis with good and interesting results, and the methods applied there might help make better sense of enrollments in Dominican schools, as well. Rainer Christoph Schwinges, *Deutsche Universitätsbesucher im 14. und 15. Jahrhundert. Studien zur Sozialgeschichte des Alten Reiches*, vol. 123 of *Veröffentlichungen des Instituts für Europäische Geschichte Mainz, Abteilung Universalgeschichte* (Wiesbaden: Franz Steiner, 1986), esp. pp. 61-220.

If he began his philosophical and theological education just after entering the order (which is most likely) in 1346, about 1349 Johannes was chosen by his province or by its current provincial, Jordan of Quedlinburg, to study in a general school of the order. The Black Death may have caused him some months delay or perhaps discouraged an assignment to a distant part of the continent.[8] There is no known record of the act. Johannes once said that "in my time" a man at Strasbourg believed his sins were unforgivable.[9] He must have meant that he learned of this while living in Strasbourg. Perhaps he studied at the general school there.[10] If on the other hand, he was sent to a more distant

---

[8]For Jordan, Kunzelmann, *Geschichte*, 5:332. For the plague in Germany, Peter Moraw, *Von offener Verfassung zu gestalteter Verdichtung: das Reich im späten Mittelalter, 1250 bis 1490*, vol. 3 of *Propyläen Geschichte Deutschlands* (Berlin: Propyläen Verlag, 1985), pp. 264-66, 444 (bibliography). The general chapter of 1351 allowed students to study at a general school of their own province. Ypma, *La formation*, p. 155. The required minimum period of study in a provincial school was three years; the complaints of general chapters, however, imply that students tended to move before the three years were completed. The required minimum, therefore, was probably, in practice, more often the longest time students would stay. Ibid., pp. 148, 149 (general chapters of 1326 and 1338).

[9]Johannes recalled this in the *expositio literalis* of Peter Lombard's *Sentences*, which I will later argue was composed during his magisterium at Oxford and later revised. For the versions of the commentary see Trapp, "Notes." The exposition on book two of the Lombard exists in three manuscripts (see the Bibliography), one of which preserves an earlier version of the commentary on book two, Siena, Biblioteca Comunale, G.V. 16 (also indicated in this study with the sign 'S'). The Siena manuscript appears to be the work of a general school lecturer (so Trapp, which opinion I will be compelled to follow). The remaining two manuscripts that contain the commentary on II *Sent.*, Klosterneuburg Stiftsbibliothek Ms. 304 (K) and Erfurt Wissenschaftliche Allgemeinbibliothek Amplon. F. 117 (E2) and Amplon. Q. 118 (E1), preserving the magisterial exposition (to be discussed in due course), contain the story of the Strasbourg man at II *Sent.*, d. 43, where Klenkok defines the sin against the Holy Spirit (Mt. 12.31) as not merely perseverance in a mortal sin, but the belief that God's mercy is not sufficient to forgive such a sin. That sin is attributed to Cain (Ge. 4.13). This is the text of E1 (f. 96rb) with variants from E2 (f. 29vb) and K (f. 133r) noted after:

> Et temporibus meis quidam homo apud Argentinam similis[a] conceptus fuit, cui cumque fratres et religiosi et alij dicebant de Dei misericordia, semper respondit quod sciret se esse dampnandum propter peccata sua, nec Deus miseriturus esset sui. Custodiat nos Deus a tali concepto.

> meis] audiui quod *add* K. similis] silens K. fuit] habuit K. cui cumque] quicumque K. fratres] *om* E2, K. et] *om* K. dicebant] dicerent E2. quod sciret] *om* K. se] *om* E2. a tali] consimili K.

> a. i.e. like Cain.

[10]A general school there is first mentioned at the general chapter of 1306. AA 3(1909-1910):55. Kunzelmann, *Geschichte*, 2:18-19. There were general schools relatively close at Erfurt, in Klenkok's own province (founded after 1300 and certainly operating at the time; Kunzelmann, *Geschichte*, 5:13-15; Overmann, *Urkunden*, 3:61 no. 79) and at Cologne in the neighboring province of Cologne and Belgium (founded in 1290 and certainly operative at the time; Kunzelmann, op. cit., 1:157, 251; 4:9-10; AA 3[1909-1910]:55). Evidence for a general school at Magdeburg (in Klenkok's Saxon-Thuringian province) is known for the period from 1320 to 1341 (Zumkeller, *Urkunden*, 1:52; Kunzelmann, op. cit., 5:107; 4:50; Overmann, op. cit., 3:23, 29; Kunzelman, op. cit., 5:108), but then not again until 1390 (Kunzelmann, op. cit., 5:110-11).

province, Bologna was a favored destination.[11] A few years later, while commenting on the first book of *Sentences*, he did mention that he had been in Italy (without disclosing the time, place, or purpose), where a Franciscan lector of Paris reported that he had heard a Parisian woman preach about how she learned that God is everywhere: she went throughout her house and asked if God were there, and in each place a voice answered, "I am here" (he tells the story in support of a theological argument without amusement, clearly respecting the beguine preacher).[12] And a few years after that, Johannes referred to snake handlers at Bologna in a way suggesting that he was an eyewitness.[13]

Although the passage referring to the Parisian beguine has been taken as evidence of a Bolognese education and although the reference to Bolognese snake handlers may seem to confirm this, neither reference offers positive evidence that Klenkok lived or studied in that city. An Italian education can be ruled out on other grounds. Two decades later, Johannes named a Saxon Augustinian (with whom he then found himself in bitter conflict) as his teacher: Rudolf Block. Block went to Paris about 1359, read the

---

[11]The prior general's student assignments (i.e. those exceeding the ordinary privilege of 1 to 3 students [see n. 19, below] per general school from each province) of the neighboring province of Cologne to *studia generalia* provide the best available evidence: 0 students to Brouges, 0 to Mainz, 1 to Erfurt, 1 to Vienna, 2 to Strasbourg, 4 to Prague, 13 to Padua, 20 to Rimini, and 50 to Bologna (assignments to other *studia*, like Paris and Oxford, may, for the present purpose, be excluded). There was a clear preference to send students away from Germany. Teeuwen and de Meijer, "Documents," passim.

[12]I *Sent.* d. 14. The passage is quoted from three manuscripts of Klenkok's commentary on the *Sentences* by Damasus Trapp, "Notes," pp. 384, 389. I checked the passage against the fourth extant manuscript, which Trapp was not able to examine, and found the text to be the same. Erfurt, Wissenschaftliche Allgemeinbibliothek, Amplon. Ms. 117, f. 8rb. Because in another instance Klenkok referred to a Bologna burial custom (IV *Sent.*, d. 45, cited by Trapp, loc. cit., p. 385), Trapp concluded that Klenkok's Italian sojourn was in that city, which he further took as strong evidence that Klenkok studied there. Trapp also suggested that the Franciscan or presumably Franciscan lector was Friedrich of Regensburg (alias Francis of Ratisbon), who allegedly studied at Bologna as well as Paris and Oxford and who cited Klenkok's *Sentences* commentary (ibid., p. 384, note). He believed that Friedrich and Klenkok were associates at Oxford. William Courtenay has recently challenged Trapp's association of Friedrich with Oxford, his identification as a Franciscan, and his personal contact with Klenkok, which leaves the identity of the anonymous Franciscan lector in the dark. William J. Courtenay, "Friedrich von Regensburg and Fribourg Cordeliers 26," *Die Philosophie im 14. und 15. Jahrhundert. In Memoriam Konstanty Michalski (1879-1947)*, vol. 10 of *Bochumer Studien zur Philosphie* (Amsterdam: B. R. Grüner, 1988), pp. 603-13 (Prof. Courtenay kindly provided me with a pre-publication copy of the essay, for which I am grateful).

[13]In his *Postilla* on Ac. 28.3, where the apostle Paul is struck by a viper, Eichstätt 204, f. 191rb-191va:

vippera. Genus serpentis, de cuius proprietatibus uide Bartholomeum et Plinium. Ex hoc hodie quidam apparuerunt qui uipperas et serpentes sine lesione contractant, et alios docent quod hoc facere ualent, et tales se[a] dicunt de generi beati Pauli, sicut in Bononia plures uidi. Ysidorus xii. *Ethimologiarum*[b] dicit, uippera dicitur quasi ui pariens, quia pulli corrodunt uiscera matris in partu, et mater interficit patrem in coitu.
    a. *corr* se! b. Isidorus, *Etym.* xii.10, PL 82:443.

Sentences, and became master of theology in 1363 on the initiative of his prior general and the appointment of Pope Urban V.[14] Documents pertaining to his first assignment and to his promotion mention that Block had been teaching at general schools in Germany for years, but of that early part of his career, we know only that he was a lector at Magdeburg in 1341.[15] The Magdeburg school may have been closed shortly after that year, for nothing is known of it for another half century (note 10, above), and no evidence exists to suggest where Block may have gone, if the Magdeburg school did close (the closest alternative general school, at Erfurt, was probably occupied by other lectors); but he must have remained in Germany.[16] Johannes himself became master at Oxford in 1359, and therefore he could only have been a student of Block's at a school somewhere in Germany before either of them had entered a university.[17] Johannes Klenkok studied in a general school somewhere in Germany. As for the two references to Italy, Johannes, as we shall see, later became a Parisian bachelor, and it is quite possible that he knew the Franciscan lector from that time, in which case his Italian sojourn, where he could then have met his acquaintance, occurred well after his studies in a general school. As for the snake handlers, Klenkok might have visited Bologna before or after becoming an Augustinian for any number of reasons, and the spectacle would

---

[14]CUP 3:197, 122, no. 1284, 1299. Klenkok, *Decadicon*, ed. Scheidt in *Biblioteca*, a. 21, p. 96: "doctor meus Rudolfus Block." Contrast his earlier edition of the treatise to bishop Albert of Halberstadt: "pater meus Rudolfus Block, doctor et magister." B. J. L. De Geer, "Klenkok's Decadicon," *Nieuwe Bijdragen voor Rechtsgeleerdheid en Wetgeving*, 18(1882):367-409, here 407. A personalized title does not necessarily indicate a personal relation. For example, Klenkok also called Gregory of Rimini "magister meus" in his *Questio in canonice beati Johannis* delivered at Oxford (Oxford, Bodleian, Hamilton Ms. 33, f. 258ra) which corresponds to his indebtedness to the writings of Gregory, thus indicating an intellectual propinquity that is evident throughout Klenkok's work. Gregory was famous; such a claim made sense. Block was not famous, and no such intellectual indebtedness to Block is evident in Klenkok's writings. The title indicates a sense of familiarity with Block and suggests an actual relation between the two.

[15]E. Ypma, "Notice sur le 'studium' de Paris au cours de la deuxième moitié du quatorzième siècle," *Augustiniana*, 17(1967):14-36, here 33-34. CUP 3:107 no. 1284.

[16]24 July 1350, "Johannes et Conradus lectores" (perhaps also "Henricus et Bruno"), listed in a 20-pound donation of capital to the Erfurt cloister by Heinrich of Friemar, from which he was to receive annually two pounds interest until he died. Overmann, *Urkunden*, 3:61 no. 79.

[17]Bütow, with evidence only of Block's promotion to master, drew the same conclusion. "Lebensgeschichte," pp. 544-48. Trapp thought Klenkok studied at the general school in Prague, but he overlooked Klenkok's relation to Block. "Notes," p. 360, cautiously followed by A. Zumkeller, *Erbsünde*, p. 22. There is no evidence to support this supposition, and a conspicuous lack of evidence for Rudolf Block as lector there. Jaroslav Kadlec, *Das Augustinerkloster Sankt Thomas in Prag vom Gründungsjahr 1285 bis zu den Hussitenkriegen, mit Edition seines Urkundenbuches*, vol. 36 of *Cassiciacum* (Würzburg: Augustinus-Verlag, 1985), pp. 52-57 (although Kadlec accepts Trapp's supposition, as well as the claim that Klenkok studied canon law at Bologna).

be an attraction for anyone on tour. Knowledge of this certainly does not mark him as a Bolognese intimate.

An Augustinian general school employed two lecturers: a *lector principalis* to comment on the Bible, to conduct disputations on philosophical subjects he deemed appropriate, and to lecture on a book of the arts; and a *lector secundarius* to lecture on philosophy and to comment on Peter Lombard's *Sentences*—two books per year, four books biennially. Each normally delivered two lectures a day.[18] The students, who hailed from twenty-four provinces of the Augustinian Order, usually pursued, for two or three years, a course that roughly corresponded to the more rigorous six years of hearing lectures required of secular students at Paris before admittance as bachelors of the Bible.[19] The writings of lecturers betray practical biases. As *professor sacre paginis* in Erfurt, Heinrich of Friemar wrote a famous commentary on the ten commandments and a treatise on the celebration of the mass; as *lector principalis* in Erfurt, Jordan of Quedlinburg interpreted the gospel of Matthew and wrote a treatise on the Lord's Prayer derived from the lectures, and as lector in Magdeburg, he composed sermons for the liturgical year.[20] The standard Lombard and Bible were also supplemented with lectures on moral and legal casuistry—the administration of penance and the cure of souls, handled theologically and canonistically.[21] Lecturers were polymaths

---

[18]Ypma, *La formation*, pp. 152, 155, 156.

[19]Venício Marcolino, "Der Augustinertheologe an der Universität," *Gregor von Rimini. Werk und Wirkung bis zur Reformation* (Berlin and New York: Walter de Gruyter, 1981), pp. 127-94, here 131-41, 144-45. The general chapter of 1338 stipulated a five-year maximum attendance at a general school, which Ypma mistakenly took as the norm. Ypma, *La formation*, pp. 39, 152 (cf. Marcolino, for the corrections). For the number of provinces, A. Zumkeller, "Augustiner-Eremiten," TRE 4:730. Each province could originally send three students to each general school (general chapter of 1295, which established the first general schools outside of Paris; Ypma, *La formation*, p. 150); Thomas of Strasbourg reduced the number to one student of each province to each general school, excepting the province of France, which could send seven students to the general school at Paris. Additional students required approval of the prior general. Ypma, "Notice," p. 14.

[20]Clemens Stroick, *Heinrich von Friemar. Leben, Werke, philosophisch-theologische Stellung in der Scholastik*, vol. 68 of *Freiburger theologische Studien* (Freiburg: Herder, 1954), pp. 12-20, 34, 38, 59. Jordanus de Saxonia, *Liber vitasfratrum*, ed. R. Arbesmann, W. Hümpfner, American series vol. 1 of *Cassiciacum* (New York: Cosmopolitan Science and Art Service Co., 1943), pp. xxx, xxxi. Zumkeller, *Manuskripte*, pp. 125-63 no. 285-337.

[21]Leonard E. Boyle, "The *Summa confessorum* of John of Freiburg and the Popularization of the Moral Teaching of St. Thomas and of Some of his Contemporaries," *St. Thomas Aquinas, 1274-1974. Commemorative Studies*, ed. A. A. Maurer, et al., vol. 2 (Toronto: Pontifical Institute of Mediaeval Studies, 1974), pp. 245-68, reprinted in Boyle, *Pastoral Care, Clerical Education, and Canon Law* (London: Variorum, 1981), no. 3. Kurtscheid in n. 3, above. The most prevalent handbooks of canon law in Germany were composed by the Franciscans Johann of Erfurt, Heinrich of Merseburg, and Astenasius, the Dominican Johann of Freiburg, and the Augustinian Heinrich of Friemar. These were frequently supplemented with marginal additions, revised, and incorporated into other editions, changes which largely reflect their use in convents and convent schools. Emil Seckel, *Beiträge zur Ge-*

of divinity; students learned the abstractions that produced the substance of their religious identity and its ambitious program to manage the world as a house of God, while gaining some acquaintance with the codices, their tables and formularies, that made the work doable. They also copied books, either for themselves or for the libraries of their future convents.[22] They openly displayed their progress in sermons and disputations; responses in disputation measured the students' ability; a final examination before the general chapter or an appointed examiner tested them in logic, philosophy, and theology and determined whether the title of lector should be conferred.[23]

It may be assumed that Johannes passed through quickly, which was common, in a mere two years, with an eye to a university and eagerly assembling material for his own baccalaureate.[24] The plague may have depleted the order of teachers, hastening promotions and appointments of new lectors to schools.[25] If so,

---

schichte beider Rechte im Mittelalter, vol. 1, *Zur Geschichte der populären Literatur des römisch-kanonischen Rechts* (Tübingen: J. C. B. Mohr, 1898; reprinted Hildesheim: Georg Olms, 1967), passim. Ferdinand Doelle, "Die Rechtsstudien der deutschen Franziskaner im Mittelalter und ihre Bedeutung für die Rechtsentwicklung der Gegenwart," *Geisteswelt des Mittelalters*, 2:1037-64. Handbooks were glossed as convent lectures; e.g. a "Glossa super poeniteas cum reportatis lectis bonis lecta per Meinhardum sublectorem in Erfordia" (so, the explicit), Stadtbibliothek Mainz, Hs. I. 166, ff. 90v-98r. Sometimes the original was, thereby, rendered unrecognizable; e.g. the *Summa juris canonici* of Heinrich of Merseburg (frequently revised, Seckel, op. cit., pp. 199, 262-63, 332, 334; no. 171, 119), completely reworked by an anonymous lector, in Stadtbibliothek Mainz, Hs. II. 330, ff. 1r-59v. The lector explained his method (f. 3r):

> Cum summam Heinrici fratribus legerem, et quosdam casus lectioni intersererem quos textus eiusdem summule non habebat, fratres multi modis precibus ac[a] importunis instancijs me rogauerunt ut eosdem casus uerbis breuibus ac simplicibus annodarem, ad quos fratres simplices pro expediendis pluribus prolixitatibus uerterent, qui non possent se ad confitentes sibi in lacera silua de iure canonico aliquid expedire.
> a. *corr* et.

Heinrich of Friemar also wrote a *Tractatus de poenitentia*, which may have originated as convent lectures. Stroick, *Heinrich*, pp. 71-73. For the idea of the compatibility of theology and canon law and its origins, see Herbert Kalb, "Bemerkungen zum Verhältnis von Theologie und Kanonistik am Beispiel Rufins und Stephans von Tournai," ZRG, KA 72(1986):338-48.

[22]Zumkeller, *Manuskripte*, pp. 105, 110, 116, 123, 125, 179, 215, 220, 233, 244, 330, 347, 349, 350, 352; no. 222, 237, 254, 278, 279, 284, 376, 448, 463, 467, 485, 514, 684, 747, 748, 752, 755, 762.

[23]For the assignment of examiners, Ypma, *La formation*, p. 151 (general chapter of 1318). General chapters of 1338, 1341, and 1345 reasserted the need for sufficient knowledge of logic, philosophy, and theology before promotion to lector; the chapter of 1345 and Thomas of Strasbourg's additions insisted that students not be exempted from the required disputations and sermons; ibid., pp. 154-55. There were also friars who made fraudulent claims to having attained academic degrees and official positions. Ibid., p. 152 (French provincial chapters of 1329 and 1330).

[24]Marcolino, "Augustinertheologe," pp. 148ff., for pre-university preparation of baccalaureate lectures.

[25]Franz Roth, "Deutsche Generalkapitel," *Cor Unum*, 12/1 (1954):18-22, esp. 19, for allowance of the reception of illiterate novices at the general chapter of 1351; similar concessions may have been made at various stages of the educational program. The best evidence for such hastening of students through degrees exists for the Dominicans, who

Johannes may have acquired the rank of lector prematurely, after as little as a year of study, but he is perhaps more likely to have withstood his final examination in 1351 or 1352—whether at the general chapter held at Basel over Pentecost in 1351, before the general prior, or before an examiner in Saxony is impossible to determine.[26] He would then be assigned to teach in a provincial school or as *lector secundarius* in a general school. The latter seems to have been the case, for part of an early redaction of his commentary on the *Sentences* is still preserved in a manuscript of Siena. It must have been composed before Johannes went to university, and it therefore shows that he then performed the task that most properly belonged to the *lector secundarius* of a general school, but no evidence suggests where it might have been.[27] He anticipated an appointment to a university. In the early redaction, he churned out a thorough literal exposition of the text, with an eye toward 'classical' sources, like the *Glossa ordinaria* to the Bible, Augustine, Ambrose, and of course, the Lombard, deriving patristic references from the canon law (he, like other mendicant theologians, used one of the numerous canonistic handbooks for his references). Although he would soon exploit university libraries to check his references against the original sources and to amplify his uses of them, his most mature exposition of the *Sentences* attempted to improve the work of his intellectual youth, not supersede it.[28] He laid his foundations in a general school.

---

after the plague, energetically attempted to increase their number of scholars. Benedictus Maria Reichert, *Acta capitulorum generalium ordinis praedicatorum*, 3 vols. (Rome: Typographia polyglotta s. c. de propaganda fidei, 1898-1900), 2:349-50 (general chapter of 1353). Consider also W. J. Courtenay, "The Effect of the Black Death on English Higher Education," *Speculum*, 55(1980):696-714, esp. 707 and 713, for university evidence and for the loss of parish teachers in England.

[26]If he was promoted after a year, he may be the lector Johannes mentioned in n. 16, above. The acts of the general chapter of Basel of 1351 contain no allusion to his promotion (AA 4[1911/12]:276-78); the register of Thomas of Strasbourg, prior general at the time, is not extant; no names of Saxon examiners appointed by general chapter or general prior for this period are known.

[27]Siena, Biblioteca Comunale, G.V.16, ff. 20v-35v. Trapp drew this very reasonable conclusion. "Notes," p. 366, followed by Zumkeller, "Erbsünde," p. 23.

[28]This observation is based upon a comparison of II *Sent.* dd. 4, 29, and 44 in the *redactio lectoris* (S, ff. 23ra-23rb, 31rb-31va, 35va) with the same distinctions in the magisterial exposition (E1, ff. 87va-88ra, 97vb-98ra, 107va-107vb; E2, f. 15vb, 23ra, 29vb-30ra; K, f. 98r-98v, 117r-117v, 133r-133v). In all his commentaries on the *Sentences*, Johannes used the handbooks and glosses of canonists for accessing the canon law; in the second and third editions of his *Decadicon*, written later in life, he cited Johannes of Freiburg's *Summa confessorum*, which shows that he used at least one popular handbook, as well. John Baconthorpe is the best studied fourteenth-century theologian to have used handbooks extensively. De Geer, "Klenkok's," p. 27. Scheidt, *Decadicon*, pp. 79, 86. Walter Ullmann, "John Baconthorpe as Canonist," *Church and Government in the Middle Ages: Essays Presented to C. R. Cheney on His Seventieth Birthday* (Cambridge: Cambridge University Press, 1976), pp. 223-46; reprinted in Ullmann, *Scholarship in the Middle Ages* (London: Variorum, 1978),

Johannes was soon chosen to study at a university. Since he was eventually promoted to *magister* at Oxford (3 August 1359), his best biographers have concluded that he was assigned as a bachelor there.[29] In fact, evidence confirms that such an assignment was made but not carried out according to plan. The general chapter of Perugia, in 1354, assigned a Johannes of Saxony and a Dionysius of Milan to read the *Sentences* at Oxford.[30] Since Johannes was of the Saxon-Thuringian province, should have begun his baccalaureate about that time, and had to be approved and assigned as his order's contribution to a particular university by the general chapter, it is safe to assume that he is the Saxon mentioned here, even though "Johannes" was a terribly common name. According to a letter of Gregory of Rimini, prior general, of 17 June 1358, Johannes and Dionysius were unable to begin their lectures, because the English province filled their places with local candidates. Gregory complained that it had happened before, and in this year, 1358, a proxy for Dionysius of Milan (apparently no longer able to begin himself) appointed by Gregory's predecessor, Thomas of Strasbourg (who died the previous year), was still unable to assume his proper place.[31]

---

no. 10. Beryl Smalley, "John Baconthorpe's Postill on St. Matthew," *Medieval and Renaissance Studies*, 4 (1958):91-115, reprinted in eadem, *Studies in Medieval Thought and Learning* (London: The Hambleton Press, 1981), pp. 289-343. Ernst Borchert, *Die quaestiones speculativae et canonicae des Johannes Baconthorpe über den Sakramentalen Charakter*, new series vol. 9 of *Veröffentlichungen des Grabmann-Instituts* (Munich: Schöningh, 1974). Boyle, "Summa," pp. 263-64.

[29]Trapp discovered the date of promotion in an explicit to Klenkok's III *Sent.*, "Notes," pp. 360, 400 (his conjecture about the text's origin as a marginal note is somewhat plausible, but by no means certain). Trapp correctly deduced a baccalaureate beginning 1354. Bütow also placed the baccalaureate at Oxford, but with conjectural dates that have proved about five years too late. "Lebensgeschichte," pp. 545-52.

[30]The text has not been preserved in the extant acts of that general chapter (AA 4[1911/ 12]:307-10) but in a letter of 1358 written by the current prior general, Gregory of Rimini, to the English prior provincial. AA 5(1913-1914):124-26, here 124-25: "Item, diffinimus, quod infrascripti fratres mittantur ad Angliam et eo citius quo poterunt, sine preiudicio eorum, quos ad Sententias licentiarunt dicte provincie universitates, ad lecturam Sententiarum promoveantur secundum ordinem quo hic nominantur, videlicet: fratres Ioannes de Saxonia et Dyonisius de Mediolano, Oxonie; fratres Galvanus de Padua et Gerardus Aymerici, Cantabrigie, etc."

This identification was once suggested by Francis Roth, but Adolar Zumkeller, assuming that the entire baccalaureate was at Oxford, dismissed the identification without further consideration. Zumkeller, *Erbsünde*, p. 22, n. 71. Bachelors' lectures lasted one year (W. J. Courtenay, *Adam Wodeham: An Introduction to His Life and Writings*, vol. 21 of *Studies in Medieval and Reformation Thought* [Leiden: E. J. Brill, 1978], p. 175), hence Klenkok was to read 1354/55 and Dionysius, 1355/56.

[31]Ibid., pp. 123-24: "Post hec [i.e. definitionem capituli generalis Perusia celebrati] vero frater Andreas de Mediolano per venerabilis memorie fratrem Thomam predecessorem nostrum prenominato Dyonisio fuerit subrogatus ad dictam lecturam pro eis loco, tempore et ordine, pro quibus dictus frater Dyonisius extiterat diffinitus, consequens esse constat, quod sicut predicti fratres Iohannes et Dyonisius non potuerunt de iure Sententias

In the meanwhile, it seems that Johannes went to Paris. Johannes once recalled very clearly the recantation of a Parisian bachelor that occurred "in my time"; the bachelor was a fellow Augustinian, and the event made a strong impression on Johannes, for he referred to the withdrawn doctrines at least three times in his magisterial lectures at Oxford.[32] The recantation occurred in May 1354, which suggests that either Johannes had

---

Oxonie legere cum preiudicio illorum, qui ante tempus dicte diffinitionis fuerant ad huiusmodi lecturam per dictam provinciam ordinati, ita nec post dictam diffinitionem potuerunt aliqui alii ad legendum ibidem Sententias ante fratrem Andream per dictam provinciam deputari."

Gregory then insists that, on pain of excommunication, Andreas be given his due. See also the letters to the provincial prior and to Andreas of Milan of 20 January 1358, ibid. Andreas will later appear in a reference to a conflict with another Augustinian master, Giovanni of Piacenza, from the general chapter of 1371. AA 4(1911/12):475.

[32]II *Sent.* d. 42 (I reproduce E1, f. 95va-95vb, with variant readings from E2, f. 29rb, and K, f. 132r-132v, noted at the end):

Osbertus autem quidam doctor uniuersitatis nostre, scilicet Oxonie, posuit quod quodlibet peccatum, per quod peccans non crederet se amissurum gratiam Dei, esset ueniale . . . Ymo unus baccalarius tempore meo fuit Parysius coactus reuocare illius positionis conclusiones in ista materia, unde caute est ambulandum. De istis autem dante Deo scribam plenius in questionibus super isto secundo.

Osbertus] Ospertus E2. autem quidam] *om* K. scilicet] legit Sentencias K. Dei] *om* E2. Ymo] *om* E2. fuit Parysius] Parisius fuit E2. illius positionis conclusiones] conclusiones illius positionis K. ista materia unde] illa materia bonum K, illa materia unde E2. caute est] est causa K. ambulandum] abulandum E1, abulandi K. dante] date K. in questionibus super isto secundo] isto secundo in questionibus K.

Trapp also noted this passage and two others that refer to the errors, in I *Sent.* d. 1 and IV *Sent.* d. 14, and although he correctly identified the opinion referred to in I *Sent.* d. 1 and IV *Sent.* d. 14 as that of the Augustinian Guido who recanted at Paris 16 May 1354 (CUP 3:21-23 no. 1218), he did not seem to realize that II *Sent.* d. 42, quoted here, also refers to the same person. Thus he incorrectly conjectured that the anonymous bachelor mentioned in II *Sent.* d. 42 was a disciple of Osbert, and he overlooked Klenkok's unmistakable allusion to have been at Paris about the time of the recantation. "Notes," pp. 388, 400; idem, "Augustinian Theology of the Fourteenth Century," *Augustiniana*, 6(1956):227-28. Nothing, apart from coincidence of ideas, associates the anonymous bachelor with Osbert, an Oxford Carmelite whose relationship to Paris is tenuous, at best (BRO 3:1481). Guido actually set his doctrine against a Carmelite bachelor (CUP 3:22) who, if Osbert had first been a Paris bachelor, actually could have been Osbert before going to Oxford to become a master; but consider also the anonymous Carmelite mentioned by Johannes de Falisca, P. Glorieux, "Jean de Falisca. La formation d'un maître en théologie au quatorzième siècle," *Archives d'histoire doctrinale et littéraire du moyen age*, 33(1966):23-104, here 84, 89. In any event, Klenkok raises the condemnation of Guido in order to mark the boundaries of an acceptable argument against Osbert, by referring to what was actually Guido's failed attempt to nail the Carmelite (although, at I *Sent.* d. 1, he thought the Parisian judgment might be fallacious; Trapp, "Notes," p. 388, which produces the text from E1, K, and S, and which I checked against E2, unavailable to Trapp, and found to be substantially the same). Trapp's further identification of the bachelor with Albertus Ranconis de Ericinio, who he suggests was a student of Osbert at Paris, does not correspond with Albertus' biography (he became bachelor of theology only c. 1363). Cf. Jaroslav Kadlec, *Leben und Schriften des Prager Magisters Adalbert Rankonis de Ericinio*, new series vol. 4 of BGPTM (Münster: Aschendorff, 1971), pp. 1-10, esp. 6. According to Charles du Plessis d'Argentré, a similar question was raised by a Franciscan named Amand of Valenciennes in 1350 in a disputation entitled "De peccato ueniali aliqua," which he found in the library of the Sorbonne. C. du Plessis d'Argentré, *Collectio judiciorum de novis erroribus*, 3 vols. (Paris: Andreas Cailleau, 1728), 1:334 (where the disputation is associated with the aftermath of the radical Scotism of Jean de Ripa—his date for Ripa, 1350, is off by two decades).

gone to Paris before his official appointment to Oxford or shortly thereafter, when the embarrassment of the affair remained rife (the latter would presuppose an almost immediate discovery that the English had filled the vacancy reserved for Johannes; conceivably, the stolen vacancy could have been admitted by the English *definitor* at the chapter itself, soon after the passage of the act appointing Johannes and Dionysius or soon after the conclusion of the meeting).[33]

The general chapter of 1354 appointed Johannes as bachelor of the *Sentences*, the first Oxonian degree. Apparently, he was expected to pass through both baccalaureates (of the *Sentences* and of the Bible), and so, presumably, he would now begin with the first Parisian degree in theology as bachelor of the Bible.[34] Appointments were made six months before the beginning of tenure to allow time for preparation, so we may assume that Johannes was in Paris in the late spring, was examined by four doctors for admission as a *baccalaurius biblicus*, and delivered his *principium* at the opening of the next academic year.[35] Unlike their commentaries on the *Sentences*, bachelors seldom preserved their early exegetical works, which reproduced the most standard glosses in a marathon-like attempt to cover as much as half a Bible in a mere nine months.[36] The normal course also required providing a response in a disputation and two occasional lectures (*collationes*) or one lecture and a sermon.[37] This conceivably could be accomplished by the end of the year, if the bachelor had come to Paris well prepared, as the friars usually did. We would, then, expect that Johannes was ready to advance to *sententiarius* in the fall of 1355.

---

[33]A papal bull of Innocent VI dated 1355 restricts Augustinian promotions to the grade of master to the universities of Paris, Oxford, and Cambridge. AA 5(1914):97-98. The tenor of the bull suggests the difficulty of controlling the mendicant students, so that it may not be surprising for Klenkok to have gone to Paris even without proper authorization (although it remains uncertain when, precisely, he would have gone there).

[34]At Paris, biblical lectures (of bachelors and masters) preceded lectures on the *Sentences*, although appointments directly to *Sententiarius* were possible and, among the mendicant orders, fairly common. Marcolino, "Augustinertheologe," pp. 136-41. At Oxford, a bachelor of divinity lectured one to two years on the *Sentences* and then one year on the Bible. A. G. Little, *The Grey Friars in Oxford*, vol. 20 of *Oxford Historical Society* (Oxford, 1892), pp. 42ff.

[35]H. Rashdall, F. M. Powicke, A. B. Emden, *The Universities of Europe*, 3 vols., revised edition (Oxford: Oxford University Press, 1936), 1:474-75.

[36]Secular bachelors, however, lectured on the entire Bible over two consecutive years. Friars were originally required to lecture two years over the entire Bible. The time was reduced to one year, but successive bachelors were to cooperate with their predecessors, so that the entire Bible could be presented over any two-year period. See Marcolino, "Augustinertheologe," pp. 131-41. Nothing is known of Klenkok's lectures as *baccalaureus biblicus*.

[37]Ibid., pp. 131-36. Cf. Rashdall, *Universities*, pp. 476-77.

The common practice in the Augustinian Order allowed bachelors one year in Paris before beginning lectures on the Lombard—a time to rake the libraries and taste better the current academic culture in public lectures and disputations.[38] Friars with ambitions to the master's book and ring would feel pressure to impress with clever, orthodox arguments. The lectures were delivered over the brief course of an academic year, and accordingly, only select pieces of the *Sentences* were treated in an analysis of questions and alternative solutions.[39] Johannes is likely to have prepared for his lectures in 1355/56 and to have delivered them in 1356/57. The common practice of bachelors and the constraints of time apparently forced him to depart from the form of exposition he had previously begun in a general school: he presented, instead of a textual exposition, questions on the second book of *Sentences*.

The commentary has been discovered by Damasus Trapp in a manuscript which mistakenly attributed the work to a contemporary Augustinian, Facinus of Ast.[40] The Klenkok lectures made

---

[38]Marcolino, "Augustinertheologe," pp. 144, 145.

[39]The Augustinians received the privilege of reading the *Sentences* for only one year about 1340 (Franciscans and Dominicans had obtained it earlier); secular bachelors began the practice about 1350 (before which they lectured two years). Ibid., pp. 165-67. See also Courtenay, *Adam*, pp. 177-78, for Oxford.

[40]Eichstätt, Staatliche Bibliothek, Ms. 471, ff. 157v-186r. Trapp, "Notes," pp. 362, 363, 367-73. Zumkeller has, through additional comparisons of Klenkok's own citations of the work, confirmed Trapp's identification. *Erbsünde*, pp. 23-26. Trapp believed it represented magisterial lectures delivered at Prague around 1370, when Klenkok is frequently presumed to have been a master there (which I shall deny in due course). Zumkeller, on the basis of his comparisons of citations of the questions in Klenkok's own *Expositio litteralis in IV. libris Sententiarum*, concluded that the composition of the questions took place concurrently with that of the literal exposition. Since the literal exposition was composed at Oxford, the questions, Zumkeller concluded, should also have been composed at Oxford. This is a plausible but, it seems to me, ultimately unsatisfactory view. Zumkeller's evidence, to which I can add one more citation (at II *Sent.* d. 44, again referring to the subject matter of q. 25), may be summarized as follows (Zumkeller's citations may be found in op. cit., pp. 25-26; II *Sent.* d. 44 may be found in E1, f. 107va-107vb; E2, ff. 29vb-30ra; K, ff. 133v-134r). Two of the five citations are in the perfect tense, presupposing a previous completion of the questions, and three of the five citations are in the future tense, suggesting that they were incomplete; that is,

at	II *Sent.* d. 4,	q. 6	is incomplete
at	II *Sent.* d. 36,	q. 14	is complete
at	II *Sent.* d. 42,	q. 25	is incomplete
at	II *Sent.* d. 44,	q. 25	is incomplete
at	IV *Sent.* d. 26,	q. 13	is complete

If these citations represent a chronology of writing questions concurrently with the literal exposition, they manifest an odd one: that Johannes had hardly begun the questions at the beginning of his magisterial lectures on the second book of *Sentences*, had completed 14 questions by d. 36, had not reached the twenty-fifth question shortly after, at d. 42, but probably completed the entire enterprise by the middle of the fourth book of *Sentences*. He would, then, have maintained a terrific pace through the first 14 questions, but dropped off dramatically in the next questions (although qq. 14-25 are about the same length as the rest). It is even more difficult to imagine how a composition of questions on the second

some impression, for they not only proved to Augustinian supe-
riors his worthiness for magisterial recommendation, but they
also gained him a little notoriety: his obsession with the literal
text and traditional sources is reflected in his meticulous attention to a comprehensive and thoroughly cross-referenced view of
the Lombard's four books, supplemented with patristic and only
safe contemporary arguments, characteristics winsome enough
at Paris in the wake of the Mirecourt condemnations (1346,
1347).[41] An inquisitive Gerhard Groote, hearing lectures in Paris
before becoming bachelor of arts in 1357, apparently then learned
of Johannes and his definition of venial and mortal sins, treated
in questions 24 and 25 of Klenkok's *Questiones* (a subject made
acute by the trial and recantation of the Augustinian predecessor
noted earlier). Johannes will later expand this material to address
the arguments of an Oxford theologian and work through much
of the same material in his Oxonian lecture on the forty-second
distinction of the second book of *Sentences*.[42] From Deventer in

---

book simultaneous with a literal exposition of the four books would fit into the University
curriculum. Although perhaps possible, there is no apparent explanation for a decrease in
momentum or two simultaneous expositions. It is rather more likely that questions were
first composed at Paris and expanded at Oxford, then published in an expanded form (q.
6 appears to have been added in its entirety, and q. 25, either supplemented with the refutation of Osbert or added in its entirety—for this question, see also note 42, below). As
one may also see in the *Postilla* on Acts, Klenkok customarily added extensive cross references to his writings, and these suggest he revised texts for publication. This explanation better accounts for the prominence of Parisian judgments and theologians in the
questions. The British theologians, apart from Osbert, were Parisian favorites: Ockham,
Bradwardine, and Buckingham; Trapp, "Notes," pp. 378-81 (for the citations of British
theologians), and Courtenay, *Adam*, pp. 137ff., and idem, *Schools*, pp. 163-67 (for English
theology at Paris). Writing questions for bachelor's lectures also corresponded to the universal practice of theological bachelors. Marcolino, "Augustinertheologe," pp. 158-60.
Courtenay, *Adam*, pp. 177-78. And although Klenkok habitually referred to his other writings in most of his works, the questions (like the *redactio lectoris* of II *Sent.*) contain no
known cross references, strongly implying that they were written before his other works
(a reference to the *redactio lectoris*, however, would confirm that the questions are later
than it; at present, I know of none).

[41]Courtenay, *Adam*, pp. 135-40, for an excellent, brief description of Paris theology, 1349-
1364 (but following Trapp's view of Klenkok's Oxford baccalaureate). Questions 14, 18-20
have been edited by Zumkeller, *Erbsünde*, pp. 536-41, 507-30, and they provide a reliable
representation of the text. Klenkok refers, in q. 10, to the articles of Mirecourt condemned
by chancellor Robert of Bardis in 1347 (perhaps he felt especially convinced of their propriety for the role played by the Augustinian master, Ugolino of Orvieto, in Mirecourt's
condemnation). Trapp, "Notes," p. 379. CUP 2:432 n. 29, 61-14. For the *Questiones*, see also
the next footnote.

[42]For Groote at Paris, R. R. Post, *The Modern Devotion. Confrontation with Reformation and
Humanism*, vol. 3 of *Studies in Medieval and Reformation Thought* (Leiden: E. J. Brill, 1968), p.
98; CUP 3:92, 93 n. 31. Cf. A. G. Weiler, "Grote, Gerhard (1340-1384)," TRE 14:274-75.
Trapp's index of the questions treated in Klenkok's *Questiones super II Sent.*, lists q. 24 as
the final one (f. 183v-185r; "Notes," pp. 378-81). In actual fact, a twenty-fifth question is
contained in those folios and should be added to the list. It begins, at f. 184va, "Utrum
peccatum ueniale solum puniatur corporaliter, et arguitur quod non. Peccatum ueniale est

1378, Groote recommended Klenkok's doctrine of sin to Wilhelm Vroede, who was studying at Prague, and he tried to redress some problems that Vroede then raised from it.[43]

Nothing is known of Klenkok's fellow bachelors, the Augustinian master under whose supervision he lectured, preached, and disputed, or any other mendicant master in 1356/57. His lectures were probably preceded by those of the Augustinian recantor noted above—named only Guido in the record and tactfully ignored by later bachelors of his order (Klenkok's reference is the sole exception)—in 1353/54, and by those of the Augustinian, Rudolfo of Castello in 1355/56.[44] Master Jean of Hesdin, Hospitaler, who had left Paris in 1349 and returned sometime before 1362, might have been a regent at the time, yet nothing is known of this accomplished exegete's teaching at Paris between 1349 and 1362.[45] The Scotist, Jean of Ripa, who probably lectured as Franciscan bachelor in 1354/55, referred to Rudolfo of Castello; Klenkok must have been familiar with the Franciscan's intense application of terminist logic to epistemology and doctrines like the beatific vision, but he seems never to have cited the Fran-

---

in facte malicia, igitur in facte [sic] et eternaliter puniendum est . . . " This is the question containing the refutation of Osbert. Zumkeller followed Trapp's index and considered the Osbert passage part of q. 24 (Trapp's index of questions is otherwise accurate).

[43]Willelmus Mulder, ed., *Gerardi Magni epistolae*, vol. 3 of *Tekstuitgaven van Ons Geestelijk Erf* (Antwerp: Uitgever Neerlandia, 1933), pp. 17-22, Ep. 8. R. R. Post believed that Vroede learned of Klenkok in Prague and brought his work to Groote's attention. *Modern*, pp. 100-01, 109-10. The basis of the claim is the fact that the letter answers Vroede's queries (p. 20: "ut scribitis Clincok dixisse," said Groote). But Groote shows some familiarity with Klenkok's thought, and he likes it more than one would expect, had he known it only second hand (particularly attractive was Klenkok's use of Augustine [ibid., pp. 19, 20] and his defense of the view that a venial transgression performed by deliberate intention and in full knowledge of its sinfulness becomes a mortal sin [ibid., p. 19]). Since Groote's letters show that he assiduously guided Vroede's reading, it is better to assume that he had earlier recommended Klenkok's works, in which Vroede found problematic ideas and wrote to Groote about them; Groote sticks with his recommendation: "valde libenter viderem Clincok vel alium rationabiliter de hiis tractantem" (ibid., p. 22). Bütow took this letter as evidence that Klenkok taught in Prague, as though Groote were recommending a Prague master to Vroede, misdating the letter to 1373, and even knowing that Johannes could not have been at Prague in 1373! "Lebensgeschichte," p. 561 and n. 77, followed by Trapp, "Notes," p. 362. Klenkok's lectures and reputation at Paris are the most plausible sources of Groote's knowledge of Klenkok's thought.

[44]CUP 3:21-23 and note, for Guido. A Samuel of Janua had probably read *Sentences* as an Augustinian bachelor in 1352/53. AA 4(1911/12):278. No work of Rudolfo is known to be extant, but through references in Facinus of Ast, John of Ripa, and Johannes Hiltalingen of Basel, he is known to have become a master in 1360 and is therefore presumed to have been a bachelor about 1355. Trapp, "Augustinian," pp. 246-47, 268.

[45]B. Smalley, "Jean de Hesdin O. Hosp. S. Ioh.," *Recherches de théologie ancienne et médiévale*, 28(1961):285-330, reprinted eadem, *Studies in Medieval Thought and Learning*, pp. 345-92, here 346-48.

ciscan or specifically addressed his argument.[46] But both avoided naming peers.[47] Nevertheless, Johannes left an impression on students like Groote, and an Augustinian, Johannes of Basel, who attained the grade of lector at Avignon in 1357, taught at Strasbourg, and became bachelor at Paris in 1366, followed Klenkok's theology in considerable detail, using his arguments for and against Gregory of Rimini and drawing from works that were only recently composed in Saxony.[48] Yet Paris did not make Johannes a famous theologian.

Because he eventually became master at Oxford, we know that Johannes moved there, and this presumably occurred soon after the completion of the baccalaureate, probably in the late spring or summer of 1357. Such a move was not unusual,[49] and Johannes had a claim to a place in England, because of the general chapter's original assignment. If he did move in 1357, he enjoyed the usual

---

[46]Trapp, "Augustinian," pp. 239-42. Jean de Ripa, *Lectura super primum Sententiarum*, ed. A. Combes, 2 vols., vols. 8, 16 of *Textes philosophiques du moyen âge* (Paris: J. Vrin, 1961, 1970), 1:xxxi-xxxii, for the date of his baccalaureate. Also F. Ehrle, *Der Sentenzenkommentar Peters von Candia des Pisaner Papstes Alexanders V*, Beiheft 9 of *Franziskanische Studien* (Münster: Aschendorff, 1925), pp. 268-77. Cf. A. Combes, "Presentation de Jean de Ripa," *Archives d'histoire doctrinale et littéraire du moyen âge*, 23(1956):145-242, esp. 158-59 [Combes revised de Ripa's dates in the preface to the edition]. For his Scotism, see also A. Combes, "La métaphysique de Jean de Ripa," in *Die Metaphysik im Mittelalter*, ed. P. Wilpert, vol. 2 of *Miscellanea Mediaevalia* (Berlin: Walter de Gruyter, 1963), pp. 543-57. His refences to peers in baccalaureate disputations are painfully oblique. Jean de Ripa, *Quaestio de gradu supremo*, ed. A. Combes, vol. 12 of *Textes phil. du moyen âge* (Paris: J. Vrin, 1964), p. 88 (for date), p. 172: "Sed contra ista duo correlaria, quidam socius meus probabiliter posset instare"; p. 189: "Nam contra ipsa videtur procedere quidam alius socius, qui tertiam conclusionem primi sui articuli posuit sub hac forma: 'Licet non quecumque a Deo vel a creatura distinguuntur realiter distinguuntur, quecumque tamen aliquo modo distinguuntur, realiter distinguuntur.' " Jean's *determinationes*, if composed the year following the commentary on the *Sentences*, would originate 1355/56. Jean de Ripa, *Determinationes*, ed. A. Combes, vol. 4 of *Textes phil. du moyen âge* (Paris: J. Vrin, 1957), p. 13 (but see also idem, *Lectura*, 1:xxxi-xxxii, for date of the commentary). For Paris theologians from 1345-1363, consider also Johann de Falisca (Glorieux, "Jean," pp. 50-54).

[47]Klenkok would normally have addressed his *socii* in disputation. Since we have no determinations from him, we have no references. His *Exposicio litteralis*, with the exception of Guido, O.E.S.A., only refers to Oxonian associates. It remains possible that allusions or references to Jean of Ripa can be found in Klenkok's *Questiones*; q. 3 on creation and divine omnipotence seems a more likely place to find such references than most other questions.

[48]Kunzelmann, *Geschichte*, 2:206-13. Trapp, "Notes," pp. 367-76. Idem, "Augustinian," pp. 246-47 (Johannes of Basel cited Klenkok 87 times; Jean of Ripa, 76 times; Gregory of Rimini, 133 times; Ugolino of Orvieto, 193 times [the most frequently cited contemporary author]; among others). Klenkok, as will be seen, was a professor in Saxony during Hiltalingen's baccalaureate. However, it is not certain that Hiltalingen used Klenkok's works in Paris. Courtenay has noted references in Hiltalingen's *Sentences* commentary to authors writing after Hiltalingen's baccalaureate, which strongly suggest that the commentary was revised and expanded around 1375. Courtenay, *Adam Wodeham*, pp. 141-42.

[49]Consider CUP 2:213, 269, no. 756, 818. A move from Oxford to Paris may have been more difficult, requiring papal intervention. Ibid., 3:149, 157, no. 1321, 1329; consider also ibid., pp. 110-11 no. 1291.

two years of preparation preliminary to becoming a master.[50] Some of this time would be spent as respondent in disputations against bachelors and all the regent masters of theology, and Johannes apparently also lectured on at least part of the *Sentences*, for the explicit of two manuscripts of the second book of his *Exposicio litteralis* lists him as "the least of the bachelors and other students," that is, not yet a master (but anxious to provide a useful and salutary commentary).[51] Once he was formally invited to become the Augustinian *magister regens*, up to a year may have elapsed before he actually began.[52] Inception, by his own testimony, came on 5 August 1359.[53] If he had begun lecturing on the *Sentences* at Oxford during a preceding year, which seems to have been the case, he continued to do so now, and with greater freedom: after cautiously avoiding the hot and current Oxonian conflicts in the first two books of the *Sentences*, in books three and four he stabbed at champions against the friars—the Benedictine regent, Uthred of Boldon, and the archbishop of Armagh, Rich-

---

[50]The standard applied by the order to Paris must have been valid at Cambridge and Oxford, as well. Marcolino, "Augustinertheologe," p. 144. Klenkok's absence from the letters of Gregory of Rimini to the English provincial prior in 1358 might also imply that he had, by then, gotten his spot at Oxford.

[51]See Trapp, "Notes," p. 400. See also Trapp, "Notes," p. 392. For requirements imposed by the convocation of regents upon transfer students, see Rashdall, *Universities*, 3:145ff. Trapp saw Klenkok's self-designation, "minimus," here, in the incipit of the *Exposicio litteralis*, and in other works, as a "heraldic mystification" of the name "Klenke" (= "Kleinchen" and "minimus," according to Trapp), following a fourteenth-century practice of hiding a name in a pun in a *collatio*. Ibid., p. 382 and idem, "Augustinian," pp. 269f. In actual fact, "Klenke" means clasp, latch, or crossbar, and is related to the word "Klette," not "Klein." J. Grimm, W. Grimm, *Deutsches Wörterbuch*, 16 vols. (Leipzig: S. Hirzel, 1873), 5:1147. Agathe Lasch, Conrad Borchling, *Mittelniederdeutsches Handwörterbuch*, 3 vols. + (Neumünster: Kark Nachholtz, 1956+), 2:581. The family name "Klenke," although it came into use among the Klenkoks in the mid-fourteenth century (Müller, *Amt*, pp. 26, 46 for examples; contrast Bütow, "Lebensgeschichte," p. 542, who enjoyed only the evidence provided by Scheidt in *Biblioteca*), was never used by Johannes. "Minimus" was a common self-designation made exceedingly popular by the apostle Paul (1 Cor. 15.9; Klenkok pointed out Paul's use of the designation in *Postilla super Actus apostolorum*, f. 169va) and has nothing to do with one's name. E.g. Jordanus de Saxonia, *Liber vitasfratrum*, epistola introductoria, p. 1; Johannes of Freiburg in Boyle, "Summa," p. 250. See also Courtenay, *Adam*, p. 173.

[52]Little, *Grey Friars*, pp. 45ff.

[53]In one explicit to IV *Sent.*; Trapp, "Notes," pp. 360, 400 (Klosterneuburg, Stiftsbibl. 304, f. 195r). It is impossible to determine when Klenkok added this note to the text. Trapp believed it was added as soon as Klenkok had finished the requirements for inception, which presupposes that the *Exposicio litteralis* represents the baccalaureate lectures and that the note would not have been added later. There is, however, no reason to assume that the writing of the date in the explicit had to occur on that date. Erfurt, Allgemeine Wissenschaftliche Bibliothek, Amplon. fol. 117, f. 66va, which Trapp was not able to examine, contains a scribal ending which notes that Johannes was Oxford inceptor and that the copy was completed on the eve of the Feast of the Blessed Virgin (8 December) 1419 (Trapp knew the year from the published catalogue of Schum, "Notes," p. 365).

ard FitzRalph.[54] The required exegesis was performed in a typical, almost perfunctory way, with analytical questions used to interpret a very small part of biblical literature—the first Johannine letter.[55] Five magisterial sermons are extant, but the quodlibets are lost.[56] We may presume that these works occupied him for the two statutory years, as has usually been done.[57] He was, therefore, *magister regens* of the Austin friars from the late summer of 1359 to the spring or early summer of 1361.

Times were not propitious for friars in England. Richard FitzRalph had challenged the privileges of the mendicant orders at Avignon in 1350 without success, but he brought his dissatisfaction back to Armagh and vented it in a book that he began in the *Midi*, *De pauperie salvatoris*, which he published in Avignon and Oxford in 1356. The book presented his ultimate assault on

---

[54]The first criticism of Uthred (regent since 13 October 1357) occurs at III *Sent.* d. 35 and another, at IV *Sent.* d. 15—along with criticism of an unnamed Oxonian bachelor and of Richard FitzRalph. Trapp, "Notes," pp. 398-99, 402. BRO 1:212-13. Cf. the criticism of the Augustinian friar, Guido, in I *Sent.* d. 1, II *Sent.* d. 42 (n. 32, above), and the criticism of Parisian judgment in I *Sent.* d. 1 (E1, ff. 119va-120va; E2, ff. 1va-2rb; K, ff. 68v-69v; S, ff. 1vb-2rb, and also observed by Trapp, op. cit., p. 388). Klenkok seems to avoid offense in the first two books, which can suggest greater caution of a transferred bachelor before the decision of the convocation of regents to invite him to incept. Penn R. Szittya has noted that Uthred produced a *questio* against the friars, "Utrum paupertas mendicitatis, que est ultima in divisione facta in predicacionibus, ponat offendiculum verbo Dei" (BN Ms. Lat. 3183, fols. 160v-168v). P.R. Szittya, *The Antifraternal Tradition in Medieval Literature* (Princeton: Princeton University Press, 1986), p. 109. The *questio* may be contemporaneous with Klenkok's criticism.

[55]*Questiones super totam materiam canonice Johannis*, Oxford, Bodleian Library, Hamilton Ms. 33, ff. 247ra-258va; the manuscript was completed in 1394, according to Trapp ("Notes," p. 363) at Erfurt, but there is no apparent evidence of the place of the copy's origin (the explicit gives only the date). In the *Postilla super Actus apostolorum*, considering a question on the possibility of sinlessness in this life, Klenkok referred to the lectures on 1 Jn.: "quid sentencia in hoc dubio dicebam super canonicam primam Johannis in lectura magistrali." Eichstätt, Ms. 204, f. 132vb.

[56]Erfurt, Allgemeine Wissenschaftliche Bibliothek, Amplon. Q. 118, ff. 108ra-117rb. Sermons 1-3, 5 (ff. 108ra-114ra, 115vb-117rb) treat Christian struggle with the devil. Sermons 3 and 5 include some Christology: the victory of Christ (sermon 3) and issues like why the Son was chosen to fight the devil, and not the Father or Spirit (sermon 5). Sermon 4 treats Mariology, especially Mary's role in devotion and her *compassio* with Christ (ff. 114ra-115vb). The incipits are given in Trapp, "Notes," p. 365, and in Zumkeller, *Manuskripte*, pp. 249-50 no. 533. Zenon Kałuza has discovered references (made at Paris) to an anonymous "subtle" Augustinian at the school of the Austin friars in Oxford, in a manuscript of Thomas of Cracow; the text (a question) can be dated to sometime before 1360. *Thomas de Cracovie. Contribution à l'histoire du collège de la Sorbonne* (Wrocław: Ossolineum, 1978), p. 72 n.29; idem, "Le problème du 'Deum non esse' chez Étienne de Chaumont, Nicolas Aston et Thomas Bradwardine," *Mediaevalia Philosophica Polonorum*, 24(1979):3-19, here 8. There is some possibility that these represent quodlibets of Klenkok, but they may also be questions on the first book of *Sentences* (or quodlibets) of a bachelor perhaps contemporary with Klenkok's magisterium (Courtenay called the questions an anonymous *Sentences* commentary, but Kałuza's references do not identify them so specifically; Courtenay, *Schools*, pp. 315-16 and n. 12; 338-39). The references do not manifest any transparent affinity with what I know of Klenkok's works.

[57]Trapp, "Notes," p. 361. One-year regencies are also known. See Courtenay, *Adam*, p. 50 n. 25.

the friars, with a cleverly formulated accusation that the mendicant orders, by virtue of their sinfulness, could not legitimately exist.[58] Publication of the book met an unsurprising conjuncture in a London church council of 16 May 1356, where complaints of parochial clergy against the friars were carefully formulated and sent to Avignon. FitzRalph went to London only weeks after the council on diocesan business, and he was asked to preach the parochial cause, which he did in a sequence of sermons delivered over the next months, finishing 25 March 1357 (the dean of St. Paul's, Richard Kilvington, also preached against the friars). Representatives of the four mendicant orders met at London Grey Friars 7 March 1357, and they countered FitzRalph's assault with an *appellacio* accusing the Irish archbishop of twenty-one errors.[59] The *appellacio* probably served as the source of most polemic against FitzRalph by friars in England over the next years, while FitzRalph's more intricate arguments, finally presented by him at the curia in his *proposicio* of 8 November 1357, were deconstructed by mendicant theologians in Avignon.[60] At Oxford, the Augustinian regent from 1357 to 1359, Geoffrey Hardeby, offered a serious but circumspect response to *De pauperie salvatoris*, yet he appears to be the only mendicant to have addressed that work; others responded only to the London sermons.[61]

The agitation between friars and other clergy at the university was more acute than Hardeby's measured response might suggest. Irritants were many. Privileged friars circumvented the standards of the university by winning exceptions from without: this may have been behind the suspension of the Augustinian professor, John Kedington, in 1357; it certainly inspired, in 1360 or 1361, the derisive condemnation of "wax doctors" who were,

---

[58]Katherine Walsh, *A Fourteenth-Century Scholar and Primate: Richard FitzRalph in Oxford, Avignon, and Armagh* (Oxford: Basil Blackwell, 1981), pp. 387ff.

[59]Ibid., pp. 406ff. Idem, "The 'De vita evangelica' of Geoffrey Hardeby, O.E.S.A. (c. 1320-1385). A Study in Mendicant Controversies of the Fourteenth Century," AA 33(1970):151-261, 34(1971):5-83, esp. 33:166-68. "Super cathedram," the papal bull regulating relations between friars and diocesan clergy, was sent to the abbot of Westminster, the prior of St. Bartholomew's, and the archdeacon of London in August 1357. BF 6:305 no. 724.

[60]K. Walsh, "Archbishop Richard FitzRalph and the Friars at the Papal Court in Avignon, 1357-1360," *Traditio*, 31(1975):223-45.

[61]Walsh, *FitzRalph*, pp. 413ff. Idem, "De vita," p. 182. Hardeby's response to *De pauperie salvatoris*, presumably originating in quodlibets, is preserved in books 5-11 and 14-17 of Hardeby's *De vita evangelica*. See ibid., pp. 198, 204f. Klenkok, however, offered discussion of Oxonian debates, referring anonymously to a friar and to two opinions of a bachelor (or perhaps two separate bachelors), and the friar did raise the Augustinian theory of dominion by grace, which became controversial in FitzRalph's adaptation of it in the *De vita euangelica*. IV *Sent.*, d. 15, E2, ff. 46vb-48ra; K, ff. 167r-167v; S, ff. 63rb-66rb. In the same distinction, he also argued for the possibility of temporal punishment of mortal sins, against FitzRalph: E2, f. 46rb; K, f. 166r-166v; S, f. 62rb-62va.

the convocation of regents declared, mostly mendicants getting by on privileges and exemptions and seducing boys into their religions.[62] The regents finally named three who had benefited from royal graces—Richard Lymynster, O.F.M. (incepted 1359), John Nuton, O.P. (who preceded Richard), and Giuliort of Limousin, O.F.M. (who attained opponency by royal privilege). The friars, in education as in much that they did, knew how to exploit extraordinary allegiances; many mendicant promotions came at the instigation of a party intractable—the papacy. These three were only an extreme example of the more common mendicant doctors made of wax, and the convocation's point-blank accusation reflects discomfort with the friars' tremendous aptitude at getting in through, as it were, back doors.

Once inside, they agitated. A mendicant master known only as John was forced to apologize publicly to all regents for dishonoring the Canterbury monk, John Bodi, in 1357.[63] In 1358, the university forbade mendicant recruitment among students.[64] That same year, a friar John, apparently master in theology, claimed that mendicants have more right to tithes than parochial clergy, that royal supremacy supersedes the rights of ecclesiastical lords, and that the university is a "gymnasium hereticorum."[65] He was forced to make public apology on a Sunday after the university sermon in St. Mary's, retracting his opinions, and he was required to pay a hefty fine of one hundred shillings.

Thrust and parry over FitzRalph's doctrine thrived in this volatile atmosphere. FitzRalph, by means of a new application of the Augustinian doctrine of dominion by grace, had argued that the friars violated their vows of poverty and humility by the private use of goods (and by encroachment on those of others, namely parochial clergy) and by their evasion of episcopal rule: they are, FitzRalph concluded, in a state of sin, and, as such, they enjoy no rights. He also regarded the privileges that supported them as

---

[62]William Page, ed., *The Victoria History of the County of Oxford*, vol. 2 (London: Archibald Constable, 1907), pp. 145-46. Henry Anstey, ed., *Munimenta Academica or Documents Illustrative of Academic Life and Studies at Oxford*, 2 vols., vol. 50/1-2 of *Rerum Britannicarum Medii Aevi Scriptores or Chronicles and Memorials of Great Britain and Ireland during the Middle Ages* (London: Longmans, Green, Reader, and Dyer, 1868), vol. 1, *Libri cancellarii et procuratorum*, pp. 207-08 (misdated 1358). See also ibid., p. 206. BRO 2:1132, 1147, 1380. For the date, consider the years of the procurators mentioned at the beginning of the entry, Richard Toulworth (1358-59, 1360-61) and Robert Derby (1360-July, 1361). BRO 1:571; 3:1886. Also, Herbert B. Workman, *John Wyclif. A Study of the English Medieval Church* (Oxford: Clarendon, 1922; reprinted Hamden, Connecticut: Archon Books, 1966), 1:92-93.

[63]*Libri canc.*, p. 203.

[64]Ibid., pp. 204-05.

[65]Ibid., pp. 208-10 (in a winter determination; he is also called "doctor"). For the chancellor, proctor, and date, BRO 1:568; 2:970.

equally sinful.[66] The chancellor and regents of Oxford, already in March 1357 in a letter to Innocent VI, complained that FitzRalph's doctrine gave rise to disputations over a futuristically "Wyclifite" question: did the possession of property entail the damnation of the church?[67] Bachelors—mendicants might seem likely—reversed the trajectory of the archbishop's argument by altering some of its premises. If one assumes a certain definition of the gospel, as, for example, Spiritual Franciscans had done, the entire church failed to observe poverty and might be damned. Some might have sincerely posed the argument, but they might also have used it to demonstrate the potential havoc of FitzRalph's position.

Once FitzRalph had brought the English controversy to Avignon in November, 1357, Augustinian friars played an important role in the mendicant defense over the next three years, but in Oxford, where discussion was also intense, the friars did not form a united front or undertake an organized campaign. This may have been due to the ability of the convocation of chancellor and masters, with secular clergy among them, to check party conflicts among students, bachelors, and fellow doctors.[68] In a letter of 20 January 1358, Gregory of Rimini, prior general, demanded that the masters and lectors of the English province answer FitzRalph and that the confessors and preachers scrupulously follow the stipulations of proper approval and licensure, that is, that they adhere to the regulatory bull of pope Boniface VIII, "Super cathedram."[69] Hardeby's quodlibets suggest that the prior general's demand would inspire no more than a circumspect response, which may have been the best a cautious mendicant regent could do in a volatile environment. Johannes Klenkok was equally circumspect, waiting until the end of his lectures on the third book of the Lombard to challenge a non-mendicant colleague, Uthred of Boldon, and a wildly untraditional conclusion drawn from Uthred's view of cognizance and culpability—that ignorance of the culpability of a deed exempts an individual from its consequences, so that, for example (and

---

[66]Walsh, *FitzRalph*, pp. 380-84, 395, 399-405.

[67]25 March 1357. Walsh, "Vita," p. 182. Wyclif was master in arts and hearing lectures in theology at the time. BRO 3:2103-04. Walsh, *FitzRalph*, pp. 412, and 377-79 for the relation of Wyclif to FitzRalph.

[68]As in the events recorded at note 62, above. Gregory of Rimini made supplication to the pope against mendicant enemies and asked the order's cardinal protector to support it in the papal audience, 20 January 1358. Later that year, 16 November 1358, he imposed a tax on the provinces to raise financial support for the Avignon campaign against FitzRalph. AA 5(1914):257, 271-72.

[69]Walsh, "Vita," p. 182 and n. 202.

this was quite important to Uthred), non-Christians in pagan societies may not be punished for their lack of belief in the Christian gospel.[70] At distinction 14 of the fourth book, Klenkok accused his regent associate ("Ulcredus de Dunelmo magister monachus qui mecum legit Sentencias") of Pelagianism for claiming that it is possible to find the way to salvation by natural ability, without the assistance of God.[71] At the next distinction, he discussed some of the controversy over poverty recently occupying doctors and bachelors: he denied FitzRalph's view, expressed in a London sermon, that mortal sins could not be redressed by temporal penalties, because transgressions against the infinite good must receive eternal punishment; he answered the proposition of one anonymous "secular bachelor" claiming the superiority of the status of any "simple" doctor, rector, or archdeacon to those in religious vows; he refuted another proposition by the same or another secular bachelor and its source, the archbishop of Armagh, claiming that mortal sin deprives the sinner of dominion.[72] These

---

[70]Note 54, above. Klenkok also referred to the Dominican, Thomas Stubbs, who is better known for his continuation of the *Chronica pontificum Eboracensis*. BRO 3:xliii. II *Sent.* d. 39, E1, f. 104rb-104vb, E2, f. 27vb, K, f. 129r, S, ff. 27va-28ra. Trapp, on the basis of this reference, put Stubbs in the Oxford Blackfriars 1354/55, under the assumption that Klenkok referred to him as a bachelor during that academic year. Klenkok's reference indeed suggests that Stubbs responded to him or with him in a disputation; if this occurred at Oxford, it occurred three years after Trapp's date, when Klenkok, as a transfer student, responded in disputations before being admitted as a master (hence, Stubbs is actually witnessed at Oxford Blackfriars sometime between 1357 and 1359). The reference only indicates that Stubbs confronted Klenkok in a previous year—although less likely, it could have occurred while Klenkok was a bachelor at Paris, in which case Stubbs would also have studied there. Trapp also noted that this doctrine of Uthred corresponded to question 6, article 6 of the anonymous *Monachus Niger* of Fribourg, Cordeliers, Ms. 26, but the opinion also represents a preliminary form or a part of Boldon's doctrine of the "clara visio" (at the moment of death, all people receive a clear vision of God and a free choice between good and evil, on the basis of which they are judged). For the distinction between that Black Monk and Uthred, see Courtenay, *Adam*, pp. 90-95, esp. 94 n. 199. Trapp, "Notes," pp. 398-99. Idem, "Augustinian," pp. 207-10, 238. M. D. Knowles, "The Censured Opinions of Uthred of Boldon," *Proceedings of the British Academy*, 37(1951):305-42. W. A. Pantin, *The English Church in the Fourteenth Century* (Cambridge: Cambridge University Press, 1955), pp. 168f.

[71]Trapp, "Notes," p. 402. Idem, "Augustinian," pp. 237-38. The reference to "reading" the *Sentences* might be taken to refer to the work of a *sententiarius*, but Klenkok declared himself to be incepted at the end of the previous book of the Lombard; Boldon had incepted in 1357 (see BRO in n. 54, above); both were therefore lecturing on the *Sentences* as masters.

[72]See the passages of IV *Sent.* d. 15 noted in n. 61, above. Trapp also noticed Klenkok's discussion of FitzRalph's view of the remission of mortal sin, "Notes," p. 402. The sermon in question is probably that of 17 July 1356, preached at St. Paul's cathedral. Consider Walsh, *FitzRalph*, p. 411, for that sermon. The subject also figured prominently in the *appellacio* of the London mendicants of 7 March 1358 (ibid., p. 417), and Klenkok probably knew of it from there. Klenkok's discussion supports the mendicant status quo on poverty, but at one point, he conveys his disinterest: "De illa questione non curo, sed credo

passages contain Klenkok's consideration of a doctrine argued passionately by his colleagues, and it will occupy him again in his exegesis of the Book of Acts a few years hence. For the present, it should suffice to point out that Klenkok's most certain contribution to academic debates at Oxford lies with his terse criticisms of Boldon, and not with his developed, but certainly not exhaustive arguments against the *Armacanus*, as FitzRalph was known: Johannes posed the earliest criticism of Boldon's views of the salvation of unbaptized people, of grace, and of sin.[73] Over the next years, Uthred will nurture his sympathies for FitzRalph's cause and further develop his peculiar preoccupation with the future of non-Christians (peculiar vis à vis his contemporaries' views of final judgment). About 1366, a Dominican, William Jordan, tried to knock down the Benedictine master's views and in 1368, with a Franciscan, John Hilton, successfully saw twenty-two of Uthred's opinions censured by an archiepiscopal commission.[74] It was hardly a coup. The commission refused to name Uthred a heretic, and the friars probably sustained other hostilities within the university.[75] The tensions of 1356 to 1360, however, continued to stir the university throughout the next decade, and Klenkok's early response to Boldon must have seemed

---

quod sancta mater ecclesia Dei credit in hoc sperans saluari" (curo] multum *add* S. sancta mater] *trans* S. Dei] *om* S. credit] *add* S.). E2, f. 47vb-48ra; S, f. 66ra (this is from part of the distinction that is missing from K).

[73]Although it is possible that Geoffrey Hardeby also responded to Uthred in 1360, Katherine Walsh showed that it is improbable, because Hardeby's disputation was more directly aimed at an Augustinian canon, which Boldon was not. "Vita," p. 190. Cf. M. B. Hackett, "The Spiritual Life of the English Austin Friars in the Fourteenth Century," *Sanctus Augustinus Spiritualis Magister*, 2 vols. (Rome: Analecta Augustiniana, 1959), 2:421-92, here 444. For Klenkok's lack of influence against FitzRalph, consider Hiltalingen's dissatisfaction with Klenkok's arguments, but his seeming allowance of the arguments of a Parisian bachelor who read the *Sentences* in 1361/62 or 1362/63, Etienne Gaudet. Trapp, "Notes," p. 371 for Hiltalingen's reading of Klenkok's criticism of FitzRalph in the literal exposition of IV *Sent*. d. 15, and Zenon Kałuza, *Thomas de Cracovie*, pp. 68 n. 20, 139, for Etienne Gaudet. Trapp thought that Hiltalingen was defending FitzRalph against Klenkok (op. cit.), but it may be noted in passing that Hiltalingen, in the passage quoted by Trapp, referred to Gaudet's argument explicitly, to avoid being seen as entirely of FitzRalph's mind. William Courtenay has also noted Klenkok's role as critic of Boldon, *Schools*, p. 353 n. 69.

[74]Knowles and Pantin in n. 70. Trapp pointed out that Klenkok's criticism of Boldon's doctrine of grace was answered in Boldon's *Contra querelas fratrum* (without naming Klenkok). "Augustinian," pp. 237-38. For his doctrine of grace and the commission's censure, see also Ocker, "Augustinianism in Fourteenth-Century Theology," *Augustinian Studies*, 18(1987):81-106, here 92-94.

[75]A Dominican bachelor who was prevented from taking degrees at Oxford, because he prosecuted an unknown question on behalf of his order at Avignon and in England, may have been a mendicant casualty. Bliss, *Petitions*, 1:536 (the papacy granted him the right to incept at Paris). Consider also the Carmelite in CUP 3:149 no. 1321.

to retain its relevance.[76] It certainly called attention to the black monk's vulnerable areas.

If the few references in the *Exposicio litteralis* offer a fair representation of Klenkok's position in the Oxford debates—and any final judgment is handicapped by the absence of his quodlibets, where sparring was most likely to occur—they could misleadingly portray a reserve that just escapes passivity.[77] The constraints of Oxford's constitution, with its subjugation of everyone to the entire assembly of chancellor and masters, required political savvy, particularly among those who more frequently exercised the system with extraordinary assignments and promotions.[78] The recantation of master John a year before Klenkok's inception was the nearest example of the convocation's readiness to subjugate individual members of the theology faculty. The Augustinian regent avoided direct response to challenges against the existence of friars. A closer look at his Oxford writings shows that he preferred to make hits indirectly, in doctrinal areas that increasingly belonged to Augustinian theologians, thereby following interests and commitments intrinsic to the cultural tradition of his order, maintaining the (by the late 1350s) rather common voice of the order in the theology faculties, and avoiding confrontations that might compromise his effectiveness as protagonist of his students among the regents of the university. Mostly, he accused Osbert, English Carmelite and master (who is known for his defense of human freedom and his opposition to the theology of Thomas Bradwardine) of Pelagianism, but he also had FitzRalph and Uthred in mind when he wrote the texts against his mendicant colleague.[79] For example, FitzRalph's view of an infinite degree of

---

[76]Consider the use of Klenkok's refutation of Boldon by Johannes Hiltalingen, the Monachus Niger, and the anonymous commentary on the *Sentences* in Fribourg, Cordeliers, Ms. 26, gathered by Trapp, "Augustinian," pp. 207-39 (but on Trapp's ascription of the last work to Friedrich of Regensburg, cf. Courtenay, "Friedrich").

[77]A cross-reference to an Oxonian quodlibet in the *postilla* on Acts does indicate that at least one of them treated mendicant poverty. The *postilla* is prefaced with a question and twenty-nine arguments. The question is this (Eichstätt 204, f. 118ra): "Utrum in potestate ligandi soluendique apostolorum sint ad apostolice uite regulam obligati, et arguitur quod non." Argument 19 appears ibid., ff. 119vb-120ra, and it begins, "Apostoli tenebantur seruare precepta decalogi, . . . sed a hoc non tenentur eorum successores." The response appears ibid., f. 122ra, where Klenkok refers the reader to an Oxford quodlibet, adding only a brief comment on an example that appeared in the argument (concerning the execution of thieves).

[78]Rashdall, *Universities*, 3:148, for the constitution. Walsh, "Vita," p. 203, describes Hardeby's polemic as "strangely detached from the Oxford intellectual scene of his own time."

[79]Osbert, like at least one other Carmelite theologian (John Brammart), criticized Thomas Bradwardine—Osbert, for the Mertonian's restrictions on human liberty (John Brammart, similarly; John Baconthorpe and Franciscus Bacon were Carmelites who cited Bradwardine favorably). B. Xiberta, *De Scriptoribus Scholasticis Saeculi XVI. ex Ordine Car-*

punishment, which is criticized by Klenkok in his *Exposicio litteralis* (note 61, above), is also raised in his questions on the Johannine letters, without naming the archbishop. There, the refutation is supported with references to question 25 of the *Questiones super secundum Sententiarum*, which Klenkok expanded or composed at Oxford and added to the questions of his baccalaureate lectures in Paris and which names the Carmelite Osbert as the enemy, not FitzRalph. The Johannine question considers the eternal punishment of sins classified as venial in terms closest to those of FitzRalph, even though allusions to the *Armacanus* are obscure and references to him by name, absent. But Osbert is clearly identified several times.[80] When he addressed FitzRalph's view of dominion (by which the archbishop argued for the withdrawal of mendicant privileges and the dissolution of the orders), he took care to point out that a secular bachelor brought the problem to him, presumably having raised it in a disputation which the Augustinian regent "determined."[81] Similarly, Klenkok offered more extensive discussions of the views of Boldon in his questions on the Johannine epistles, sometimes alluding to Uthred's views, sometimes naming him, but keeping the black monk's ideas in close proximity to Osbert and his alleged Pelagianism.[82] Boldon, like Osbert, is given serious and fairly thorough consideration, but there is a perceptible reluctance to isolate Boldon and FitzRalph as enemies of the friars, and a consistent

melitanorum (Louvain: Revue d'histoire ecclésiastique, 1931), pp. 174 n. 1, 258, 279, 282, 407, 430, 439, 445. Osbert is presumed to have lectured on the *Sentences* by 1354. Klenkok's literal exposition of *Sentences* contains the first known references to Osbert, and this date rests upon the assumption that Klenkok composed the work during a baccalaureate at Oxford alleged to have begun in 1354. Since Klenkok's literal exposition actually dates from his magisterium (or perhaps begun shortly before the magisterium), Osbert's magisterial lectures, which are opposed by Klenkok, might be no earlier than about 1358. Contrast Trapp, "Augustinian," p. 227; Courtenay, *Schools*, p. 335 n. 18, 338 n. 30.

[80]*Questiones super totam materiam canonice Johannis*, f. 249va, "Alij dicunt quod pro tanto punitur eternaliter, quia est contra bonum infinitum"; f. 249vb (on the distinction between mortal and venial sins), "de hijs vide super secundo Sentenciarum mea ultima." The doctrine is attributed to FitzRalph by name only in IV *Sent.* d. 15. The question in the *Questiones super II Sent.* is given in note 42, above. Cf. Osbert's claim, as challenged in the same question and in II *Sent.* d. 42 (Zumkeller, *Erbsünde*, p. 25): "quodlibet peccatum, per quod peccans non crederet se amissurum gratiam Dei, esset ueniale."

[81]IV *Sent.* d. 15, E2, f. 47rb; S, f. 64va (also within the section of d. 15 missing from K).

[82]*Questiones super tot. can. Joh.*, f. 250va-vb, examines the relation of culpability to knowledge (by examining the case of Jewish disbelief in Christianity) without naming Uthred; at ff. 253vb-254ra, he names Uthred ("Sed queritur utrum quilibet per legem nature inimicum diligere teneatur, et est opinio magistri Ulcresus [*lege* Ulcredi] de Dunelmo tenentis quod sic"). He then draws six conclusions, and provides a long sequence of rebuttals, answers to the question, and conclusions, in the course of which he refers again to Uthred at f. 255rb ("Ad argumenta magistri que uidentur pro re quod diligere inimicum sic diligere nature inmutabili . . . "), but placing Osbert's views in this general context, as well (f. 256bva-vb). Uthred may have been the object of much of the arguments.

tendency to couple criticism of the non-mendicants with criticism of a Carmelite. This is consistent with Klenkok's commitment to an agenda largely created among the Augustinian Hermits some twelve or thirteen years earlier at Paris by Gregory of Rimini.[83] But it also represents what could only be a deliberate avoidance of the debate instigated at the English university by FitzRalph. Nevertheless, these jousts affected Klenkok's thought, even if only to confirm his views as a friar and an Augustinian, as will be seen in his lectures on Acts. At Oxford, Johannes became publicly located in the scholastic milieu as a defender of Gregory of Rimini, but that location would only underscore his relation to a mendicant order; it did nothing to press his influence into other groups as, for example, the metaphysics of John Duns Scotus or the linguistic philosophy of William of Ockham had done for them.[84]

The formation of Klenkok as a mid-century theologian required joining the debates raging between clerical parties. As he became another keeper of Christendom's universal culture, the university master also became an advocate of a religious community. This partisanship reveals a purpose of theological science in human society—the self-assertion of clerical communities in competition with one another. It is important to recognize the role of the defense in theological education, in order to appreciate the power of what would otherwise appear to be biblical and theological arcana, like the rights of Adam and Eve in paradise or the relation of Jesus and the apostles to what little property they used, things that were lavishly proven in opposite ways since the grand assault of Guillaume of St. Amour on the friars at the University of Paris one hundred years before. Klenkok was a minimalist in debate and preferred to argue over theories of property and government rather than from the famous, tiny matters of biblical history beloved of Franciscan defenders of mendicant poverty. But these preoccupations had nevertheless become imprinted upon his intellect and would soon drive him to find new tensions in the ways people live, to assault Saxon traditions. They signal the participation of his mind in the religious strife of his age.

---

[83]For Gregory's career, Marcolino, "Augustinertheologe." For Augustinianism in the order, Zumkeller, *Erbsünde*, pp. 433-42. The literature on this subject is voluminous and need not be considered here. See Ocker, "Augustinianism," pp. 82-86; Courtenay, *Schools*, p. 315.

[84]But Cistercians are known to have written commentaries based upon Gregory of Rimini and Ugolino of Orvieto's commentaries on the *Sentences* in the late fourteenth century. Trapp, "Augustinian," pp. 251-55.

III. SASSEN NICHT SCHENDEN

With the statutory years completed, Johannes, as was usually the case, returned to his home province of Saxony and Thüringen, where his title and his skills were exploited in the offices of lector and provincial.[1] We may assume that Klenkok returned to Germany soon after the close of the academic year in 1361, just missing an outbreak of the plague in England.[2] He was at least forty-one years of age. The provincial chapter of that Pentecost, held at Grimma, may have assigned him to teach in a school.[3] A document of January, 1363 contains his name as provincial prior, which suggests that he had been elected to that office by the provincial chapter held the previous Pentecost in 1362; a document of June 1367 also contains his seal as provincial, and the provincial chapter held at Gotha 28 May 1368 elected him to another term: he was either provincial for several consecutive terms or for two sets of terms between 1362 and 1369.[4] As provincial, he would receive some laity into the order's confraternity, in the one known case in which Klenkok did this, receiving a man and wife with the man's sister and her children. He would participate in financial transactions, like sales and the receipt of donations, that involved more than one convent of the province.[5] He would participate in property disputes between convents, like a conflict between the cloister of Lippstadt and the cloister of Cologne (in the neighboring province) over a disputed satellite house in Dortmund; the provincial consented to the settlement.[6] He held the "power of the keys," penitential authority, over the friars in his jurisdiction, so that cases not settled by priors ought not circum-

---

[1]Of the 16 known provincials of the province in the fourteenth century, 4 were lectors, 5 were masters of theology, 1 was bachelor of theology, and 9 had no known academic degree. Kunzelmann, *Geschichte,* 5:322-40.

[2]Wyclif, master of arts, left Oxford about the same time. Workman, *John Wyclif,* 1:152.

[3]L. Schmidt, ed., *Urkundenbuch der Stadt Grimma,* part 2, vol. 15 of *Codex Diplomaticus Saxoniae Regiae* (Leipzig: Giesecke und Devrient, 1895), p. 244 no. 348, records a transaction with an abbess by Conrad, prior provincial, at the provincial chapter, 16 May 1361. Kunzelmann, *Geschichte,* 5:334.

[4]Zumkeller, *Urkunden,* 2:604-08, no. 933, 938. Kunzelmann, *Geschichte,* 5:335.

[5]Zumkeller in previous note.

[6]Kunzelmann, *Geschichte,* 4:26f. n. 98, 5:189.

vent him.[7] An ambiguous controversy between a lector, Johannes Gunther of Stargard, and the cloister of Stargard failed to reach a settlement satisfying that well-bred conventual. As provincial prior, Klenkok imposed a judgment that confirmed the position of the cloister against him, but Gunther brought an appeal directly to the general chapter at Avignon, with a complaint against the provincial, Klenkok, in 1368. For this, with his "unjust vexation" of "master Johannes," the general chapter imposed silence upon Gunther.[8] The provincial chapter, held concurrently at Gotha and over which Klenkok presided, reasserted the constitutional requirement forbidding appeals that circumvent the hierarchical order of prior, provincial, general prior, and general chapter.[9]

Such must have been the business which commonly occupied the provincial as he performed his visitations and presided over provincial chapters, all of it deceptively jejune. His juridical role within the province was considerable, perhaps most similar to the role of bishop in a diocese, although it was neither indelible nor as absolute because possession of the office, its status, and its privileges covered a limited period of time and was subject to the election of the provincial chapter (just as the election of priors was subject to conventual chapters). Rather than exercising an authority intrinsic to the person, the provincial prior occupied a position at a point of contact between the separate cloisters of a geographical area and the government of the whole, and in this context, to preserve order was not merely to maintain hierarchical structures of authority and subordination, but to preserve an equilibrium between individuals and communities within the society of a mendicant order through communication. It was a crucial juncture, where a very large religious body, with its peculiar interests and commitments within a universal church, converged with the existence of small but established religious communities in towns, with their consistent sets of religious roles

---

[7]Gregorius Ariminensis, *Registrum generalatus*, p. 304 no. 564. AA 4(1911/12):454.

[8]In 1366, the duke of Pommern asked Pope Urban V to promote Gunther, a Paris lector who had read at Prague for three years, to master. The outcome is not known, but it shows that Gunther had access to nobility, which probably implies that he was himself of higher birth. J. Kadlec, "Das Augustiner-Generalstudium bei Sankt Thomas zu Prag in vorhussitischer Zeit," *Augustiniana*, 17(1967):396. For the general chapter, AA(1911/12):454.

[9]*Acta pauca capitulorum quorundam prouincialium prouincie Thuringie et Saxonie*, Clm 8491 (note 30, p. 15, above), f. 165v. Also noted by Kunzelmann, *Geschichte*, overlooking its relation to the Gunther affair. Certain privileges made lectors and, especially, masters the equal of priors, e.g. they all enjoyed a voice in the provincial chapter, and masters and priors could give benedictions "extra refectorium." Ypma, *Formation*, p. 151 (general chapter of 1324). See also the *Constitutiones Ratisbonenses*, ii, in AA 1(1901) (also copied in the fifteenth-century *Acta pauca*, f. 162v).

and their polymorphic concerns over the minute contingencies of their immediate environments. As a master of theology, Johannes was expert in the abstractions that distinguished his mendicant society in a mental universe, and as a prior, he participated in the life of particular communities precisely where they interacted with the structures and concerns that transcended local preoccupations.

Johannes also taught in a general school in the province as *lector principalis* probably until 1370, and he may have held both offices, provincial and lecturer, at the same time.[10] It has long been recognized that the province of Saxony and Thüringen had two *studia generalia*, one at Magdeburg and one at Erfurt. Otto Franklin concluded that Klenkok taught at both, and Klenkok's biographers have since concurred.[11] But the Magdeburg cloister— owning a small library only six years old and a church still incomplete in 1361 (when Klenkok likely returned to Germany)— may not have hosted an operating general school at the time, as mentioned earlier.[12] Klenkok's alleged presence in Magdeburg has rested largely upon his controversy with the city's *Rat*, but nothing about the controversy indicates that he lived in town, as shall be seen. The evidence for an Erfurt residency is conclusive,

---

[10]The *additiones* of Thomas of Strasbourg forbade provincial and local priors to exercise the office of lector, except by license of the general chapter. But it must have been common to combine the offices and was, perhaps—at least immediately after the Black Death— necessitated by a lack of suitable candidates: the general chapter of 1351 lifted the prohibition. Ypma, *Formation*, p. 155. A prominent but late example of lectures by a provincial prior and general prior is Augustinus Favaroni of Rome, who lectured on philosophy as provincial and on the Pauline letters as general. Salesius Friemal, *Die theologische Prinzipienlehre des Augustinus Favaroni von Rom O.E.S.A. (+ 1443)*, vol. 12 of *Cassiciacum* (Würzburg: Augustinus-Verlag, 1950), pp. 21-22. Willigis Eckermann, "Augustinus Favaroni," TRE 4:739-40.

[11]For the two schools, A. Höhn, *Chronologia provinciae Rheno-Suevicae Ordinis Fratrum Eremitarum Sancti Patris Augustini* (Würzburg, 1744), p. 246. Homeyer put Klenkok in the Magdeburg convent, on the assumption that his controversy with that city (to be discussed shortly) implied his residency there. *Johannes*, p. 382. Otto Franklin placed Klenkok in Erfurt and Magdeburg and was followed by Bütow and Trapp. Franklin, "Johannes Klenkok," *Festgabe für Oskar von Bülow* (Tübingen, 1884), p. 6. Bütow, "Lebensgeschichte," p. 553. Trapp, "Notes," p. 361. Zumkeller adduced evidence for both cities, but the evidence for Magdeburg—Klenkok's contact with Walter Kerlinger—falters, because Kerlinger lived in Erfurt, as will be seen.

[12]Note 10, p. 19, above. The cloister's church was completed in 1366. Kunzelmann, *Geschichte*, 5:110. Jordan of Saxony, provincial, and Rudolf, prior, purchased 44 volumes (counting parts of divided works separately, e.g. "Augustinum super Psalterium tres partes" as 3) from the Premonstratensian cloister of Magdeburg, Unser Lieben Frau, on 31 January 1355. On 28 February 1355, Rudolf purchased 5 volumes from the abbot of the Benedictine cloister outside the Magdeburg walls, St. Johannes. Gustav Hertel, *Urkundenbuch des Klosters Unser Lieben Frau zu Magdeburg*, vol. 10 of *Geschichtsquellen der Provinz Sachsen und angrenzender Gebiete* (Halle: Otto Hendel, 1879), p. 196 no. 217. H. Holstein, *Urkundenbuch des Klosters Berge bei Magdeburg*, vol. 9 of *Geschichtsquellen d. Prov. Sach. u. angr. Geb.* (Halle: O. Hendel, 1879), p. 159 no. 214. Kunzelmann took the first transaction as the foundation of the cloister library. Kunzelmann, *Geschichte*, 5:109.

because Johannes himself, in his convent lectures, referred to the city as "here," and a student, Gander of Meppen, later wrote that his master had been *regens* in Erfurt about 1367.[13] Two other known students can be safely ascribed to this period of Klenkok's career: Angelus Dobelin and Johannes Merkelin, the latter probably as *lector secundarius* with Klenkok.[14] Gander furnishes the only substantive description, however brief, of Klenkok's teaching: "and I was a student under him, not, except seldom, in theology, but in the arts."[15] Other young contemporaries, like Gander, affectionately gushed about Klenkok: Gander named him "gloriosus doctor" and declared, "I've not known a better and more learned master in theology"; Angelus called him "reverendus pater meus singularis" and declared himself "the least disciple and once his son." But only Gander mentioned that he taught theology and the arts.[16] It is an interesting claim confirmed by a passing reference by Johannes to his own comment

---

[13]The "here" passage was noted by Trapp, "Notes," p. 359. The same distinction of the *Sentences* commentary (where this passage occurs) comments "apud nos in Saxonia et in Anglia." Erfurt, Amplon. 117, f. 53rb (Siena, Bibl. Comm., G.V. 16, f. 77rb-77va preserves the reference in a distinct form "apud nos in Saxonia Brabancia"). The same distinction also contains a reference to the Oxford controversy in the perfect tense (Erfurt, Ampl. 117, f. 51va). The reference by Gander occurs in a sermon of the Feast of the Ascension from which it was extracted by Johannes Schiphower in the early sixteenth century and included in his treatise on the immaculate conception. W. Eckermann, "Quelle," pp. 210-12. For Gander, see also F. Landmann, *Das Predigtwesen in Westfalen in der letzten Zeit des Mittelalters. Ein Beitrag zur Kirchen- und Kulturgeschichte*, vol. 1 of *Vorreformationsgeschichtliche Forschungen* (Münster: Aschendorff, 1900), p. 67. Gander does not appear in Johannes Baptist Schneyer, *Repertorium der lateinischen Sermones des Mittelalters*, 9 vols. (Münster: Aschendorff, 1969-1980), nor in Stegmüller, RB, nor in Zumkeller, *Manuskripte*. It is not certain whether Gander belonged to an order. Landmann assumed that he was a secular priest, because Schiphower did not name him a monk. For the use of "magister meus," consider Ehrle, *Sentenzenkommentar*, pp. 260ff.; Courtenay, *Schools*, pp. 172-73; Zumkeller, *Gnade*, pp. 432ff.

[14]D. Trapp, "Angelus de Dobelin, Doctor Parisiensis, and His Lectura," *Augustinianum*, 3(1963):389-413, esp. 389-90, presents Dobelin's references to Klenkok but attributes the relationship between them to a time of Klenkok's presumed residency at Prague. The evidence is a letter of Johannes of Neumarkt, chancellor of Karl IV, recommending Angelus' promotion at Paris to master; the chancellor calls Dobelin "singularem amicum meum et socium apud cancellarium" (cited ibid.). Because Angelus worked in the imperial chancellory in Prague, Trapp assumed that the two friars encountered each other in that city. Zumkeller has since shown that Angelus could only have gone to Prague after attaining the grade of lector, after which he was probably assigned lector in the Augustinian general school at Prague, and he therefore concluded that Angelus could only have studied with Klenkok in Erfurt or Magdeburg (assuming also that Klenkok taught in both cities). *Erbsünde*, pp. 136-37. For Merkelin, Bütow, "Johannes Merkelin," pp. 6, 8-12, G. Uth, "Die Augustiner in Polen vor der Gründung der selbständigen polnischen Ordensprovinz (1547)," AA 33(1970):263-308.

[15]Eckermann, "Quelle," pp. 210-12: " . . . et studens fui sub eo non tamen in theologia, nisi raro, sed in artibus."

[16]Gander: "meliorem et doctiorem magistrum in theologia non vidi." Angelus: "minimus discipulus et filius suus quondam." Cited in Trapp, "Angelus," p. 390.

on book one of the *Peri Hermenias*.[17] He may also have used the work of someone else, with or without his own additions, which would render identification of his philosophical lectures, should they still exist, very difficult, if not impossible.[18] Johannes Schiphower, in the first known list of Klenkok's works, makes the intriguing claim that they included "Quodlibeta varia iuris totius," but he probably meant the compilations of texts of Erfurt disputations on the *Sachsenspiegel*.[19] Thus, Klenkok's scholastic activity in Erfurt included the arts—which in a mendicant school meant grammar, logic, and dialectics—and the canon law, which would normally focus on penitential casuistry, but in Klenkok's case also included constitutional matters. An interest in philosophy and law is evident in his theological and biblical lectures.[20] There, Johannes digressed to miscellaneous philosophical topics while lecturing on the Bible, and he added copious references to the canon law in all his writings—with a long casuistic digression added to distinction 15 of the fourth book of *Sentences*.[21] The com-

----

[17]Eichstätt 204, f. 124rb. The text is not extant and no one else is known to have ever referred to it (the reference has not been known to Klenkok's biographers). All that is known of the text is the reference by Klenkok.

[18]A Middle High German translation of the Ps. Aristotelian *Secretum secretorum* in Wernigerode is ascribed to Johannes Klenck, son of Patricius. Zumkeller, *Manuskripte*, p. 240 no. 522. Johannes was a common name in the Klenkok clan (Müller, *Amt*, p. 404), as everywhere, and the identification of this one as a son of Patricius excludes the possibility that this is a work of the Augustinian friar. Johannes Klenkok may have read the philosophical commentaries of Augustinians, like Augustinus of Ancona, Angelus of Carmerino, or Heinrich of Regensburg (Zumkeller, op. cit., pp. 61, 67-68, 165-68, no. 11, 120-21, 344-46), or anything considered good, to his students. The catologue of Amplonius Ratinck of Bercka (1410/12), the donor of the famous Amplonian collection of Erfurt, included two references to *sophismata* by Klenkok (in no. 7, 11). These, if properly attributed, probably originated in Klenkok's Erfurt lectures; they are not known to be extant. Lehmann, *Bibliothekskataloge*, 2:16-17.

[19]Johannes Schiphower wrote of Klenkok: "Quodlibeta etiam varia iuris totius, canonum legumque, doctor scripta reperitur compilasse." Eckermann, "Quelle," pp. 210-12. They were *quodlibeta iuris totius*, because they treated the conflict between secular and ecclesiastical law and, therefore, involved both laws (*ius totum*). The *Sachsenspiegel* disputation will be discussed below.

[20]The extant works not composed in the earlier stages of his career can be ascribed to Klenkok's Erfurt years: the *postilla* on the Acts of the Apostles, his latest extant theological work, additions to the literal exposition of the fourth book of *Sentences* (see next note), the various editions of his *Decadicon* against the *Sachsenspiegel*, and an Erfurt disputation on the *Sachsenspiegel*. An additional *postilla* on the Gospel of Matthew, cited in his commentary on Acts and listed by Schiphower, and a treatise on original sin and the immaculate conception mentioned by Schiphower, is not known to be extant. For Schiphower, Eckermann, "Quelle," pp. 210-12.

[21]In the *postilla* on Acts, for example, one finds discussions of the meaning of propositions and, with that, problems of grace, predestination, divine foreknowledge, and propositions concerning future contingents (Eichstätt 204, f. 123va-123vb); the behavior of judges (ibid., ff. 150va-152rb); forcible conversion (ibid., ff. 161va-162rb); and ecclesiastical property (ibid., ff. 158va-160ra)—among other things. The long discussion of legal cases in IV *Sent.* d. 15 is preserved in E2, ff. 48ra-56rb, and S, ff. 66rb-83vb. Consider also Valens

mentary on Acts portrays the work of the *lector principalis* especially well, and its exhaustive cross references to other theological works, the canon law, and some philosophy, reveal a use of biblical lectures to handle all the various subjects commonly treated in the general school. Digressions to law and the arts were integral to his work as an interpreter.

The regard of young contemporaries—Gerhard Groote, Johannes Hiltalingen, Angelus Dobelin, Gander of Meppen, and Johannes Merkelin—indicates the status of the theologian: they considered him a major voice, and some, like Gander, Merkelin, and Dobelin (the latter two, known to have been Augustinian friars; Gander might not have been), expected to gain respect for their association with him. Hiltalingen (also an Augustinian friar), who never claimed to have been a student of Klenkok but who persistently considered his arguments and frequently followed his conclusions in his bachelor's lectures at Paris before 1371, took material from the university writings, the commentary on Acts, and a treatise against the *Sachsenspiegel*.[22] Dobelin quoted the university writings and the commentary on Matthew.[23] Both aligned themselves with Klenkok's promotion of theological trends largely established by Gregory of Rimini in his Paris lectures of 1343/44 and continued by Ugolino of Orvieto in his Paris lectures of 1348/49: an adaptation of Ockham's metaphysics, the criticism of Scotist views of merit and grace, double predestination, criticism of Bradwardines's view of causality, and a particular approach to justification.[24] Hiltalingen and Dobelin knew Klenkok as the defender rather than as an originator of ideas; it must have been especially important that he had recently answered theologians like Boldon. To those not committed to the Augustinian school, Klenkok's tireless integration of theological analysis and ecclesiastical law may have seemed the greater contribution. Gerhard Groote, who thought of Klenkok together with the *Glossa ordinaria* to the *Decretum*, regarded his view of

Heynck, "Studien zu Johannes von Erfurt," *Franziskanische Studien*, 40(1958):329-60, here 331, who notes that IV *Sent.* d. 17 usually occasioned treatises on contrition (e.g. Thomas Aquinas, Pierre of Tarentaise, Richard of Middleton, Peter John Olivi, Petrus de Trabibus).

[22]Trapp made excerpts and provided some brief comments on 78 of these citations. "Notes," pp. 367-76. See also idem, "Hiltalingen's Augustinian Quotations," *Augustiniana*, 4(1954):412-49.

[23]Zumkeller, *Erbsünde*, p. 142.

[24]Ibid., pp. 142-214. Idem, "Der Augustinertheologe Johannes Hiltalingen von Basel (+1392) über Urstand, Erbsünde, Gnade und Verdienst," AA 43(1980):59-162. Marcolino, "Einleitung," in *Gregorii Ariminensis lectura super 1. Sent.*, 1:xii. For the Augustinian school, Courtenay, "Augustinianism at Oxford in the Fourteenth Century," *Augustiniana*, 30(1980):60-70; Zumkeller, *Erbsünde*, pp. 437-42; Ocker, "Augustinianism."

intention, cognizance, and degrees of culpability as a unique defense of a doctrine earlier taught by Augustine and maintained by Bertold of Brescia.[25] Some anonymous lectures of the early fifteenth century on Heinrich of Merseburg's *Summula iuris canonici* used "frater Johannes," along with patristic literature and other medieval theologians and canonists, to bring Heinrich (a middle to late thirteenth-century Franciscan lector at Magdeburg) up to date. The most specific of the references to friar Johannes— to the commentary on the fifteenth distinction of the fourth book of *Sentences*—can be traced to Klenkok's Erfurt addition.[26]

---

[25]Ep. 8, *Gerardi Magni epistolae*, p. 19.

[26]For Heinrich of Merseburg, R. Naz, "Henri de Mersebourg," DDC 5:1093 and Seckel in n. 21, pp. 22-23, above. The version of the *Summula* used in the lectures, which are actually a complete rewriting of the text, has the following note by the explicit (f. 59v): "In uigilia Elizabeth anno 1402." The text is written in two cursive gothic hands typical of the turn of the century, in a very clean, small script. The presence of only a few incidental corrections (mostly words added by the scribe above the line, probably as he wrote the draft) and the hurried appearance of the whole suggests a *reportatio* that had not been subsequently proofread and corrected. The reference to friar Johannes and the passage in Klenkok's IV *Sent.* d. 15 (in italics at the end of the excerpt), with textual notes at the conclusion of each passage, follow:

1. (*Summula*, f. 14r-14v) Nota tamen si clericus habet res, habet aliquas ex patrimonio uel artificio uel que date sunt ei intuitu persone. De hijs potest facere testamentum uel eciam dare cui placet. Sed si habet ex beneficio uel que date sunt intuitu ecclesie, de hijs non potest facere clericus quamdiu uiuit, nec testamentum facere nec modicum et moderate dare. Hec frater Johannes lib. iv. Sentenciarum distinctione xv..

que date sunt] *ms add et del* ei. non potest facere clericus] *ms* non potest facere clericum.

2. (IV *Sent.* d. 15, S f. 71rb, E2 f. 50rb-50va) Sequitur de peculio clericorum. Peculium est possessio rei priuate quam quis habet qui non est sui iuris quoad alia, sicut peculium castrense habet filius non emancipatus id quod in bello acquisiuit, peculium aliud aduenticium quod fortune sibi aduenit. Clericorum autem peculium dicitur eorum patrimonium uel quod operibus manuum acquisiuerunt, et loquor de clericis non de religiosis, quia religiosi non possunt habere peculium. Professi enim sunt non habere proprium, quia tria sunt de professione sue religionis: non habere proprium, uiuere in castitate et in obediencia usque ad mortem, nec ab hijs soluitur religiosus si in statu episcoporum assumatur. Patet satis *Clementinarum* "de statu monachorum" cap. i. et infra, et secundum glossam Petri* et secundum Innocentium. Isto eciam modo serui habent peculium, quia siquis seruus manumittitur, incurrit et peculium manumissus nisi expresse interdicatur, *Decreti* cap. "de libertis" in glossa. *Item de peculio, clerici possunt testari quidquid non acquisiuit occasione ecclesie nec de bonis ecclesie. Omnia enim talia tenetur clericus ecclesie derelinquere, patet* Decretalium *"de testamentis," "cum in officio," secundum Innocentium et Hostiensem.*

sic peculium] E2 sicud peculium. castrense] S castranse; E2 castiense. Peculium aliud] E2 *om* aliud. fortune] E2 fortuite (*leg* fortuito). aduenit] S uenit. patrimonium] E2 matrimonium. quia tria sunt] S que tria sunt; E2 habet enim tria sunt. sue religionis] E2 *om* sue. assumatur] S assumeritur. glossam Petri et secundum Innocentium] S *om* Petri et secundum. quia siquis] S quia si. incurrit] E2 intelligitur. manumissus] E2 missis. quidquid] E2 quodam. acquisiuit] E2 acquisiuerit. Hostiensem] E2 glossam.

*Petrus de Stagno? (see Johann Friedrich von Schulte, *Die Geschichte der Quellen und Literatur des canonischen Rechts*, 3 vols., [Graz: Akademische Druck- und Verlagsanstalt, 1956 reprint of Stuttgart: Ferdinand Enke, 1875], 2:201-02.)

The other references to "frater Johannes" are not specific; one of them may refer to Klenkok's *Postilla* on Acts, where Klenkok raises the matter of remuneration for masses in terms more intricate than the *Summula*, hinging his argument on the intention of the donor and the priest (whereas the *Summula* argues from a priest's intention alone). The passages follow:

Such practical literature of the later fourteenth century may hide much unknown data about the nature and extent of Klenkok's influence.[27] Amplonius Ratinck of Berka collected copies of the commentary on the *Sentences*, the magisterial sermons, and *sophismata* attributed to Johannes, which were included in the library he donated to the University of Erfurt in the early fifteenth

---

1. (*Summula*, ff. 34v-35r). Sed frater Johannes dicit, cum ab huiusmodi anniuersarium faciendo sacerdos non teneatur, quia eciam ex pacto licet accipere aliquod, cum locare potest opera sua, nunquid potest aliquis legere psalterium pro anima alicuius pro denarijs? Respondetur, si legens psalterium intendat uere uendere spiritualia, symonia est. Si autem recipere intendit stipendium laboris, licitum est. xii. questio ii. "caritatem"* et libro fratris Johannis.
Decretum, C.xii, q. ii. 45. CICan 1:701-02.
2. (*Postilla super Actus apostolorum*, f. 159ra-159rb). Queritur utrum omnibus satisfaciat [sacerdos] per unam missam. Uidetur quod sic, quia omnibus audientibus satisfacit per unam, si audiant unam. Ergo omnes deuocionem habentes ad unam similiter habebunt quibus [] unam.[a] Sed contra ponatur quod unus recommendat sacerdoti missam de sancto Petro, alius de sancto Augustino. Talis sacerdos non uidetur satisfacere.[b] Item, quilibet intendebat concedere opera sacerdotis singulariter uel laborem contrahendi uel tale quid. Ergo non debuit sacerdos eas locare altari. Item alias similiter si aliquis daret alicui pecuniam ut edifficaret unam ecclesiam, et alius similiter, talis satisfaceret per unam solam ecclesiam utrumque. Sic eciam obligatus mille hominibus ad dicendum, pro quolibet psalterium unum omnibus satisfaceret. Respondeo, intencio conferentis respicienda est et accipientis exprimenda, unde si quis offerret sacerdoti denarium, 'dicatis pro me missam hodie', si sacerdos acciperet pro alio dicens, 'libenter orabo pro te, et unus iam obtulit michi ut dicam hodie pro eo missam', et si offerens contentatur, sufficit. Et ex hoc uidetur quod numquam deberent accipere denarios pro missis quibus ut celebrent sufficienter est promissum. Dico ergo breuiter quod nisi offerens dicat quod sufficiat sibi quod oret pro eo sicut pro alio in eadem missa, non tunc accipitur munus eius.
audientibus] *rep ms.* item alias] *corr ms* altari. dicens] *corr marg* dicit. tunc] *corr marg* ille.
a. The scribe apparently made an omission, but the argument is clear: those who did not pay for the mass will have the merit of truly hearing it. b. I.e. two people purchase two different masses. The priest says one, and the other person's request is excluded. To the argument that rectors of churches receiving tithes as a pension for performing the sacraments is simoniacal, Klenkok notes: "dico talia oblata sunt ex dono libero ut inde sustententur [sacerdotes], nec ibi uenduntur sacramenta nec aliqua talia. Si uir sacerdos peteret pro administracione eukaristie uel altaris sacramenti pecuniam certam, symoniacus esset" (ibid., f. 159va). IV *Sent.* d. 15 treats the matter in a slightly different form: E2, f. 46va-46vb; K, f. 167r, S, f. 63ra-63rb. The anonymous lectures on the *Summula* also refer to Wilhelmus (Durand?), Baldwinus (Brandenburgensis?), Alexander (papa IV?), Reinerus (de Pomposis?), Ambrose, Augustine, Gregory the Great, Gandulphus, Hugh of St. Victor, Pierre (of Tarentaise?), Raymundus (of Peñafort?), and Hostiensis. The lector defends the authority of abbots and the pastoral privileges of religious orders, which suggests a monastic provenance.
[27]In the late fifteenth century, Schiphower knew all the writings of Klenkok known to us (except the commentary on the *Peri hermenias*, which is also not extant) and a treatise on original sin which proves the immaculate conception (the last work is mentioned in no other source; Eckermann, "Quelle," pp. 210-12). Also in the late fifteenth century, Gottschalk Hollen cited Klenkok in several works. W. Eckermann, *Gottschalk Hollen O.E.S.A.* (+1481). *Leben, Werke und Sakramentenlehre*, vol. 22 of *Cassiciacum* (Würzburg: Augustinus-Verlag, 1967), pp. 74, 151, 209, 247, 317. Although Adolar Zumkeller has found intellectual continuity between fifteenth-century Augustinian professors at Erfurt and Klenkok, he appears to have found no direct citations or indirect references after those of Angelus Dobelin. *Erbsünde*, passim.

century.[28] Klenkok's criticism of Scotus remained appreciable to at least one confrère of Lower Saxony in the later fifteenth century, but especially in practical subjects of pastoral theology.[29]

Klenkok's greater reputation grew at Erfurt, where members of his order, like Dobelin and Merkelin, could still absorb the abstractions that helped form the distinctive features of a religious community, but where the more universal value of Klenkok's thought was most readily found in his use of the canon law, providing a conceptual framework by which Augustinians could understand themselves as comfortably integrated into ecclesiastical society, but also solving, tersely and pointedly, problems common to all church professionals. The extent of the influence of a friar of lower Saxony at Oxford may have been impeded by the ability of English Augustinians to dominate their university or by the simple fact that Klenkok spent no more than four years there and probably up to eight or nine years in Erfurt.[30] The city on the Gera was an administrative center of the region's relatively distant temporal and spiritual lord, the archbishop of Mainz, and it enjoyed the highest concentration of schools between Cologne, Strasbourg, and Prague. Studies of works originating in the schools of arts at the four principal ecclesiastical foundations of the city—St. Maria, St. Severus, the "Scots Cloister," and St. Augustine (canons)—have uncovered the city's importance as a center of modalist grammar and logic and, with the influx of English terminism, its criticism, well before the first license to form a uni-

---

[28]Lehmann, *Bibliothekskataloge,* 2:16, 17, 60ff.; nos. 7, 11, 60 (probably E1, with the magisterial sermons).

[29]Gottschalk Hollen (died 1481), in his *Tractatus de septem sacramentis,* drew criticism of Scotus from the commentary on the fourth book of *Sentences,* based some of his sacramental theology upon Klenkok's work, and used the *Sentences* commentary as a source for at least one canonistic reference (to Henry of Segusia). Eckermann, *Gottschalk,* pp. 317, 319. Prof. Dr. Eckermann has also called my attention to a reference by Hollen to Klenkok's IV *Sent.* d. 15 and its discussion of usury (in comparison with Raŷmundo of Peñaforte), in the *Sermonum opus exquisitissimum,* 2 vols. (Hagenau, 1517, 1519/1520), dominica iii. adventus, sermo ix. G.

[30]The affair over the appointment of Johannes and Andreas of Milan demonstrates the English province's dominance at Oxford (discussed in the previous chapter). The transfer of students from Bologna to Oxford while Thomas of Strasbourg was prior general may, then, have been an attempt to weaken the province's control. Cf. Aubrey Gwynn, *The English Austin Friars in the Time of Wyclif* (London: Oxford University Press, 1940), pp. 96-105. Another possible factor in the nationalization of the Augustinian school at Oxford may have been close ties between provincial leadership and English nobility, particularly seen during the rule of Geoffrey Hardeby as provincial prior. Francis Roth, "A History of the English Austin Friars," *Augustiniana,* 8(1958):22-47, 465-96; 11(1961):533-63; 12(1962):93-122, 391-442; 13(1963):515-51; 14(1964):163-215, 670-710; 15(1965):175-236, 567-628; 16(1966): 204-63, 446-519; 17(1967):84-166. Here, 8:490-96. Walsh, "Vita," pp. 177-78. See also AA 4(1911/12):376-77, 430, 449, 476.

versity in 1379 and its actual foundation in 1392.[31] Although the three mendicant schools of the city in that period (the Carmelites had no convent school there) have not received the same kind of attention, there can be no doubt that they were equally significant—witness the reputations of the Franciscan, Johannes of Erfurt, in Scotist theology and in canon law, or of the Dominican, Meister Eckhart, and the Augustinian, Heinrich of Friemar, in theology and exegesis.[32] In 1362, people of Thüringen were already accustomed to regarding the Erfurt schools as a university ("studium generale"), "on account of the tremendous throng of students who are accustomed to pour into that place more than into any other in all of Germany"; over the four schools of arts, there already presided a "rector superior," Heinrich Totting of Oyta, who possessed the degree of master of arts from the University of Prague.[33] This was a strategic place from which to advance a career.

Johannes dug through the Saxon law while a professor in Erfurt, and he unearthed errors "contrary to the gospel of Christ and to the decisions of holy mother church, and the church of Rome."[34] His candor in the controversy that ensued offers a rare display of ideological prejudice applied to a practical problem, and his skill and persistence at applying a papalist view of the

---

[31]Jan Pinborg, *Entwicklung*, pp. 139-212. Idem, "Neues zum Erfurter Schulleben des 14. Jahrhunderts nach Handschriften der Jagiellonischen Bibliothek zu Krakow," *Bulletin de philosophie médiévale*, 15(1973):146-51. Idem, "Fourteenth-Century Schools," pp. 171-92.

[32]Pinborg, *Entwicklung*, p. 150. Ludger Meier, *Die Barfüsser Schule zu Erfurt*, vol. 38/2 of BGPTM (Münster: Aschendorff, 1958), pp. 7ff., 40, and passim, which finds Scotism the dominant theology of the Erfurt Franciscans since the early fourteenth century (but not providing a very detailed examination of the period before 1392). Also Stroick in n. 20, p. 22, and Kurtscheid in n. 3, p. 18, above. Valens Heynck, "Studien," pp. 329-60. Heinrich of Friemar's commentary on the decalogue circulated in 380 known manuscripts, "provenant surtout de l'Europe centrale où chaque couvent ou monastère en possédait un exemplaire." Guyot, "Quelques aspects," pp. 244-48, here 244 (for preparatory work toward an edition, see p. 244 n. 9). Lectors' revisions of commentaries by other authors are also an important source for the history of these schools. Pinborg called attention to a Franciscan revision of Heinrich of Friemar's IV *Sent. Entwicklung*, p. 150 n. 49; Zumkeller, *Manuskripte*, p. 157 no. 330. D. Trapp, "Augustinian," pp. 251-55, noted several revisions of the late fourteenth century not connected with Erfurt.

[33]Letter of Karl IV to the pope, quoted in Ehrle, *Peter von Candias*, p. 201: " . . . propter magnam studentium multitudinem, qui ad prefatum locum plus quam ad aliquem alium locum totius Alamannie confluere consueverunt." Heinrich Totting later studied theology at Paris. Courtenay, *Adam*, pp. 146-47. Cf. A. Lang, *Heinrich Totting von Oyta. Ein Beitrag zur Entstehungsgeschichte der ersten deutschen Universitäten und zur Problemgeschichte der Spätscholastik* (Münster: Aschendorff, 1937), p. 56.

[34]*Universis Christi fidelibus*, ed. by Homeyer, *Johannes*, p. 432a: "Quoniam etiam praedicat orthodoxa, quoniam iniqua convalescente consuetudine error pro lege custoditus est ut scribitur Sap. xiiii, hinc anno praeterito dum essem Erfordiae, quosdam errores, repugnantes evangelio Christi sanctaeque matris ecclesiae determinationibus ac Romanae ecclesiae, pro legibus reputatos et in quodam libello, qui nuncupatur Saxoniae speculum insertos, in quo libro statuta Saxonum continentur, reperi."

world made him a monk reputed, if personally only for a short time, throughout central Europe. I shall first recount the events; then, their implications.

Klenkok put the most complete account of the beginning of his controversy with the *Sachsenspiegel* in a pamphlet which he wrote in his own defense and addressed "to all the faithful of Christ." After listing the Saxon laws that conflict with papal law, he recounted:[35]

---

[35]Homeyer, *Johannes*, pp. 416-22, produces the middle low German version of Klenkok's "Universis Christi fidelibus," which is used here (the Latin version, quoted in the previous footnote, suppresses the accusation against Kerlinger and the allegation that the Magdeburg *Rat* pressured the cloister, and it also claims that Kerlinger asked Klenkok to write up the errors and their refutation in order to send them to the curia for papal action. The German also presents less developed arguments than the Latin version and neglects, unlike the Latin, to mention a debate in Halberstadt, all of which suggest that it antedates the Latin version). The first passage is on p. 416:

Dit sint de stŭcke an deme Sassenspegel de mek dŭncket sin tegen de christen ee und weder gotlich gheistlich und keyserrecht. Dar umme ich broder Johan Clenkok orden der enzedel sŭnte Augustini unwerdich genomet eyn lerer der hilgen schrift, sprak to mester Walter Kerlinger predekers orden eime wroger des orden in der christenheit van des paves macht, dat he provede of itlich stŭcke, de hir na gescriven stan ind halden sind vor recht in deme Sassenspegel, icht sin weder de christen ee, vnd weret dat en des dŭchte, dat he dat beterde. Do bat mek deselve mester, dat ich eme de stŭcke schreve und redde weder de stŭcke, dat dede ich dor gotlike warheit ind salicheit der seile vnd horsam der christen ee, ind ich dede des mesters bede und schref dat ich ene bede, of ich ierne unrecht geschreven hedde, dat he dat beterde. Dar na nam de selve mester dat bok dat ich eme schreven hadde unde ghaf dat den erborn Ratluden to Maydeborch, und de selven ratlude hebbet gekart er unhulde tegen mek hir umme.

The second passage, from the conclusion, is on pp. 421-22:

Do en mester Walter predekers orden vorgenant geantwortet hadde dat bok, dat ich dor des selven mesterrs bede gescreven hadde weder artikele de hir vorgesat sint, sammeden (se) uppe dat Raithus to Meideborch drei Raide, dat waren 36 Raitlude, dar to hundert ere Koremann der stat van Meideborch, und vorbodden dar to de aildesten brodere van unsen clostere der Augustinere, und kundigheden vor den allen, dat ein broder eres orden de ere overste were hedde geschreven ein bok und ghegheven mester Walter predekers orden wrogere der kerken. In dem boke hedde de selve broder und in anderen sinen werken ghearbeidet to einer ergeringe (und) to einer vorstŭringe (der) stedden, vorsten, greven ind heren van Sassen lande. Hir umme sprak de andere Raitmester, dat sei mosten clagen ind kundigen dusse schande und smaheit, de en dusse broder gedan hedde und anderen van Sassen, stedden, heren und anderen luden. Dar umme screven de vorsproken ratlude van Meideborch vierhundert stedden eder mer und den vorsten und den heren de dar bi weren so swerlike breve, und under anderen artikelen schreven sei, dat ich mi gesat hedde weder der Sassen recht dat gewaret sevenhundert iar ses iar min, do et koning Karl de Grote gaf den Sassen mit witschap des paves, der vorsten und der heren, uppe dat de sassen christen worden und bleven. Und einen artickel schreven sei, dat hir umme solden stedde ind heren sorchvoldig wesen, dat mi des nicht gestadet enworde, dat ich der Sassen recht kreinkede. Hir antworde ich to, ich were ein Sasse geboren und en welde Sassen nicht schenden, dan gerne wolde ich, dat in mi ind in allen anderen luden unrecht worde vornichtet. Wi leset dat de paves ind de keiser hadden gesat vor ein recht: de eine maget nodigede eder entforde mit gewalt, dat he de na nicht en mochte to echte nemen, dat weder schref sunte Jheronimus, dat na gotliken rechte de man mochte de maghet to echte nemen, dar umme wandelden de paves ind keiser ere gesette. (Hic modicum deficit) Wol is mi geschreven van Meideborch, dat de vorgenanten ratlude mer sin upp mek vorbittert und vortornet, dan de van Meideborch weren uppe eren ertzebiscop heren Borcharde des greven sone van Scrapelo den sei mordeden. Vele anderer swarer sake hebben de

These are the errors of the *Sachsenspiegel* which seem to me against the Christian gospel and both divine spiritual and imperial law. That is why I, brother Johann Clenkok, Order of the Hermits of Saint Augustine, unworthily called a teacher of Holy Scripture, told master Walter Kerlinger, Order of Preachers, an inquisitor of the order in Christendom by papal authority, that he might consider some excerpts—written here and held for lawful in the *Sachsenspiegel*—whether they be against the Christian gospel and, if so, that he might correct them. Then the same master bade me, that I write him the excerpts and refute them. That is what I did, by divine truth and sanctity of the soul and obedience to the Christian gospel, and I carried out the master's wish and wrote that I asked him that, if I had written anything unjust, he should reprove it. Then soon after, the same master took the book that I had written and gave it to the honorable city counsellors of Magdeburg, and the same counsellors turned their displeasure against me because of this.

It is not at all clear that Kerlinger betrayed Johannes. The Latin version of the text shows how Klenkok believed that Kerlinger asked for his refutation of the *Sachsenspiegel* in order to acquire a papal censure of the questionable laws—which the counsellors of Magdeburg also believed and feared (note 36)—and now he found himself betrayed by Kerlinger's transmission of the arguments to the city council. What then occurred, however, had nothing to do with Kerlinger, as Klenkok himself explained in the conclusion to his self-defense:

When the above-mentioned master Walter of the Order of Preachers had handed over the book which I had written at the request of the same master against articles here laid out, there assembled in the *Rathaus* in Magdeburg three sessions of council. There were thirty-six counsellors with a hundred angry citizens of the city of Magdeburg. They summoned there the noblest brothers of our cloister of the Augustinians and announced before all that a brother of their order who is their superior had written a book and gave it to master Walter, Order of Preachers, inquisitor of heretics. In the book [they said] the same brother, and in others of his works, created injury and embitterment in the cities and among the princes, counts, and lords of the Saxon land. The other *Ratmeister* [that is, of the new city] said that they [the Magdeburg Augustinians] must complain against and denounce this scandal

vorgenanten ratlûde theghen mek ghedan. Doch bidde ich io Gode vor sei und beghere en des besten. Dusse stûcke do ich kûndlich allen guden lûden und bidde, es ich ierne unrecht geschreven eder gesproken hebbe, dat sei leifliken nicht hetliken mine rede beteren. Ok is swar dat de selven ratlude screven, dat de Sassen christen sin geworden und bleven dar umme dat en koning Karel dusse stûckevor recht gheve. Ich hope dat sei cristen geworden sin and bleven nicht hir umme, dan dor Godes recht und erer ewighen salicheit und heil erer zele.

and insult which this brother had committed against them and other Saxons—cities, lords, and other folk. That is why the aforementioned counsellors of Magdeburg wrote such heavy letters to four hundred cities or more and to the princes and lords associated with them. And they wrote, among other allegations, that I spoke against the Saxon law which, 694 [sic] years ago, king Karl the Great gave the Saxons with the consent of the pope, the princes, and the lords, so that the Saxons would become Christians and so remain. They wrote one article—that for this reason, cities and lords should take care that I not be allowed to weaken the Saxon law. To this I answer: I was born a Saxon, and I do not want to disgrace Saxony, rather would I that in me and in all other people injustice were destroyed. . . . In fact, I have received word from Magdeburg that the aforementioned counsellors are more embittered and irritated with me than the people of Magdeburg were with their lord archbishop Burchhardt, the son of the count of Schraplau, whom they murdered. The aforementioned counsellors have done many other terrible things against me. I pray to God for them and wish them well. These excerpts I declare to all good people, and I ask, if I have written or spoken anything unjust, that they kindly and not hatefully correct my speech. It is also terrible that the same counsellors write that the Saxons have become christians and so remain because king Karl gave these excerpts for law. I hope they have become Christians and so remain not on that account, but through God's law, and their eternal happiness and salvation, their goal.

The meeting of the Magdeburg *Rat* and their letter to the cities probably occurred in the late winter or early spring of 1368.[36]

---

[36]A summons of the Hildesheim *Rat* to three knights and their neighbors to meet on Pentecost to examine the book of a monk against the Saxon law appears in a register without a year but among entries from 1368. Hans Bütow, knowing that Klenkok was provincial prior when the controversy broke out but thinking that Klenkok was elected to provincial prior on Pentecost 1368 and not *re*elected, concluded that the place of the entry in the register is misleading and opted for a beginning date of the controversy in 1369. Bütow, "Lebensgeschichte," p. 557 and n. 64 for the source of the register entry, followed by Trapp, "Notes," p. 360. Since Klenkok was actually elected provincial prior on Pentecost 1367, the Hildesheim entry stands in a very plausible place and can be taken at face value. The Hildesheim *Rat*'s response to the Magdeburg letter, which this entry certainly represents, must have occurred shortly after receiving the Magdeburg correspondence. The sessions of the Magdeburg *Rat* must, therefore, have occurred in the late winter or early spring of 1368. A copy of the Magdeburg letter is edited by Emil Steffenhage, *Catalogus codicum manuscriptorum bibliothecae Regiae et Universitatis Regimontanae*, 2 vols. (Königsberg: Schubert Seidel, 1861, 1867, 1872), 1:72-73. Since it is not widely available, I reproduce it here:

"Uniuersis rectoribus, Judicibus, Consulibus Ciuitatum et villarum Jure saxonum gaudentibus seu utentibus Consules vnionumque rectores ciuitatis Magdeburgensis, vnser willige dinste alle czeit boreit, wir begeren euwir vorsichtikeit czu wissen, das eyn monch geheysen Cleynekoch, provincial yn sachsen vnde doringen landen der swarczen monche sinte augustinus regele, den man heyset heremiten, hat bucher getichtet vnde geschreben wedir sachsen recht, das vnser eldern wol sebendehalb hundert ior sechs ior myn haben gehat, dat koning karle der grose mit rechte vnde volbort des bobistes vnde der fursten yn

Only a short time earlier, a few months at most, Klenkok approached Kerlinger, who operated out of the Dominican cloister of Erfurt, and composed his first criticisms of the *Sachsenspiegel*, his *Decadicon* (so named for its ten original articles).[37] Kerlinger might have been immediately suspicious of Klenkok's concern

---

den czeiten dem lande gap vnde bestetigete, uff das die sachsen Cristen wurden vnde cristen (ge)louben behilden, das sint von vele keysern, koningen vnde fursten vnde von velen gutten leuten gehalden ist. Jtem wedir dis recht hat der monch eyn buch gemacht, des wir vsschriffte haben, das nenet her den Codicon, vnde hat is gesant eynem meister der prediger orden, das her is sulde an vnsern heiligen vater, den pobist, brengen. Jn dem buch spricht der monch: ffursten, herren, groffen, freyen, ale dy lantstete, dorffer, vorsteer vnde regirer, dy sachsen recht haben, synt yn irthume, vngelouben vnde yn vnrechtikeit vordustert mit dem buche, do der sachsen recht ynne geschreben steet, vnde die Jenne, dy is gemanet werden vnde dor uff nicht lassen, sulle man so vngelobissche vnde vncristene leute uff der hort bornen, vnde disser rede vil gleich, der wir euch alle nicht schreyben konnen. Noch deme mole ir denne sachsen rechtis gebrauchet, Bitte wir euch, das ir dor czu sorgfeldigk seit vnde vorkundiget das vort den, dy bey euch besessen synt vnde sachsen recht haben, das sie dor czu gedencken, ap der monch vnser sachsen recht vor ergern adir nedern welde, das is ym keyne stat nochuolgen wurde. Ap der monch das aws seynem eygenen houpte hat, adir von ander leuthe geheise vnde rothe, wisse wir nicht, wenne vns dunket, en bewege allir meist dor czu, das noch sachsen rechte dy monche keyn erbe nemen mussen, vnde das yn dy leute ueren, das sie czeug seyn Jres erbes vnde guttis, vnde erbelouff nicht genemen mogen. Datum."

For the legendary assertion that Charlemagne gave the Saxons their law, consider Sigurd Graf von Pfeil, "Karl der Grosse in der deutschen Sage," in *Das Nachleben*, ed. W. Braunfels, Percy Ernst Schramm, vol. 4 of *Karl der Grosse. Lebenswerk und Nachleben* (Düsseldorf: L. Schwann, 1967), pp. 326-36, esp. 326-27.

[37]Kerlinger came from an established Erfurt family long known to have had close relations with the Dominican cloister, and, in addition, in 1369, he was elected provincial of Saxony (the acts of the provincial chapter of Ruppin in that year were preserved in part on a binding and edited by A. Zacke, *Ueber das Todten-Buch des Dominikaner-Klosters und die Prediger-Kirche zu Erfurt* [Erfurt: Carl Villaret, 1861], pp. 8, 10, 131). We know that Kerlinger operated out of Erfurt from the curia's attempt, after his death in 1373, to get 1,500 gold florins of the inquisitor's proceeds that he had deposited with the city council of Erfurt (the papacy was directed there by the Dominican province). Beyer, *Urkundenbuch Erfurt*, 2:553 no. 757. Gustav Schmidt, *Päbstliche Urkunden und Regesten*, 2 vols., vols. 21-22 of *Geschichtsquellen der Provinz Sachsen* (Halle: Otto Hendel, 1886, 1889), 2:332, 333, 334. Although this document has been long known, its implications for Kerlinger's policy and residency have been overlooked. Cf. Paul Flade, "Römische Inquisition in Mitteldeutschland," *Beiträge zur sächsische Kirchengeschichte* (1896):58-96, here p. 75 n. 4; McDonnel, *The Beguines and Beghards in Medieval Culture* (New Brunswick: Rutgers University Press, 1954), p. 563. That Klenkok himself was not in Magdeburg at the time has already been pointed out by Bütow. "Lebensgeschichte," p. 557. Schiphower's hagiographic account— that Klenkok escaped out of the city in a basket, like the apostle Paul (ibid., p. 557; Homeyer, *Johannes*, p. 382; Ac 9.25)—was probably based on an earlier account that simply claimed that Klenkok was expelled from the city: P. Lehmann, *Mitteilungen aus Handschriften, Sitzungsberichte der Bayerischen Akademie der Wissenschaften, philosophisch-philologische Klasse*, 1929 (Munich: Bayerische Akademie der Wissenschaften, 1929), 1:44. This is based probably on Klenkok's own claim that he suffered many things on account of the Magdeburg *Rat*. We know that Klenkok originally contacted Kerlinger only a short while before the meeting of the Magdeburg *Rat* because of a comment in his "Universis fidelibus"—that he had discovered the errors of the *Sachsenspiegel* "in the previous year" in Erfurt (note 34, above). Because "Universis fidelibus" mentions a meeting with Albert of Halberstadt that took place after April 1369 (note 44, below), the original list of errors was composed in 1368. Because the Magdeburg *Rat* met in late winter or early spring of that year, the first edition of the *Decadicon* and Klenkok's first contact with Kerlinger must have occurred in early 1368.

with discrepancies between the canon law and the favored code
of central and eastern Europe, because of the strategic disad-
vantage of Klenkok's campaign. The success of Kerlinger's inquisition had much to do with the participation of cities, which
received one-third of the proceeds from confiscations, and Kerlinger is known to have even put the inquisitor's third in a city
council's trust.[38] Since city councils were frequently inclined
to support their beguines, it was necessary to make the inquisition beneficial to councils. Kerlinger would hardly do anything
rash to alienate the Magdeburg counsellors—especially at Magdeburg, where he may have had difficulty garnering support,
and especially now, when he was arduously destroying beguin-
ages in Thüringen, Saxony, Braunschweig, Mecklenburg, and
Hessen, wherever he could find them and gain the necessary
local support.[39]

There is no reason to believe, however, that Klenkok was
"treacherously denounced to the City Council of Magdeburg" by
Kerlinger.[40] To the contrary, Kerlinger's action deeply unsettled

---

[38]Previous note. P. Fredericq, *Corpus Documentorum Inquisitionis Haereticae Pravitatis Neerlandicae*, 5 vols. (Ghent: Martinus Nijhoff, 1885-1902), 1:212-13 no. 210. Schmidt, *Bettelorden*, pp. 92-93.

[39]Fredericq, *Corpus*, 1:206-07 no. 209. In 1368, he reportedly ordered 400 beguines to return to the world in Erfurt; 200 complied and carried penitential crosses; 200 did not and
were exiled. He forced the exile of beguines from Eisenach, Mühlhausen, Wismar, Lüne-
burg, and Rostock. Martin Erbstösser, *Sozialreligiöse Strömmungen im späten Mittelalter*, vol.
16 of *Forschungen zur mittelalterlichen Geschichte* (Berlin: Akademie Verlag, 1970), p. 114 n.
239. *Lübeck*, 3 vols., vols. 19, 26, 28 of *Die Chroniken der deutschen Städte* (Göttingen: Vandenhoeck und Ruprecht, 1967 reprint of the first ed., Leipzig: Solomon Hirzel, 1884),
1:539. Günter Peters, "Norddeutsches Beginen- und Begardenwesen im Mittelalter,"
Niedersächsiches Jahrbuch für Landesgeschichte, 41/42(1969/70):50-133, here 106-09. P. Flade,
Das römische Inquisitionsverfahren in Deutschland bis zu den Hexenprozessen, vol. 9/1 of *Studien
zur Geschichte der Theologie und der Kirche* (Leipzig: Dietrich, 1902), pp. 119-20 (which also
includes later examples of the dissolution of property). Karl IV, in 1369, said that the be-
guinages of the provinces of Magdeburg and Bremen and in the lands of Thüringen, Saxony, and Hessen were entirely destroyed. Fredericq, *Corpus*, 1:208-10, 212, 216, 219-20,
here no. 213, 1:219-20. He said this to justify his own support of Kerlinger's inquisition,
and the claim probably originated with Kerlinger himself. Of course, if it were literally
true, it is not clear why Kerlinger sought the support of the king and emperor, but the
claim must nevertheless have had some basis in successes. Kerlinger had been busy in the
preceding years. A chronicle claimed that he was, about 1367, particularly active around
Magdeburg and Erfurt, and that many heretics were burned in and about Erfurt—both
men and women. "Collationes Chronici Magdeburgensis a Meibom . . . editi cum codice
manuscripto in Archivo Electorali Saxonico Dresdae exstante . . . ," in vol. 3 of *Scriptores
Rerum Germanicarum praecipue Saxonicarum*, ed. Johannes Burchard Menken (Leipzig:
Johann Christian Martin, 1730), col. 371. Of these executions, we know only of that of
Johann Hartmund at Erfurt in 1367. Robert E. Lerner, *The Heresy of the Free Spirit* (Berkeley:
University of California Press, 1972), pp. 134-41. A papal letter of 1364 specifically called
upon the city of Magdeburg (as well as the archbishops of Mainz and Magdeburg) to
support the inquisition, and this may imply that the city was reluctant to cooperate (pre-
vious note). For council support of beguines, Peters, "Beginen-," pp. 104, 106-09, esp. 109;
McDonnel, *Beguines*, pp. 566, 568.

[40]Trapp, "Notes," p. 361.

the counsellors, who could take no comfort in Kerlinger's position in the matter and who did not know whether Klenkok's position was privately held but certainly feared that it might find widespread concurrence, which is readily apparent in the conclusion to their letter to their daughter cities (note 36, above). All of this suggests painful circumspection on Kerlinger's part, but in view of the counsellors' reaction, it seems likely that the inquisitor had confronted them with the implications of Klenkok's claims, even though he could not afford to press the issue himself.

Nor was it likely that Klenkok should find support in the church of Magdeburg. Her archbishops, whose tumultuous relationship with the city is most vividly seen in the murder of Burchard of Schraplau in 1325, were not prepared to jeopardize a generally sensitive position over the law that undergirded the immensely influential *Schöppenstuhl*, the most powerful urban court of appeals within the Empire.[41] Albrecht of Bohemia, whom Karl IV saw transferred to the archiepiscopal see in 1368 against the will of the cathedral chapter, exchanged the usual promises with the city—his respect of their freedoms and their faithfulness to their (ostensible) lord. But he spent the next three years fighting his cathedral canons, only to resign in 1371.[42] When his successor, Peter of Bohemia, exchanged promises with the city, he even conceded the authority of the Saxon law in his courts.[43]

Klenkok turned elsewhere. Johannes received an audience with Albert of Saxony, recently consecrated (1366) to the see of Halberstadt, whose cathedral lay some fifty kilometers to the south-southwest of Magdeburg and about one hundred and twenty kilometers north of Erfurt.[44] Albert was a Parisian master

---

[41]Thus, a property dispute documented 23 April 1363 between the city of Magdeburg and Rolof of Saxony—over rents to a house sold to the old city of Magdeburg by the archbishop, even though he had previously sold rents to part of the house to the abbess of Gernrode (who subsequently sold her rents to count Rolof)—was settled in the court of the imperial bailiff according to the Saxon law, and the terms of the settlement were guaranteed by the archbishop (who relinquished all rights to the house, to the city). Hertel, *UB Magdeburg*, pp. 293-95 no. 460.

[42]Ibid., pp. 317-18 no. 492-93. Gottfried Wentz, Bernt Schwineköper, *Das Erzbistum Magdeburg*, vol. 1 of *Die Bistümer der Kirchenprovinz Magdeburg*, in *Germania Sacra* (New York: Walter de Gruyter, 1972), pp. 293-95 no. 460.

[43]Hertel, *UB Magdeburg*, p. 328 no. 514-15.

[44]For Albert, the following note. After the meeting, Klenkok wrote a new preface to the *Decadicon* addressed to Albert, which is published by B. J. L. De Geer, "Klenkok's," pp. 386-409. It is identical to the final edition of the *Decadicon* published by Scheidt, excepting a preface to Albert in De Geer's version and a letter to cardinal Pierre de Vergne in Scheidt's version. A reference to a conflict between the count of Lippe and the count of

who had to his credit fine works on Aristotle, mathematics, and logic and who had served nine years as rector of the Paris arts faculty (1353 to 1362). Klenkok must have known of Albert from his own Parisian years, and he probably also knew that three years in Avignon (1362 to 1365) made the new bishop a kind of curial intimate: Albert did procure the papal license for the foundation of the University of Vienna in 1365 and became her first rector.[45] Rudolf Block also appeared in Halberstadt—from what city he came and whether he came by Albert's invitation or under his own initiative is not known. Klenkok and Block debated the *Sachsenspiegel* before the bishop—whether in a private hearing or in a formal disputation is impossible to determine. In the course of this, two other positions were also put on the table: the written opinion of Jordan of Quedlinburg, an old Augustinian professor who in some cloister of the province was struggling past failing eyesight to complete a major collection of sermons, and the argument of Wilhelm Harr, a Benedictine of unknown provenance (whether present or corresponding is not clear).[46] Harr argued against the validity of mendicant claims to property.[47] Closer to the general principles at issue, Block and Quedlinburg argued for a separation of laws: what is legal in civil law might not be legal in the canon law, but such conflict is acceptable.[48] Block also said that the alleged granting of the law by Charlemagne to the Saxons when they converted to Christianity, with its accommodations of Saxon custom, was strategic—it kept the land away from the greater evil (rejection of Christianity)—and lent the law its validity. Klenkok already knew this argument from the letter of the Magdeburg *Rat* to the cities.[49] Quedlinburg added (presum-

---

Tecklenburg, which is first testified on 5 April 1369, indicate that the audience with Albert occurred after that date. De Geer, op. cit., pp. 375-76. Böhlau, "Lebensgeschichte," pp. 559-60. Contrast Homeyer, *Johannes*, pp. 391-92.

[45]E. Neuenschwander, "Albert von Sachsen," *Lexikon des Mittelalters*, 3 vols. + (Munich and Zürich: Artemis Verlag, 1980-1986+), 1:289-90.

[46]Trapp believed a formal debate was held. "Notes," p. 361. For Jordan, Jordanus de Saxonia, *Vitasfratum*, pp. xix-xx; Kunzelmann, *Geschichte*, 5:40-41. Klenkok's rebuttals of Block and Quedlinburg were written in the version of the *Decadicon* that he subsequently sent to Albert and later sent, with very minor revisions, to Pierre de Vergne. De Geer, "Klenkok's," pp. 405, 407-09. Scheidt, *Biblioteca*, pp. 92-93, 96-102.

[47]Contending that a donor has "more right" to property given to friars than the friars who had received it. De Geer, "Klenkok's," pp. 403-05. Scheidt, *Biblioteca*, pp. 90-93. The argument arose in conjunction with the *Sachsenspiegel*'s denial of feudal rights to novices in religious orders who do not take vows but return to the world. *SLdr* I.xxv.3; 1;93. Cf. *Decretum*, XX.i.10; *Dec. Greg.*, III.xxxi.20. CICan 1:845; 2:577. Note also the conclusion of the letter of the Magdeburg *Rat*, n. 36, above.

[48]De Geer, "Klenkok's," p. 409. Scheidt, *Biblioteca*, pp. 98-99.

[49]The claim appears to be an adaptation of Johann Buch's doctrine—that the *Sachsenspiegel*, at least in part, translates a privilege granted to the Saxons by Charlemagne. See Heinrich Siegel, *Die deutschen Rechtsbücher und die Kaiser-Karls-Sage*, vol. 140, Abhandlung

ably in his correspondence) that conflicts between the laws were permissible, as long as the civil law does not damage the Faith by contradicting the gospel.

Theirs must have been a frustrating, if superficial, challenge to Johannes, for rather than address the legal particulars of his criticisms, Rudolf and Jordan simply denied the relevance of the conflict of laws and its implications for the social order. At Block's defense of Caroline authority, Johannes dared reproof and appealed to their spiritual kinship:

You could consider, Reverend Master, if it might seem to you that errors as well as deductions move you. If so, I demand that you, by your holy office [of professor of sacred theology], remedy these matters. And if something in these expressions of mine will have been found displeasing, your learned prudence should correct my expression. His is it not, of whom it is not legitimate to have spoken falsehood. You know that I would devote a temporal life to this cause, if I could [thereby] profess what, in the law of God, is the unity of an orthodox people. Frequently did I write, preach, dispute against the aforementioned errors, which I shall continue to do, laying hope upon him who is the cord of peace and unity in oneness with you, to receive, by your prayers, eternal life as a reward.

And to Jordan punctiliously, "To the contrary I declare: what is opposite the gospel is against the gospel."[50] The law of the church is built upon the gospel—in fact, upon two specific texts, "quod in ore duorum uel trium . . . " and, to Peter and his successors, "quodcumque ligaueris . . . "; how could one contradict the law of the church and not assault the gospel?[51] Johannes was sure that he merely defended an indivisible Christian society.

---

9 of *Sitzungsberichte der philosophisch-historischen Classe der kaiserlichen Akademie der Wissenschaften* (Vienna: Carl Gerold's Sohn, 1899), pp. 3-12, 14, 15, and passim, for the popularity of the story since the late fourteenth century. Siegel believed an entry for the year 810 in the *Magdeburger Schöffenchronik* (composed after 1373) contains the first definite reference, apart from Buch, to the story. The Magdeburg letter and Rudolf Block should now be regarded as the earliest references.

[50]De Geer, "Klenkok's," pp. 407-08; Scheidt, *Biblioteca*, p. 99: "Consideretis ergo, reverende Magister, si vobis videatur, an errores et deductiones vos moveant. Si sic est, requiro vos per sanctum officium vestrum ut remedium in his fiat. Et si quid in his dictis displicuerit, vestra docta prudentia corrigat dictum meum. Illius non est, cujus dictum errorem esse fas non est. Scientes quod vitam temporalem ad hoc ponerem, si valerem profiteri quod in lege Dei plebis esset unitas orthodoxae. Contra praedictos errores frequenter scripsi, legi, praedicavi, disputavi, quod et faciam, sperans ab illo, qui pacis et unitatis est vinculum una vobiscum, vobis suffragantibus aeternam vitam recipere pro mercede." And concerning Jordan: "Contra statuo, quod oppositum est Evangelio est contra evangelium."

[51]Scheidt, *Biblioteca*, p. 99. Mt. 16.19; 18.16.

Interestingly, Rudolf and Jordan, at least as Klenkok presents them, offered arguments that did not supersede those of the Magdeburg *Rat* (note 36). Albert of Saxony, in his only known contribution to the debate, put in a word for Klenkok's side: the idea that something might be at once just according to civil law and unjust according to canon law sounded like theses condemned at Paris only a short while ago—that a philosophical truth may be a theological falsehood and vice versa.[52] Klenkok was sure to record Albert's contribution. Yet the outcome of the debate in the bishop's audience was inconclusive, which was, to Johannes, a loss, for it left him convinced of the rightfulness of his cause but without support from even his two confrères. He might later have his revenge against the bishop's ultimate neutrality.[53] Now, soon after the meeting, he added some revisions to his *Decadicon* and recorded his refutations of Harr, Block, and Quedlinburg and sent it to Albert, but apparently to no avail.

The meeting in Halberstadt occurred after early April 1369, probably soon after, but nevertheless more than a year past the three sessions of the Magdeburg *Rat*. It was a fraction of Johannes' campaign. According to the counsellors of Magdeburg, in their letter of early 1368, Klenkok had already undermined the *Sachsenspiegel* in other works, apart from the *Decadicon* (note 36), and that pertinacious Augustinian indicated his position at Halberstadt—that by then he had well exploited his offices of lector and provincial by pen and by mouth against the Saxon law and had no reason to stop. By pen, there was the *Decadicon* itself, which he copied in Latin and Middle Low German, the German

---

[52]De Geer, "Klenkok's," p. 409. Scheidt, *Biblioteca*, pp. 98-99. CUP 2:576-87 no. 1124. Philotheus Böhner, Etienne Gilson, *Christliche Philosophie von Ihren Anfängen bis Nikolaus von Cues*, 3rd ed. (Paderborn: Ferdinand Schöningh, 1954), pp. 629-30, for a concise account of Latin Averroism, the source of the philosophical doctrine, in the fourteenth century. Johannes repeated the argument, adding something of his own: what is repugnant to the just individual can only be injustice, but according to Block, a just person might be repelled by justice or what is just according to the allegedly alternative law, in which case the individual is actually unjust or the initial law is unjust.

[53]15 March 1372, when Klenkok was in Avignon as papal penitentiary, Gregory XI wrote to Herbord, prior of St. Severus, Walter Kerlinger, and Rudolf, Augustinian friar and professor of theology, charging them to call Albert, bishop of Halberstadt, publicly to renounce his heretical doctrine, namely that celestial movements determine all human actions. Nobles and others of the region, influenced by Albert's teaching, allegedly neglected the invocation of the help of God and the saints on this account. The Erfurt prior and the two professors were to move against Albert with threats of excommunication and the suspension of his spiritual and temporal governments; if he would not make public renunciation, they were to publish the recantation. Gregory mentioned that someone had told him about Albert. Gustav Schmidt, *Urkundenbuch des Hochstifts Halberstadt und seiner Bischöfe*, 4 vols. (Osnabrück: Otto Zeller, 1965 reprint of the 1889 edition), 4:150-52 no. 2816.

being the more aggressive and personal version, and which he distributed, no doubt trying to match the Magdeburg letter to her daughter cities, that is, the cities that adopted her law and relied on her *Schöppenstuhl* as their court of appeals. And there were the additions to the *Decadicon* which recorded his answers at the Halberstadt dispute. Other records of his campaign were produced, three of which have come down to us: brief treatments of the legal problem in two commentaries, which represent lectures, and a disputation with Herbord of Spangenberg in Erfurt.[54] The record of the disputation has never been published or even studied.[55] It took place in Erfurt and was based on the *Decadicon*, hence it must have occurred after that work was composed a few months before Kerlinger put it to the Magdeburg *Rat* in early 1368.[56] Herbord was a bachelor of canon law and a master (presumably of the

[54]*Postilla super Actus Apostolorum*, ff. 187vb-188rb, discusses the superiority of papal power to that of the emperor, and Klenkok there referred to another question not known to be extant: "istam materiam longius tractaui in questione una summa." This may also refer to the written record of an Erfurt lecture. IV *Sent.* d. 15, S f. 66vb; E2 f. 48rb, considers conflicts between papal and imperial laws. The earliest version of the *Decadicon* argued that "papal and Roman law" is superior to Saxon law, on the basis of the role of the Petrine see as supreme head of the church and of the unitary character of Christian society. De Geer, "Klenkok's," pp. 388-92. The later version discusses the superiority of the papacy to the emperor. Scheidt, *Biblioteca*, p. 67. These are quite different arguments with a somewhat unexpected evolution: the distinction between imperial and Roman law, and the contrast between papal and imperial law, were forced by the claim of the Magdeburg *Rat* and Block that Saxon law was legitimated by imperial law.

[55]Zumkeller, *Manuskripte*, pp. 601-02 no. 525a-d. Herbord's refutation of the *Decadicon* is found in Wolfenbüttel, Codex Guelferbetanus 314 Nov., ff. 7v-16v (following Klenkok's "Universis Christi fidelibus") and ibid., Cod. Guelf. 203 Extrav., ff. 49r-60v. Both texts are incomplete. Cod. Guelf. 203 Extrav. is missing a quire or folios which contained Herbord's response to Klenkok's errors 5 through 8 in the *Decadicon* and a quire or folio(s) containing the end of his refutations of Klenkok's error 9, the refutation of Klenkok's error 10, and the refutation of Klenkok's 5 conclusions. The other manuscript, Cod. Guelf. 314 Nov., has extensive editorial corrections and the complete refutations of Klenkok's errors 9 through 10 and the conclusions, but the scribe also omitted the refutation of errors 5 through 8, overlooking the fact of the missing quire in his source. This shows that Cod. Guelf. 314 Nov., although more complete than its relative (Cod. Guelf. 203 Extrav.), is dependent upon the incomplete manuscript and supplemented (at Herbord's answers to errors 9 and 10 and to the conclusions) by another manuscript. Klenkok's response is preserved in Cod. Guelf. 314 Nov., ff. 17r-21v. A final, irate answer by Herbord is preserved ibid., ff. 22r-31r. Contrast the description in Zumkeller, op. cit.

[56]The transcript of the disputation contains no reference or clear allusion to the disputation in Halberstadt, which may suggest that it occurred before that disputation took place. Herbord's final irate response, however, complains of Klenkok's defamation of the *Sachsenspiegel* (Cod. Guelf. 314 Nov., ff. 22r-31r), and he may owe this change of tone to the prompting of the letter of the Magdeburg *Rat*, which may suggest a date for the disputation in the late spring or early summer of 1368. However, it should be noted that the transcript of the disputation in Cod. Guelf. 314 Nov. follows Klenkok's "Universis fidelibus," which must be dated after the Halberstadt disputation. If that version of Klenkok's *Decadicon* (the letter was an edition of the treatise with self-defense) was the basis of the disputation, then the Erfurt disputation occurred after the Halberstadt disputation (after 5 April 1369) (note 44 above).

arts) who is known to have been a member of St. Mary's chapter in Erfurt, the *scholasticus* of the school in that cloister in 1366, and city scribe of Erfurt in 1369.[57] He was not to be convinced.

All of this activity did little more than call attention to Johannes. The only serious opposition came from members of specific groups—Magdeburg counsellors and citizens and a non-mendicant master. Kerlinger, if unsupportive, never criticized. The two Augustinian friars involved in the debate presented lame arguments that avoided their most serious implications. The Order of Augustinian Hermits' commitment to papal absolutism (this was the order of Giles of Rome, Augustinus Triumphus, and Jacob of Viterbo) may have precluded an earnest defense of the separation of laws and their respective governments, and it is not surprising that Klenkok's province, after the conflict broke out, confirmed him in the office of provincial. Nor did any bishop support or condemn Klenkok's campaign, perhaps because many of them were also in the awkward position of benefiting from papal power (largely due to the way Karl IV and territorial princes capitalized on papal reservations to overcome the stronghold of local aristocracies or other rulers on cathedrals), yet bishops were local lords still needful of local support and, consequently, not likely to benefit from subversions of regional tradition.[58] That Klenkok bore his cudgels alone might give the mistaken impression that his obsession was insignificant. It was merely unattractive. Ultimately, he met with success, by expanding his *Decadicon* to twenty-one propositions of Saxon law, decorating it with a letter to young cardinal Pierre of Vergne, getting the cardinal's endorsement of, at least, the majority of the accusations, and finally winning Gregory XI's condemnation of fourteen of the theses, 8 April 1374.[59] If the letter of the Magdeburg *Rat* had not made him famous, the *articuli reprobati* guaranteed his work a place in the legal controversies of late medieval

---

[57]Franz Peter Sonntag, *Das Kollegiatstift St. Marien zu Erfurt von 1117-1400* (Leipzig: St. Benno Verlag, 1962), pp. 287-89; for the office of *scholasticus*, pp. 29-37. The complexity of his own position in political relations was made apparent in 1375, when he supported the imperial and papal appointee to the archbishopric of Mainz, margrave Ludwig of Meissen, for which allegiance he was forced—by a commissioner of Ludwig's rival, the favorite of Mainz's chapter, count Adolf of Nassau—to abandon Erfurt, his house, and some property. The inventory of his house may be found in W. Friedensburg, "Ein Inventar der Habe Erfurtischer Geistlichen aus dem Jahre 1375," *Anzeiger für Kunde der deutschen Vorzeit*, 29(1882):322-26, here 323.

[58]Johanna Naendrup-Reimann, "Territorien und Kirche im 14. Jahrhundert," in *Der deutsche Territorialstaat im 14. Jahrhundert*, ed. H. Patze, vol. 13 of *Vorträge und Forschungen* (Sigmaringen: Jan Thorbecke, 1970), pp. 116-74, esp. 120-24, 149.

[59]"Salvator humani generis," *Bullarium Diplomaticum et Privilegiorum Sanctorum Romanorum Pontificum* (Turin: S. Franco, H. Fory, e H. Dalmazzo, 1859), 4:573-76.

Germany, and not always anonymously.[60] But he accomplished the reproof of those articles in Avignon, where, in 1371, he became a papal penitentiary, and not at home.

We may now take a closer look at the issues at stake in this controversy. The four versions of the *Decadicon* and the articles condemned by Gregory XI present almost identical criticisms of the *Sachsenspiegel*'s views of ecclesiastical and secular authorities, court procedure, and private law.[61] These were not esoteric forays but discussions of matters as familiar to many contemporaries as real estate law to an average home-owner now: legitimate procedure, the limitations of hereditary rights, the extent of testamentary power, the rights of novices and monks to family property, and the authority that determines superior and inferior legal norms and court decisions.[62] Klenkok's position was fundamentally a simple one. Papal authority supersedes every

---

[60]An excellent summary of the influence of the Magdeburg *Schöppenstuhl* may be found in Guido Kisch, "Magdeburg Jury Court Decisions as Sources of Jewry-Law. A Study in Source History," *Historia Judaica*, 5(1943):27-34, reprinted in Kisch, *Forschungen zur Rechts- und Sozialgeschichte des Mittelalters*, vol. 3 of idem, *Ausgewählte Schriften* (Sigmaringen: Jan Thorbecke, 1980), pp. 122-29, here 122-24. Kullmann, "Klenkok," p. 20-21. Mitteis, Liebrich, *Rechtsgeschichte*, p. 297. Homeyer, *Johannes*, pp. 396-401, 404-11. Erwin-Erhard Aidnik, "Die 'articuli reprobati' des Sachsenspiegels in altlivländischen Rechtsbüchern," *Rigasche Zeitschrift für Rechtswissenschaft*, 1(1926-1927):222-47, esp. 230-42 for the reception of only articles compatible with local tradition. Landmann, *Predigtwesen*, p. 208, for criticisms of the *Sachsenspiegel* based upon Klenkok in homiletical literature. Twenty of the twenty-one articles, "first reproved by Johannes Cleynkoc of the Order of Hermits, and by master Berniger (i.e. Kerlinger) Walther of the Order of Preachers, and by Gregory XI," appear in a collection of papal documents added to the handbook of an inquisitor of Cracow in the early fifteenth century. Wattenbach, "Handbuch," pp. 15, 26. A description of Saxony from the early fifteenth century includes a slightly embellished account of Klenkok's campaign against the *Sachsenspiegel* and his troubles with the Magdeburg *Rat*. Lehmann, *Mitteilungen*, 1:44 (and note 37, above). Elisabeth Nowak, in an otherwise thorough analysis of the textual variations that the *Sachsenspiegel* developed, did not consider the "articuli reprobati" as expurgations or appendices to manuscripts of the Saxon law (her concern was the evolution of the *Sachsenspiegel*'s *vulgata* versions [one in German and one in Latin] and glosses, which mostly antedate Gregory XI's bull, "Salvator humani generis," where the *articuli reprobati* are listed and condemned). Elisabeth Nowak, "Die Verbreitung und Anwendung des Sachsenspiegels nach den überlieferten Handschriften" (Ph.D. dissertation, Universität Hamburg, 1965), pp. 37-55.

[61]Kullmann, "Klenkok," pp. 23-117, provides the best legal analysis of the texts, dividing them into the three categories of authority, court procedure, and private law, which I have mentioned. Homeyer, *Johannes*, p. 415, provides a comparative table of the articles from two of the versions and the bull of Gregory XI (he was not able to integrate the data from "Universis Christi fidelibus," but the relevant information is given ibid., p. 432a, and he did not have the version of the *Decadicon* dedicated to Albert of Halberstadt, edited by De Geer, "Klenkok's," pp. 386-409, which actually presents the same articles as the version preserved in "Universis Christi fidelibus," only switching the place of the second and third articles). Although differences in these texts are mostly incidental, it is interesting to note that the bull of Gregory XI, on the matter of the legitimacy of bastard children, appears somewhat more restrictive than the *Decadicon*. *Bullarium*, 4:576 (art. 11). Similar conflicts in private law are known for Ireland in the same period. Walsh, *FitzRalph*, pp. 204, 272-73, 320, 330.

[62]Homeyer, *Johannes*, pp. 386-87.

other political and legal authority, and the standards of papal law therefore determine propriety and impropriety in other laws.[63] He pounced on a few traditional, Germanic particulars of the *Sachsenspiegel*—the use of ordeal and oaths; the denial of rights to illegitimate children subsequently brought, with the mother, into a legitimate marriage; limitations imposed against testators; and the ability of monks and novices to receive inheritances—his were important and progressive criticisms reflecting juridical values originating in Roman law and widely accepted in Germany only with the "reception" of Roman law in legal science after 1450.[64] Johannes was aware of this Roman factor, although he saw it as a correspondence between Jewish (that is, ancient Hebrew, not rabbinic), ecclesiastical, and imperial laws at certain points— like the freedom of testators to act without the consent of their heirs.[65] This could tempt us to see here an episode in the "early reception" of Roman law in Germany, which it was in a limited way, insofar as it underscored certain Roman elements in the canon law, but not to Klenkok.[66] He was little concerned with the scientific problem of attaining a code of justice superior to traditional codes in its norms and in its internal coherence. Nor did he share the political interests that seduced partisans of bureaucratic states increasingly to rely on Roman law (but not until the six-

---

[63]*Decadicon*, articles 1, 4, esp. 4. Scheidt, *Biblioteca*, pp. 67, 69-72. "Universis Christi fidelibus," art. 1. Homeyer, p. 432a-c. *Decadicon* to Albert of Halberstadt, art. 1. De Geer, "Klenkok's," pp. 391-92. "Salvator humani generis," art. 4. *Bullarium*, 4:575, see also p. 574.

[64]Kullmann, "Klenkok," pp. 119-20. Norbert Horn, "Die legistische Literatur der Kommentatoren und der Ausbreitung des gelehrten Rechts," Helmut Coing, ed., *Handbuch der Quellen und Literatur der neueren europäischen Privatrechtsgeschichte*, 3 vols. (Munich: C. H. Beck, 1973-1988), vol. 1: *Mittelalter (1100-1500)*, pp. 261-364, here 283-87. For the reception of Roman law see also Paul Koschaker, *Europa und das römische Recht* (Munich and Berlin: C. H. Beck, 1953), esp. 55ff., stressing the role of Roman law in effecting a common European culture; Raymundus von Wiener-Neustadt, *Summa*, pp. 51-62, for a fourteenth-century instance of reception through Christian sources (relying especially on Giles of Rome's *De regimine principum*), and pp. 116-17 for the date of composition and its Polish legal background (significant because reception occurred earlier there than in Germany); Helmut Coing, *Römisches Recht in Deutschland*, vol. 6 of *Ius Romanum medii aevi* (Milan: Collegio Antiqui Iuris Studiis Provendis, 1964), pp. 86ff.; idem, *Europäisches Privatrecht*, vol. 1, *Älteres Gemeines Recht (1500 bis 1800)* (Munich: C.H. Beck, 1985), pp. 25-34.

[65]*Decadicon*, art. 13. Scheidt, *Biblioteca*, pp. 83-84. See also pp. 86, 87. "Universis Christi fidelibus," art. 6. De Geer, "Klenkok's," p. 399. Consider also the Middle Low German version of the *Decadicon* issued in self-defense against the Magdeburg *Rat*, Homeyer, *Johannes*, p. 420, which notes a correspondence between divine and "imperial," i.e. Roman laws. Cf. *Decadicon*, art. 4 and "Universis Christi fidelibus," art. 1, which discusses papal corrections of "imperial" laws (e.g. regarding usury, concubinage, the duel). Scheidt, op. cit., p. 70. De Geer, op. cit., p. 392.

[66]For canon law and the reception of Roman law, see Helmut Coing, "Kanonisches Recht und Ius Commune," *Proceedings of the Sixth International Congress of Medieval Canon Law*, series C: subsidia, v. 17 *Monumenta Iuris Canonici* (Vatican City: Biblioteca Apostolica Vaticana, 1985), pp. 507-18.

teenth century).[67] In his mind, such a coherent law already existed in that which was based upon the gospel—in canon law.

Klenkok examined his books in the cloister. The problems of inheritance frequently vexed friars, whose penitential work often left them witnesses in and executors of testaments, and whose cloisters were recipients of inheritances. The matter of monastic inheritance is similar, for the property would accrue to the cloister, not to the individual friar, whose vows precluded his ownership.[68] The *Sachsenspiegel* merely hoped to prevent the alienation of estate property to the coffers of the church, and Johannes merely sought to protect the convent's income.

"The entire argument rests on this: that the peculiar law of a people cannot contradict universal norms, nor in turn, can secular statute contradict Christian law and ecclesiastical precept."[69] For this reason Johannes also asserted the power of popes to excommunicate emperors on any pretense: there exists no constitutional authority apart from papal law. He based this claim on a fundamental precept of the cultural commitments of the mendicant orders—that the seamless garment of Christian society is made and maintained by Peter's successors, not to the exclusion of other governments, but in a fantastic vision of the coherence of the human world:[70]

Against the aforementioned articles, this is how I argue from a single principle. All those articles are against the law of God, of the sacrosanct

---

[67]Gerald Strauss, *Law, Resistance, and the State. The Opposition to Roman Law in Reformation Germany* (Princeton: Princeton University Press, 1986), esp. pp. 48-49, 136ff.

[68]Klenkok was not concerned, as a matter of principle, with "clerical rights," but with the mendicant community. Contrast Homeyer, *Johannes*, pp. 386-87.

[69]Homeyer, *Johannes*, p. 389.

[70]*Decadicon Alberto Halbertensi episcopo*, in De Geer, "Klenkok's," pp. 388-89 (this version contains the most developed discussion of principles behind Klenkok's campaign): "Contra predictos articulos arguo unica ratione sic. Omnes isti articuli repugnant legi Dei, sacrosanctae sedis apostolicae sacrique romanorum imperii, quae defensantur pro legibus. Ergo praedictorum articulorum defensio per quemlibet christianum obedientem Deo, sacrosanctae ecclesiae sacroque romanorum imperio scismatica seu haeretica censeatur, quod probatur cum vera sit haeresis sacris legibus repugnantia pro legibus defensare, quod probatur per Augustinum in libro de arbitrio (Augustinus, *De libero arbitrio*, i.39-51. CSEL 74:13-16), quum omnis lex derivetur ab incommutabili lege divina, cui si quid repugnat, est erroneum et iniquum. Quod probat Tullius libro primo de legibus et in paradoxi stoycorum (Tullius Cicero, *De lege*, i.6-7, ed. Georg Heinrich Moser, [Frankfurt am Main: Broenner, 1824], pp. 44-59. Idem, *Paradoxa Stoicorum*, ed. Renato Badali [Milan: Arnoldo Mondadori, 1968], pp. 58-62), deducens quod omnes homines, ymmo Dii et homines unica ratione conveniunt, a qua ratione sumitur omnis lex et omne jus. Quicunque enim convenirent jure cives unius civitatis sunt, ergo totus mundus esse debet una civitas Deorum et hominum; contra quam rationem vel legem si quis aliquid pro jure defendat, contrarium erit divinae pariter et humanae civitati. Istam civitatem Christus promisit cum unum ovile et unum pastorem affore praedixit, quam civitatem Johannes in apocalypsi forma Jerusalem de coelo, id est celata conscientia, descendere contemplatus fuit."

apostolic see, and of the Roman emperor, which articles are defended as laws. Therefore, the defense of those articles must be judged schismatic or heretical by any Christian who obeys God, holy church, and the holy Roman emperor, which is proved because it is true heresy to defend as laws things that contradict the sacred laws. This is proved by Augustine in the book, *On the Free Will:* since all law is derived from the unchangeable divine law, if something should offend it, it is erroneous and iniquitous. Tullius proves it in the first book of *On the Laws* and in the *Stoic Paradoxes,* deducing that all people, or rather gods and people, come together by means of one principle from which every law and every right arises. For, all those who come together by law are citizens of one city, and therefore the whole world ought to be one city of gods and people; and if someone defends something as law against that principle or law, he [or she] will be equally against the divine and human city. Christ promised that city when he proclaimed that there would be one sheepfold and one shepherd, which city John contemplated in the Apocalypse, in the form of Jerusalem descending from heaven, that is a hidden conscience.

According to Cicero, law and justice are natural, based on reason, and common to all peoples at all times, making all the more schismatic, Johannes concludes, any contradiction of it. Cicero, however, only provides him proof of the universality of one divine law, not the ability of any society, without the Christian church, to comprehend it: ancient Rome, according to Augustine, Klenkok claims, was neither a city nor a republic "before the faith of Christ," because her people possessed, like the Saxons and their *Sachsenspiegel,* only human law.[71] The power of the papacy as supreme judiciary and pastor of Christendom, based upon a papalist reading of the Bible (Jn. 1.43, mistakenly cited as Jn. 22; Lk. 22.32; Jn. 21.17; Mt. 18.17; Deut. 17.8), will prove vital to the Saxons to overcome the deficiencies of their laws.[72]

The implications of Klenkok's campaign and his arguments could be misjudged as clerical partisanship poorly construed, for if correct in the details of most criticisms, he seems to have

---

[71]De Geer, "Klenkok's," p. 389.

[72]Ibid., pp. 390-92. The adaptation of natural law to absolute papal rule may very well be derived from Giles of Rome. Consider Aegidius Romanus, *De ecclesiastica potestate,* iii.2, ed. Richard Scholz, (Aalen: Scientia Verlag, 1961 reprint of Weimar: Hermann Böhlaus Nachfolger, 1929), pp. 149-57, esp. 149-50, 154-56. Consider also Augustinus Triumphus; see Michael Wilks, *The Problem of Sovereignty in the Later Middle Ages. The Papal Monarchy with Augustinus Triumphus and the Publicists* (Cambridge: The University Press, 1963), pp. 155-56.

missed the gist of Eike of Repgow's *Mirror of Saxony.*[73] The genius of Eike's collection—the first written collection of German laws (written in the early 1220s but only extant in a German translation of 1261/1270) and the basis of all subsequent Germanic collections—was its attention to the canon law and its conception of a Christian universe; the standard gloss by Johannes Buch accented these features.[74] Both the *Sachsenspiegel* and its gloss served as vehicles of the reception of Roman law, by their integration of canon law and, in no small measure, by giving greater currency to the idea of centralized (that is, imperial over against territorial) authority.[75] Johannes has been seen as accusing Eike and Buch of irreligion.[76] But his partisanship was more specific; he aimed at their conception of a hierocratic imperium autonomous of papal authority.[77] In so doing, he simply ignored the *Sachsenspiegel's* claim to ground its precepts in imperial law and,

---

[73]Kullmann believes that Klenkok misunderstood the *Sachsenspiegel* when he claimed that it denied the power of popes to correct feudal and private law. Kullmann pointed out that Eike allowed the power of the papacy to intervene in cases that transgress the law of God or the freedom of the church, a power expressed even more generally in the gloss by Johannes Buch; neither Eike nor Buch attempted to limit papal authority, although their view of papal power was not as universal as Klenkok's. *Klenkok*, pp. 27-36.

[74]Helmut Coing, *Römisches Recht*, pp. 45-77, esp. 69-70; 108-13, 177-81. Horn, "Literatur," p. 356. Guido Kisch, "Biblische Einflüsse in der Reimvorrede des Sachsenspiegels," *Publications of the Modern Language Association of America*, 54(1939):20-36, reprinted in idem, *Forschungen*, pp. 36-52. Idem, *Sachsenspiegel and Bible. Researches in the Source History of the Sachsenspiegel and the Influence of the Bible on Mediaeval German Law*, vol. 5 of *Publications in Mediaeval Studies* (Notre Dame, Indiana: University of Notre Dame, 1941, reprinted 1960). H. Schlosser, "Buch, Johann von," HDR 1:526-27. Dieter Pötschke, Heike Schroll, "Fragment einer Glosse zum 'Sachsenspiegel'-Landrecht aufgefunden," *Archivmitteilungen*, 38(1988):122-27, here 123. Dieter Pötschke, "Rolande als Problem der Stadtgeschichtsforschung," *Jahrbuch für die Geschichte Mittel- und Ostdeutschlands*, 37(1988):4-45. The prologue to Buch's gloss explained the value of including references to the canon law in the work: the *Sachsenspiegel* alone may not help those who appear before ecclesiastical courts. *Prologus glossae*, V., lines 197-209. Emil Steffenhagen, *Die Landrechtsglosse des Sachsenspiegels nach der Amsterdamer Handschrift*, 1. Teil, *Einleitung und Glossenprolog*, vol. 65 of *Denkschriften*, 1. Abhandlung, *Akademie der Wissenschaften in Wien, philosophisch-historische Klasse* (Vienna and Leipzig: Hölder-Pichler-Tempsky, 1925), pp. 52-53.

[75]Pötschke, "Roland," pp. 42-43. The use of Roman law by the Magdeburg *Schöffenstuhl* has also been noted. Hugo Böhlau, "Aus der Praxis des Magdeburger Schöffenstuhls während des 14. und 15. Jahrhunderts," *Zeitschrift für Rechtsgeschichte*, 9(1870):1-50, esp. 25-32.

[76]Kullmann, *Klenkok*, p. 36.

[77]It is seen in the prologue to the "Textus prologi" of the *Sachsenspiegel* and its identification of the law of Constantine and Charlemagne with divine law, and in Buch's strict separation of papal and imperial powers. Kisch, "Reimvorreden," pp. 27, 28, but cf. SLdr i.1 and ibid., p. 28 (emperor and pope should each help the other perform what the other cannot). Emil Steffenhagen, *Die Entwicklung der Landrechtsglosse des Sachsenspiegels*, vol. 12 of *Johann von Buch und die kanonische Glosse*, vol. 195/1 of *Abhandlungen der Akademie der Wissenschaften in Wien, philosophisch-historische Klasse* (Vienna and Leipzig: Hödler-Pichler-Tempsky, 1923), pp. 23-26.

through it, in divine law; the Saxon's accommodation of traditional norms and procedures to the law of the church was to
Johannes the opposite—an imposition of non-Christian norms
and procedures against the singular law of Christian society. Traditional law is entirely superseded by ecclesiastical law.

If this were a theoretical discussion of legal science, Johannes
certainly failed to recognize the canonical and Roman elements in
the *Sachsenspiegel*, even if his view of specific laws and procedures
might have remained the same. But his would have been an in-
explicably singular discussion for fourteenth-century Germany,
as the course of this controversy suggests. Regardless of attempts
to conceive law in terms of universal norms and procedures, the
content of justice had everything to do with the identity of the
court.[78] And the court was concerned only with its specific problems, not with the construction of a coherent universe of law and
order. The papal court was a unique exception, thanks to the universal recognition of papal government (however diverse the con-
ceptions of its extent and limitations), and thanks to its strength,
but it, too, remained one of many options of complaint and
appeal.[79] To challenge a court was to challenge an institution that
regulated the common life of specific groups of people in specific
contexts—economic, familial, political, and cultural. Various ecclesiastical and secular courts claimed authority over these contexts in a variety of situations. City courts and "Schöffenrecht"
knew only specific cases and their small, concrete instances of social experience.[80] The law of the city of Magdeburg, which
guided the vast majority of cities throughout central Europe, was
built of local customary law, individual privileges, and the feudal
and common law of the *Sachsenspiegel*—the latter being the pre-
dominant source; and the identification of Magdeburg law and
Sachsenspiegel was so complete that the two were sometimes con-

---

[78]Mitteis, Lieberich, *Rechtsgeschichte*, pp. 290-300. Consider the Middle High German
saying, "Der stadt recht went also verne also ere weyde went" (the city law goes only as
far as the city line). Karl Friedrich Wilhelm Wander, *Deutsches Sprichwörter-Lexikon*, 5 vols.
(Leipzig: F.A. Brockhaus, 1867-1880), 4:760.

[79]For the *Rota Romana* as a pervasive court and not "a distant court of last instance," see
Geoffrey Barraclough, "Praxis beneficiorum. A Contribution to the History of Practical Legal Literature in the Later Middle Ages," ZRG,KA 58(1938):95-134, here 127.

[80]Gunter Gudian, "Zur Charakterisierung des deutschen mittelalterlichen Schöffenrechts," *Europäisches Rechtsdenken in Geschichte und Gegenwart. Festschrift für Helmut Coing
zum 70. Geburtstag*, 2 vols., ed. Norbert Horn (Munich: C. H. Beck, 1982), 1:113-27,
here 120-21. Jan Ziekow, *Recht und Rechtsgang. Studien zu Problemen mittelalterlichen Rechts
anhand von Magdeburger Schöppensprüchen des 15. Jahrhunderts* (Pfaffenweiler: Centaurus,
1986), pp. 97-101.

sidered interchangeable.[81] The Magdeburg jurors, dominant interpreters of this law for the hundreds of cities that had adopted it, were known as guardians of the *Sachsenspiegel* (previous note). If Johannes had not initially realized the political consequence of challenging the Saxon law (which seems unlikely), the Magdeburg *Rat*, well accustomed to tolerance of their law in the courts of princes and emperors, promptly clarified the matter.[82] The controversy would then touch the ideological core of social constitution—the basis of legitimate norms and the organization of Christian society—rather than legal science per se. In that respect, it was a controversy over the application of authority to life in communities. Johannes was defending the universality of papal government.

---

[81]Nowak, "Verbreitung," pp. 233-35. Gertrud Schubart-Fikentscher, *Die Verbreitung der deutschen Stadtrechte in Osteuropa*, vol. 4/3 of *Forschungen zum deutschen Recht* (Weimar: Hermann Böhlaus Nachfolger, 1942), pp. 57-73. Albrecht Timm, "Das Magdeburger Recht an der Brücke von West und Ost," *Hamburger Mittel- und Ostdeutsche Forschungen*, 2(1960):71-96.

[82]For the toleration of urban courts, consider Horst Rabe, "Stadt und Stadtherrschaft im 14. Jahrhundert, die schwäbischen Reichsstädte," *Stadt und Stadtherr im 14. Jahrhundert, Entwicklungen und Funktionen*, ed. Wilhelm Rausch, vol. 2 of *Beiträge zur Geschichte der Städte Mitteleuropas* (Linz/Donau: Österreichischer Arbeitskreis für Stadtgeschichtsforschung, 1972), pp. 301-24, here 310-14; Emil Franz Rössler, *Das altprager Stadtrecht aus dem 14. Jahrhunderte, nach den vorhandenen Handschriften zum ersten Mal*, vol. 1 of *Deutsche Rechtsdenkmäler aus Böhmen und Mähren* (Prague: J. G. Calve, 1845), p. xxxi n. 1; Timm, "Recht," p. 87.

IV. INQUISITOR, FAMILIARIS, DOMESTICUS ET COMMENSALIS

Before 4 July 1370, Johannes Klenkok became an inquisitor of the diocese of Olomouc, resident in the new Augustinian cloister in Brno, some sixty-five kilometers southwest of the Moravian cathedral.[1] We might assume that Johannes completed his last tenure as provincial of Saxony and Thüringen at the election of a successor on Pentecost 1369, but nothing is known of the provincial chapter held that year, and it is therefore possible that Johannes was elected to yet another term. His letter "to all the faithful"—written after his meeting with Albert of Halberstadt, which itself occurred after April 1369, probably soon after—looks back on Erfurt as a previous residence, but no evidence exists to show whether he wrote from somewhere in his province (as provincial performing visitations) or from Moravia.[2] It is frequently alleged that Johannes left Erfurt for Prague, where he is presumed to have lectured on the *Sentences* and to have performed disputations.[3] The letter of Gerhard Groote to Wilhelm

---

[1]The chapter title is taken from a letter of safe conduct presented to Klenkok by Johannes of Neumarkt (note 27, below). A record of a document by Klenkok issued on 4 July 1370 was discovered by W. Wattenbach in a Bohemian formulary and published in *Anzeiger für Kunde der deutschen Vorzeit*, new series 30(1883):80. There, "in conventu fratrum heremitarum sancti Augustini in preurbio Brunnensi constitutus" and naming himself "Sacre pagine professor ordinis prelibati, inquisitor heretice pravitatis et judex supra usurarum contractibus per dyocesem Olomoucensem" appointed by ("positus") Johannes (of Neumarkt), bishop of Olomouc, he names two deputies, canons of the cathedral of Olomouc—Hinko of Betovia and a Jacob A. Klenkok probably resided in Brno rather than the cathedral city because there was no Augustinian cloister in Olomouc (although the foundation of one there had been approved by Pope Urban V in 1364). Clemens d'Elpidio Janetschek, *Das Augustiner-Eremitenstift S. Thomas in Brünn* (Brno: Päpstliche Benedictiner-Buchdruckerei, 1898), p. 18.

[2]Discussed in the previous chapter.

[3]Bütow, "Lebensgeschichte," pp. 561-63, followed by Trapp, "Notes," p. 361 and Zumkeller, *Erbsünde*, p. 22 (who believes that Klenkok was in Prague, citing the document of Brno as evidence, but admitting that it is not certain that Klenkok lectured in the university). Kadlec included Klenkok in his list of St. Thomas professors, although he found no new evidence of it. *Augustinerkloster*, p. 54. Contrast Augustin Neumann's list of known students and lectors, in *Prameny k dějinám duchovenstva v době předhusitské a Husově* (Sources of church history in the Prehussite and Hussite periods), (Olomouc: Nákladen Matice Cyrilometodĕsjské, 1926), pp. 17-18. The Augustinian convent of Prague did possess a copy of the literal exposition of the *Sentences* and, allegedly, a quodlibet; the incipit of the collection, "Utrum eterna uita," actually is that of the *Questiones super canonicas beati Johannis*, and the explicit is expressly given as that of the second (book of *Sentences*). Cf.

70

Vroede seemed to associate Klenkok with Karl IV's university, but only because the letter's recipient was there—four years after Klenkok's death and eight years after Klenkok's alleged teaching.[4] A safe conduct granted to Johannes by Karl's royal and then imperial chancellor, Johannes of Neumarkt (also known as Jan of Středa), bishop of Litomyšl (1355 to 1364) and Olomouc (1364 to 1380), seemed to prove it, and it requires more serious consideration.

We may presume that the bishop and chancellor presented the safe conduct in the early spring of 1371: it was granted that Johannes might attend the general chapter of his order in Florence, which took place on Pentecost of that year.[5] It names Johannes Klenkok "master of sacred theology, inquisitor, confidant, administrator, and our dear friend." Such effusion was appropriate in letters seeking privileges on someone else's behalf, but the language is revealing. It shows that Johannes possessed the title of master (which we know he attained at Oxford), could sit at table with the bishop and chancellor, was active in ecclesiastical administration, could give the bishop advice, and

---

Kadlec, *Augustinerkloster*, p. 426. St. Thomas therefore possessed the questions on the first letter of John and the first two books of *Sentences*. These could very easily have been copied at Erfurt, where Klenkok frequently referred his students to them (there are 69 references to Klenkok's other theological works in the *Postilla super Actus Apostolorum*, which also proves that it was written after the other works) or copied from copies brought from Erfurt; they do not imply that Klenkok lectured in Prague, because both works originated at Oxford.

[4]Note 43, p. 30, above. Bütow noted Klenkok's reference to a quodlibet on problems in English law in the version of the *Decadicon* written after the debate in Halberstadt, speculating that this may be a Prague quodlibet; it is actually the Erfurt disputation with Herbord of Spangenberg (Cod. Guelf. 203 Extra., f. 49r, and Cod. Guelf. 314 Nov., f. 16v-17r). He also noted that the Augustinian cloister in Prague possessed, in its early fifteenth-century library catalogue, a copy of a quodlibet by Klenkok with his literal *Sentences* commentary. This would also refer to the same or another Erfurt disputation. Cf. "Lebensgeschichte," pp. 562-63 n. 82. Trithemius and Ossinger listed Prague questions among Klenkok's works, which Bütow also took as evidence of Prague teaching (ibid.) and which Trapp believed to be the *Questiones super secundum Sententiarum* and assigned to the University of Prague in this period of Klenkok's life ("Notes," p. 362). Neither Trithemius nor Ossinger listed the source of their reference to Prague questions, and the attribution may very well be a conjecture on their parts or on the part of their source(s): attributing works to university masters assumes greater prestige and comes more readily to mind than attributing them to an order's general school. The Prague catalogue, preserved in the *Codex Thomaeus*, is now edited in Kadlec, *Augustinerkloster*, here p. 426. Kadlec lists Klenkok as a lector of the Prague Augustinian convent, which he bases on the previous biographical literature (the conjectures of which are denied here) and a fallacious assumption—that Johannes was the inquisitor who brought Milíč of Kroměříže to trial in Avignon. Ibid., pp. 54-55. There are several errors behind this, but it suffices to point out that Klenkok was, at the time of the process against Milíč, no longer inquisitor but resident in Avignon as papal penitentiary. His role will be discussed in due course.

[5]No. 16, *Collectarius perpetuarum formarum Johannis de Geylnhusen*, ed. Hans Kaiser (Innsbruck: Wagnersche Universitätsbuchhandlung, 1900), p. 12. David Gutiérrez, *Die Augustiner-Eremiten im Spätmittelalter*, 2 vols., trans. Beda Kriener (Würzburg: Augustinus-Verlag, 1982, 1985), 2:14, for the chapter. See also Bütow, "Lebensgeschichte," p. 563.

possessed only one office—that of inquisitor.[6] We know from
Johannes that he was installed in Brno, not in Prague and not
even in the bishop's city.[7] Johannes once wrote a letter to the Carmelite lector and sometime prior, Johannes of Hildesheim, on behalf of Johannes of Neumarkt, and this has seemed to imply that
Klenkok was active in the imperial chancellory.[8] The letter actually implies the contrary, because had it been the product of the
chancellory, we would see the imperial chancellor's name on it
(and seal upon the original), but in fact, Johannes of Neumarkt,
who responded to Johannes of Hildesheim on at least one other
occasion, asked Klenkok to answer this one, and Klenkok gives
the reason: he had presented the letter to the chancellor in the
first place.[9] That is, Johannes of Hildesheim used an Augustinian
friar to approach Johannes of Neumarkt, but this proves only that
Klenkok enjoyed the chancellor's audience, not that he lived in
Prague or worked in the chancellory. Rather, we know from Klenkok that he enjoyed the audience as inquisitor of the bishop in
Brno. There is no evidence that Johannes Klenkok ever lived or
taught in Prague, even though it may be assumed that he visited
the imperial capital.

Johannes of Neumarkt liked the Order of Augustinian Hermits,
perhaps thanks to the encouragement of Nikolas of Louny, provincial prior of the Augustinians in the province of Bavaria,
which included Bohemia. Nikolas was a favored preacher of the
imperial court, and Johannes of Neumarkt must have known him
as a young official of the royal Bohemian chancellory.[10] In 1356,
Neumarkt tried to found an Augustinian cloister in Olomouc; he
was later to become the city's bishop, and he consecrated the

---

[6]Cf. Angelus Doblin, whom the chancellor called "singularem amicum meum et socium
apud cancellarium necnon coetum magistrorum Parisiensis studii." *Cancellaria Johannis
Noviforensis*, ed. F. Tadra in *Archiv für österreichische Geschichte*, 68(1886):82-83 no. 89, and
cited in Trapp, "Angelus," p. 390.

[7]Note 1, page 70, above.

[8]Trapp, "Notes," p. 361.

[9]Ep. 55 lines 26-32, Hendricks, "Letters," pp. 234-35. Cf. Ep. 51 lines 23-24, ibid., p. 229;
a letter from the chancellor, the seal of which Johannes of Hildesheim also recorded in
his register.

[10]Nikolaus was prior provincial in 1342, 1344-53, and 1362-63. Kadlec, *Augustinerkloster*,
p. 23. Johannes of Neumarkt came to the chancellory in 1347 and became protonotary of
the imperial chancellory in 1352. J. Klapper, *Johann von Neumarkt, Bischof und Hofkanzler.
Religiöse Frührenaissance in Böhmen zur Zeit Karls IV*, vol. 17, *Erfurter Theologische Studien*
(Leipzig: St. Benno-Verlag, 1964), pp. 11-14. Kadlec, *Augustinerkloster*, p. 31. Karl IV also
generously privileged the Augustinian friars. See Alphons Huber, *Die Regesten des Kaiserreichs unter Kaiser Karl IV, 1346-1378*, vol. 8 of *Regesta Imperii*, ed. Johann Friederich Böhmer
(Innsbruck: Wagnersche Universitätsbuchhandlung, 1877), pp. 122, 126, 148, 274, 286, 303,
318, no. 1538, 1576, 1863, 3352, 3510, 3729, 3930, 3931.

church of the new cloister in Brno, dedicated to saints Mary and Thomas (donated by Johann, margrave of Moravia, and Margaretha, daughter of the prince of Troppau and Ratibor, his wife). In 1366, he forced the secular clergy of Regensburg publicly to concede the right of the Augustinians of the city and of the mendicant orders in general to preach and hear confessions—in spite of local claims to the contrary. Finally in 1368, he donated part of his library to the Augustinian Hermits of Prague.[11] His relation to the cloister of Saints Mary and Thomas in Brno supported his cultural and administrative interests. He employed its scribe to copy books for him; he filled diocesan offices with convent members; and he promoted the advancement of convent officers to high ecclesiastical office.[12] It was, then, quite natural that he should employ Johannes Klenkok, who recently displayed an adroit concern for matters canonical, as "inquisitor of heretical depravity and judge over contracts of usury for the diocese of Olomouc."[13] Promotions of lecturers to inquisitor were common.[14] The chancellor may have learned of Johannes from the prior provincial of the Bavarian province, either Hermann Stein (1363-1370) or Leonhard of Kärnten (1370-1376, 1382-1385, 1387-1395).[15] Walter Kerlinger, who visited the imperial court in July, 1369, and who also nominated inquisitors, could also have made Klenkok's name known.[16]

The inquisition in the Bohemian realm, of which Moravia and, with it, the diocese of Olomouc were a part, has been convincingly portrayed as a reign of terror that, during its best studied

---

[11]Janetschek, *Augustiner-Eremitenstift*, pp. 7-11, 18. Kadlec, *Augustinerkloster*, pp. 31-32. Kunzelmann, *Geschichte*, 3:48. Neumarkt also made supplication to the pope for indulgences for those who frequent the monastery in Brno. *Cancellaria*, ed. Tadra, no. 78 p. 75 (presumably to be dated 1356).

[12]He paid a scribe of the convent 22 gross to copy him Giles of Rome's *De regimine principum*. He appointed two conventuals as his chaplains (in 1376). He intervened with a cardinal to seek promotion of a convent lector to a titular bishopric, *Cancellaria*, ed. Tadra, no. 87, 161, 217 pp. 81, 118, 149. He also employed other mendicant friars as inquisitors, e.g. a Dominican lector of Olomouc, who subsequently absolved people of cases reserved to the apostolic see (in particular, of homicide) and extorted money in the process. When the people realized his claim to grant the absolution was fraudulent, they forced him to return the money ("non absque magna verecundia pariter et rubore"). To this Dominican's credit was also the illegal imprisonment of a man in Znoyman and the employment of a Dominican deputy to present a forged letter of the prince of Moravia to the townsfolk supporting the imprisonment. Ibid., no. 32 pp. 46-47 (a letter to a cardinal, protesting the Dominican's appeal to the curia, from 1372/78).

[13]From Klenkok's appointment of deputies, ed. Wattenbach, p. 80.

[14]Flade, *Inquisitionsverfahren*, pp. 35-38.

[15]Kunzelmann, *Geschichte*, 3:104-06, 107-16.

[16]Fredericq, *Corpus*, 1:216 no. 212: Karl IV's third letter in support of Kerlinger's inquisition, dated 17 July 1369, which mentions "other" inquisitors and two nominations.

period, saw someone accused, judged, and burned every day.[17] Klenkok's place in this is entirely obscure, for no evidence, apart from his curious claim to be judge of usurious contracts, exists.[18] The claim probably says little of his inquisition and implies that, in addition to trying heresy, he could judge cases involving rents and similar contracts as an appointee of the episcopal court.[19] We may assume that he remained in Brno, living well in the convent Johann of Moravia richly endowed.[20] He may also have lectured.[21] Bohemian inquisitors tried people for a conglomerate of ideas most frequently called Waldensian but, when treating beguines and beghards, sometimes called the heresy of the free spirit, and Johannes as inquisitor probably did the same.[22] He would also learn of the conflict between secular clergy and the mendicant orders raging in Prague, and only an indifferent friar would have been oblivious to the hostility shown the mendicant orders by parochial clergy in this province, but no evidence is known to show whether or to what extent he may have encountered the same in Brno, where both margrave and bishop supported his order without restraint.[23] Conceivably, such con-

---

[17]During the inquisition of Gallus of Neuhaus, 1335 to c. 1353/55, which has been estimated to have affected over 4,400 people, almost entirely belonging to the German-speaking minority (estimated to number 100,000 or about 1/12 of the population of the kingdom of Bohemia), of which 220 were burned. Contrast the inquisition of Bernard Gui some years earlier in southern France, in which 930 people were judged and only 69 executed or exhumed. Alexander Patschovsky, *Quellen zur böhmischen Inquisition im 14. Jahrhundert*, vol. 11 of *Monumenta Germaniae Historica, Quellen zur Geistesgeschichte des Mittelalters* (Weimar: Hermann Böhlaus Nachfolger, 1979), pp. 19-24. Patschovsky provides useful prosopography of all known inquisitors of the realm, ibid., pp. 123-30, the majority of whom were mendicant friars, mostly Dominicans, appointed by the archbishops of Prague.

[18]No other Bohemian inquisitor is known to have the same title. Ibid., pp. 123-30.

[19]But cf. Trapp, "Notes," p. 361, who took this as a description of his inquisitorial activity.

[20]The margrave of Moravia gave one village, two tenant farmers, two vineyards, two towns with forests, two mills with gardens and a plot, and two manors, in a document of 25 November 1370 which confirmed previous gifts and added a few new ones. Janetschek, *Augustiner-Eremitenstift*, pp. 20-21, for the list and the terms, pp. 22-26 for the document. It was confirmed by Johannes of Neumarkt, who also stipulated that the property in question be subject to canon law. Karl IV also contributed money and rents.

[21]Gregory of Rimini sent a lector from the convent in Prague to perform this office in Brno in 1358, which we should probably take as the foundation of a provincial school. The school is more frequently mentioned in sources from the fifteenth century. Consider Kunzelmann, *Geschichte*, 3:28.

[22]Patschovsky, *Quellen*, pp. 19-20. Klenkok's register(s) is (are) not known to be extant.

[23]The Augustinians of Prague played an important role in the controversy between the friars and Konrad Waldhausen; in fact, the articles formulated against him by the friars in 1363 circulated under the name of the Augustinian convent of St. Thomas, in Prague. Konrad represented secular clergy of Prague in a complaint against mendicant infringement of burial fees in the summer of 1369 at the papal curia, shortly before he died (November 1369, back in Prague). Although Konrad appears to have preached in the provinces of Prague and of Salzburg, it is not known that he preached in Moravia. K. Richter, "Konrad Waldhauser," in F. Seibt, ed., *Karl IV. und sein Kreis*, vol. 3 of *Lebensbilder zur*

flict could have affected his inquisition. Interest-earning transactions were varied and widespread, and as judge, Klenkok may have examined any number of contracts involving the sale or inheritance of rents and the pawning of property.[24] Of this activity, only two things are certain: Johannes began between May, 1369 and July, 1370, and he finished before 22 June 1372.[25] His short tenure allowed only contact with the chancellor's circle, renowned for its humanism—enough contact to inspire a try at a more florid epistolary style, but not enough to make him very good at it.[26] More importantly, Johannes used his connection to

---

Geschichte der böhmischen Länder (Munich: Oldenbourg, 1978), pp. 159-74. K. Höfler, *Geschichtsschreiber der hussitischen Bewegung in Böhmen*, section 1, vol. 6/2 of *Fontes Rerum Bohemicarum* (Vienna: Kaiserliche und königliche Hof- und Staatsdruckerei, 1865), pp. 21-22 (for the articles against Konrad). BF 6:395 no. 957. *Monumenta Vaticana Res Gestas Bohemicas Illustrantia*, vol. 3, *Acta Urbani V, 1362-1370*, ed. Fredericus Jenšovský (Prague: Středočeská Tiskárna, 1944), pp. 395-98 no. 637-38, p. 411 no. 666 (Karl IV making supplication for Konrad to receive license to preach in the "parts of Germany or at least in the provinces of Prague and Salzburg"). See also ibid., p. 244 no. 412 for the foundation bull of the convent of Brno, where a bull of Boniface VIII, by implication, "Super cathedram," is interpreted as requiring papal licensure of the friars (with no mention of bishops). During Leonhard of Kärnten's early tenure as prior provincial of the Bavarian province, he apparently learned of widespread hostility against his order among "nearly all" pastors and rectors of his territory (Austria, Bavaria, Moravia, Bohemia, and Poland), no doubt during his initial visitation of his province, for he made formal complaint of it to Johannes, titular patriarch of Alexandria and papal nuncio for Germany, Bohemia, Austria, Hungary, and Poland, on 18 September 1372. *Codex Thomaeus*, no. 54, Kadlec, *Augustinerkloster*, pp. 191-95. The ensuing record of complaint and restatement of mendicant privilege was also issued to the Franciscans. Ibid., p. 195 note and *Mon. Vat. Res Gestas Bohemicas Illus.*, vol. 4, *Acta Gregorii XI*, part 1, *1370-1372*, ed. Carolic Stloukal (Prague: Gregerian, 1949), no. A.5-A.7, pp. 710-16.

[24]Bernard Schnapper, "Rentes chez les théologiens et les canonistes," *Études d'histoire du droit canonique dédiées à Gabriel Le Bras*, 2 vols. (Paris: Sirey, 1965), 2:965-95 provides a fine summary of late medieval problems and views. Benjamin N. Nelson, *The Idea of Usury. From Tribal Brotherhood to Universal Otherhood* (Princeton: Princeton University Press, 1949), pp. 3-28 still provides a useful and very broad overview of medieval views.

[25]Klenkok was reelected provincial of Saxony and Thüringen in 1368 and is likely to have held that office until Pentecost 1369. Page 42, above. 4 July 1370 is the date of Klenkok's appointment of 2 deputies in Brno. Note 1, p. 70, above. The safe conduct, with which he left Moravia, must have been issued in the spring of 1371. Page 71, above. The first reference to Klenkok as papal penitentiary is dated 22 June 1372. Note 1, p. 78.

[26]Consider the letter to Johannes of Hildesheim, Ep. 55 lines 33-42, with references to Demosthenes and Cicero (a lame attempt, at best, at classicizing), and lines 6-25, with a more intricate play on the figure of Carmel. Hendricks, "Register," pp. 234-35. The style was entirely uncharacteristic of Klenkok and cannot be found in any other address by him to another individual. Consider his salutations to Albert of Halberstadt, Herbord of Spangenberg (a non-epistolary example), Pierre of Vergne, and Gregory XI (the latter two written after he left Brno and showing that he maintained his early, more punctilious style). De Geer, "Klenkok's," p. 386. Cod. Guelf. 314 Nov., f. 16v (also the explicit of Klenkok's response to Herbord, f. 21v). Scheidt, *Biblioteca*, pp. 63-67. For authors associated with Neumarkt, see Josef Tříška, "K počátkům české školské vzdělanosti a humanismu" (On the beginnings of Czech school culture and humanism), *Acta Universitatis Carolinae—Historia Universitatis Carolinae Pragensis*, 7/1(1966):49-61, here 54, 60. Klapper, *Johann*, pp. 14-29. Arbesmann, *Der Augustinerorden und der Beginn der humanistischen Bewegung*, vol. 19 of

the bishop and chancellor to acquire the safe conduct, still feeling, we may assume, afraid that the Magdeburg *Rat* had inspired the hatred to threaten his life. We do not know whether he attended the general chapter as delegate of the Bavarian province, but he led a party and enjoyed an escort of attendants.[27] Nothing is known of his activity at the chapter.[28] Although it has been assumed that, after the chapter, Johannes did not return to Brno, he most likely did precisely that.[29] Of his subsequent activity in Brno, however, no direct evidence is known.

But Johannes must have had the *Sachsenspiegel* on his mind. He brought the *Decadicon* with him to Moravia. He expanded some articles and replaced the previous preface to Albert of Saxony with a new letter to Pierre of Vergne—a Limousin who had studied canon law and went to Avignon to read supplications to the pope, was promoted to judge of apostolic cases, and was finally made cardinal 30 May 1371. Johannes sought the cardinal's approval of the *Decadicon* and asked that he present it to Gregory XI.[30] He also wrote to the pope, briefly stated the

---

Cassiciacum (Würzburg: Augustinus-Verlag, 1965), p. 103 n. 313. Kałuza, *Thomas*, pp. 55-59 (for a very fine summary of Poles affected by Prague humanism). Klenkok's place in the chancellor's circle has been much overrated. E.g. Trapp, "Notes," p. 361.

[27]*Collectarius*, ed. Kaiser, no. 16 p. 12, the safe conduct says: " . . . reconmendamus ex animo, honestatem et dileccionem uestram affectuose rogantes, quatenus sibi [Johanne] et sue familie tam de securitate conductus quam de aliis, que itineris eius promocionem respiciunt, in transitu et reditu nostre consideracionis intuitu promotivam et favorabilem velitis ostendere voluntatem."

[28]The *definitiones* of the chapter of Florence contain no reference to him. AA 4(1911/12):471-76.

[29]The safe conduct stated that it was given that Johannes attend the general chapter of his order (not that he relocate to some other city or office) asking that he be given safe passage going and returning, a clause of the letter that has been easily overlooked. Cf. Bütow, "Lebensgeschichte," p. 564; Trapp, "Notes," p. 362.

[30]Pierre held the offices of *referendarius* and then auditor of the Rota before becoming cardinal. Guillemain, *Cour*, pp. 196 n. 81, 313. Klenkok's letter is published as a preface to the final edition of the *Decadicon*; Scheidt, *Biblioteca*, pp. 65-67. In this letter, Klenkok referred to himself as "sacre pagine professor" and friar. In the letter to Gregory XI, he called himself "sacre theologie professor immeritus, Ordinis Heremitarum Sancti Augustini." The letter was written after Pierre of Vergne became a cardinal and before Johannes became a penitentiary—a title of great weight whose omission would otherwise be very peculiar. Therefore, it was written between 30 May 1371 and sometime before 22 June 1372 (the date of the first mention of Klenkok as penitentiary, as shall be seen). Notably, the letters also fail to mention that he was an inquisitor and judge of Johannes of Neumarkt, which may suggest that he no longer occupied those offices. Cf. Bütow, "Lebensgeschichte," p. 565, who held the year 1373 as a *terminus ante quem* for the final edition of the *Decadicon*. In the letter to Pierre of Vergne, Klenkok also notes that he was known to Pierre in school, but he does not explicitly say that they were at the same school at the same time. Scheidt, *Biblioteca.* p. 65. Homeyer believed that Klenkok had been Pierre's teacher, naming Paris as the place. Homeyer, *Johannes*, pp. 394-95; also Bütow, "Lebensgeschichte," p. 564. Trapp said Klenkok was his teacher in Bologna. "Notes," p. 358. This is the questionable salutation: "In Christo reuerendissimo patri ac domino suo graciosissimo, domino Petro de Vernio . . . , velut cardini ianuam, de via lata mundi ducenti animam ad artam viam salutis, portis dimissis penitus inferorum, frater Johannes Clenckok,

Sachsenspiegel's need for condemnation, and mentioned the correspondence to Pierre of Vergne.[31] He then published both letters with his text—the most common edition of the work.[32] This was before Johannes became papal penitentiary but after Pierre became cardinal, sometime between the late spring of 1371 and the early summer of 1372.

---

sacre pagine professor, noticia scolastica tironum noticie comparata, dum idem domnus esset gymnasiis ei notus, oraciones ad Christum sedulas, infra scriptorum correctionem, ac per zelum diuine legis ad ipsius legis brauium peruenire." Scheidt, *Biblioteca*, p. 65, with the correction of Homeyer, op. cit., pp. 394-95. Pierre may have known Klenkok as a professor without having been his student.

[31]Ibid., pp. 64-65. The letter was not composed as a preface to the *Decadicon* because it lacks any reference to the work and clearly assumes that Gregory shall receive it from Pierre of Vergne. Cf. Bütow, "Lebensgeschichte," pp. 564-65, who believed the letter to the pope introduced a version of the work that Klenkok personally delivered to the pope.

[32]Bütow, "Lebensgeschichte," p. 565 n. 92. There is no reason to believe that Klenkok presented the *Decadicon* to the cardinal in person. Cf. Trapp, "Notes," p. 362. Bütow believed the *Decadicon* was given by Klenkok to both Pierre of Vergne (in 1371) and Gregory XI (by 1373). Bütow, "Lebensgeschichte," pp. 564-65. De Geer recognized the role Klenkok hoped the cardinal would play in transmitting the work (although mistakenly believing that Pierre had been promoted cardinal in 1372). "Klenkok's," p. 382.

V. POENITENTIARIUS NOSTER

Before 22 June 1372, Johannes was appointed a minor penitentiary in Avignon.[1] The apostolic penitentiary was an elite society
of seventeen to nineteen monks who were almost all members of
the mendicant orders, supervised by a cardinal (not belonging to
a religious order, with one exception, during the Avignon papacy). They were immediately subject to the pope (like chaplains), bore the titles "official" and "familiar," and, in connection
with the latter, enjoyed a variety of privileges, like better access to
benefices, a special means for making supplications to the pope,
and more liberal rules on the import of grain and wine.[2] Their
status was gilded with ritual, ritual that underscored their close
association with the papal office. At the table of the pope, the
penitentiary major sat before the deacon of the Rota, followed
by a penitentiary minor, the auditor of cases, and the rest of the
minor penitentiaries; in the chapel of the apostolic palace when
the pope said mass, the major penitentiary held the holy mitre—
the deacon of the Rota might do so only in his absence or, in the

[1]The chapter title is the title used by Gregory XI to refer to Klenkok in the first known
reference to Klenkok as penitentiary. BF 6:479-82 no. 1202. This is the only reference to
Klenkok as penitentiary known to the early biographical literature. Bütow, "Lebensgeschichte," pp. 567-68 and n. 100. Trapp, "Notes," p. 362, misdated the assignment to a
commission, represented by the document noted here, to 1373, but he correctly noted that
the first reference to Klenkok in the office is from 1372 (the first reference is the assignment
to the commission; in 1373, the commission offered its conclusions. Trapp apparently con-
fused the appointment and the report). The register entry is also briefly described by L.
Mirot and H. Jassemin, eds., *Lettres secrètes et curiales du pape Grégoire XI (1370-1378) relatives à la France* (Paris: E. de Boccard, 1935), p. 857 no. 2586. Johannes may have replaced
Augustinus Münzmeister OESA, one of two other German-speaking penitentiaries at the
curia in the early 1370s, who was promoted to bishop 26 April 1372. See note 8, below. The
other German was a Theodoric of Metz O.Carm., who served 1361-1376. Timotheus Majic,
"Die apostolische Pönitentiarie im 14. Jahrhundert," *Römische Quartalschrift für christliche
Altertumskunde und Kirchengeschichte* 50/2(1955):129-77, here 167.

[2]The one mendicant cardinal to become penitentiary major in Avignon was the Franciscan, Gentile of Montefiore, in the early fourteenth century. Most minor penitentiaries
were Franciscans and Dominicans. The structure of the apostolic penitentiary in Klenkok's time dated to Benedict XII's "In agro dominico" of 1338, which organized it into two
colleges beneath the penitentiary major, that of the penitentiary minors and a college of
scribes. They were also assisted by one auditor of cases; Guillemain, *Court*, pp. 332, 335,
488-96. Boys were employed to guide penitents and carry out various odd jobs, like pub-
lishing public penances, reporting curial information (where the pope is celebrating,
when and where cardinals and curialists would participate in funerals, processions, or
other formalities), preparing the candles for the feast of purification and for the masses for
the dead.

absence of both, the eldest penitentiary minor would perform the honor. Substitutes and coadjutors were never to be seated as equals of penitentiaries.[3] The penitentiary major greeted cardinals with the kiss of peace at his palace on Easter morning; he stood after the papal chaplains in procession on Candlemass to receive candles and place a kiss upon the feet of Peter's successor.[4] As a pope lay upon his deathbed or immediately after his death, the penitentiaries chanted the office of the dead, the seven penitential psalms, and prayers; they helped wash and embalm his body and dress it in the pontifical garments; they carried it in procession to a chapel and sang the office of the dead again, with the cantors of the papal chapel, until they were replaced by the parochial clergy, the canons, and the religious of Avignon. In procession, the penitentiaries, with leading members of the chancellory and other members of the apostolic family, represented the clergy, while nobility (whoever was in town) represented the laity, proceeding as the universe of Christian society, *clerus et populus*.[5]

These rituals expressed the intimacy of the penitentiaries' role in performing the pastoral work of popes as members of his court.[6] They no longer lived in convents, said the divine office in monks' chapels, or sat in chapters; they were paid by the apostolic chamber and rented houses in town.[7] To come here was to participate in the papacy's spiritual jurisdiction of the world. Even those promoted out of the penitentiary to higher ecclesiastical office, always to bishop, did so as protagonists of papal power in sees where the pope intended to increase his influence.[8] Popes aptly referred to each of these monks as *"our penitentiary."*

---

[3]Emil Göller, *Die päpstliche Pönitentiarie von ihrem Ursprung bis zu ihrer Umgestaltung unter Pius V*, 2 vols. (Rome: Loscher and Company, 1907), 2:179.

[4]He holds the same position in procession to receive ashes on Ash Wednesday, olive branches on Palm Sunday, and the Agnus Dei on Holy Saturday. Göller, *Pönitentiarie*, 1:142-45.

[5]Bernhard Schimmelpfennig, "Die Funktion des Papstpalastes und der kurialen Gesellschaft im päpstlichen Zeremoniell vor und während des Grossen Schismas," *Genèse et début du Grand Schisme d'Occident. Avignon 25-28 septembre 1978*, no. 586 of *Colloques internationaux du Centre National de la Recherche Scientifique* (Paris: Centre National de la Recherche Scientifique, 1980), pp. 317-28, here 321-22.

[6]According to the constitution of Benedict XII (1338), the penitentiary was a purely spiritual office, in contrast with other branches of the curia. Matthäus Meyer, *Die Pönitentiarie Formularsammlung des Walter Murner von Strassburg. Beitrag zur Geschichte und Diplomatik der päpstlichen Pönitentiarie im 14. Jahrhundert*, vol. 25 of *Spicilegium Friburgense* (Freiburg: Universitätsverlag Freiburg Schweiz, 1979), p. 8.

[7]There is one known case of a penitentiary actually purchasing a house. Johannes Vinke, "Volkstum und apostolische Pönitentiarie im 14. Jahrhundert," ZRG, KA 27(1938):414-44, here 418, 437.

[8]The office of penitentiary minor was frequently a terminal position, but some were promoted to sees in Italy, Germany, and England. Majic, "Pönitentiarie," pp. 152-58

Territorial lords, kings, and queens sometimes recommended candidates for the office.[9] Although these are presumed to represent a minority of appointments, there is a chronic lack of information about the rest. One may speculate that most penitentiaries were recommended through the informal mechanisms of communication that existed between officials associated with the general chapters of the orders, cardinal protectors of the orders, or bishops with close ties to the curia.[10] The overwhelming majority were graduates of Paris; there were more theologians than canonists.[11] An attempt was made to represent all major linguistic groups.[12] Johannes Klenkok may have enjoyed the recommendation of the chancellor of Karl IV, or perhaps he attended the general chapter of Florence in 1371 to investigate options for promotion.[13] Upon recommendation, according to fifteenth-century statutes that are believed to represent long-standing practices, the candidate presented four witnesses to attest to his character and ability, and a "prior" penitentiary, with two other minor penitentiaries and a notary to make a record, conducted an examination of life, morals, and knowledge. The penitentiary major would then present Johannes to Gregory XI, at which time the day, hour, and subject of a disputation under the penitentiary major would be set. Most penitentiaries attended the examination. Upon successful completion of the ordeal, the major gave his approval; Klenkok would then perform

---

(which may overrate the frequency of promotion, but which also includes a list drawn from Eubel; these were almost exclusively mendicant friars). Guillemain, *Cour*, pp. 338-39. Klenkok witnessed several promotions. 26 April 1372, Augustinus Münzmeister OESA was placed in the see of Seckau. Majic, op. cit., p. 154. Eubel, p. 441. On 11 May 1372, a day after sending Karl IV a relic of the wood of the cross embedded in a gold cross littered with precious stones, Gregory XI wrote the emperor, Albert, duke of Austria, Pilgrin, archbishop of Salzburg, and Stephan, duke of Bavaria, commending the new bishop. G. Mollat, *Lettres secrètes et curiales du pape Grégoire XI (1370-1378) intéressant les pays autres que la France* (Paris: Éditions E. de Boccard, 1962-1965), p. 102 no. 724-28. Other promotions during Klenkok's time: Dominic of Newstead OESA to Nitra 27 October 1372; Jacob Johannis OP to Bergen, 7 April 1372; Jean Chambeire OFM to Castro, 18 July 1373; Philip Torynton OFM to Cashel, 5 September 1373; and Thomas Brienton OSB to Rochester, 31 January 1373. Majic, op. cit., pp. 154, 155, 157, 158.

[9]Sometimes attaining extraordinary appointments for a favored confessor, sometimes seeking a penitentiary for a confessor. Majic, "Pönitentiarie," pp. 150, 164, 165, 174-75. Vladimir Koudelka, "Geschichte," 25:96, 97, 98. Vincke, "Volkstum," p. 420 n. 2.

[10]The latter may have been more characteristic of appointments as scribes of the penitentiary, where the regional patterns in backgrounds suggest the influence of bishops of the south of France. Guillemain, *Cour*, p. 345 n. 441, cf. p. 336 n. 355.

[11]Majic, "Pönitentiarie," pp. 146-48. Guillemain, *Cour*, p. 336. Few had no notable intellectual qualifications. Ibid., p. 339.

[12]Majic, "Pönitentiarie," pp. 149-50. Vinke, "Volkstum," pp. 423-28, 437.

[13]There is no reason to assume that he went to Avignon in order to initiate a process against the *Sachsenspiegel*, and only subsequently was recommended to the penitentiary. Cf. Bütow, "Lebensgeschichte," p. 564; Trapp, "Notes," p. 362.

an oath promising faithful performance of the office, which was recorded on the papal bull of reception. A rite of reception was performed in the church, and the penitentiary was presented with a staff inscribed with his oath or a mention of it; the apostolic chamber entered his name in their books, which assured him of his salary.[14]

The principal task of this office was hearing confessions in the cathedral of Notre Dame des Doms, which flanked the north wall of the papal palace.[15] Johannes and his peers worked as specialists in the cases reserved to the apostolic see, and accordingly they were empowered to dispense from irregularities and hindrances to marriage; provide release, transferal, or alteration of oaths; commute penances; and grant certain privileges and favors. Their power was restricted only by stipulations that some sensitive cases be referred to the penitentiary major or to the pope himself, which left them competent to absolve a vast array of sins.[16] A characteristic of the Rota also applied, under its own terms, to this office: it claimed immediate competence over the consciences of all Christendom. It was not a court of last instance requiring approach through an irreproachable hierarchy of lower courts.[17] Anyone could come here with an onerous censure, impediment, or penance (although legal controversies belonged to the apostolic Rota).[18]

On the days of penance or on those Sundays and feast days when the city was crowded with pilgrims, the penitentiaries were in the cathedral by the ringing of prime and remained there until terce. They were to handle confessors kindly, to show no preference to the wealthy by avoiding the disadvantaged, never to take money, never to assign monetary penances, never to hire a replacement to do the job, and always to order letters of absolution or dispensation from the penitentiary scribes.[19] Johannes and his only German peer in the college, a Carmelite from Lorraine

---

[14]Göller, *Pönitentiarie*, 1:138-40; 2:125-27. Notarial records of the examinations are not to my knowledge known to be extant. For record keeping, consider also Guillemain, *Cour*, pp. 345, 562.

[15]For the church, Guillemain, *Cour*, pp. 80-81, 504, 511 and map 2.

[16]Guillemain, *Cour*, p. 335. Majic, "Pönitentiarie," p. 130. Göller, *Pönitentiarie*, 1:134-38, 2:179-80 (for a list of cases over which they were competent).

[17]On the Rota, Barraclough, "Praxis Beneficiorum," p. 127.

[18]Guillemain, *Cour*, pp. 349ff. Hans Erich Feine, *Kirchliche Rechtsgeschichte*, 2 vols. (Weimar: Hermann Böhlaus Nachfolger, 1950), 1:278.

[19]"In agro domini." Göller, *Pönitentiarie*, 1:136-38. Benedict XII's rules also stipulated that women, even if of high birth, be confessed in the church; if ill, then preferably in a church near their domicile. Penitentiaries stationed in Rome in 1374 were known to make conspicuously frequent visits to convents of nuns. Majic, "Pönitentiarie," p. 159. Guillemain, *Cour*, p. 485.

(which was part of the empire; a German dialect was spoken there),[20] must have spent many hours straining their ears for recognizable names of misdeeds and irregularities in an unsettling sea of dialects, and they would also hear messengers of rulers (which could include cities as well as royalty and nobility) who sought the resolution of spiritual penalties, like interdict, with political consequences. In addition to hearing confessions, popes occasionally assigned penitentiaries extraordinary tasks—for the most part (but with surprising exceptions) tasks that pertained to the spiritual jurisdiction of the apostolic see, which was anxious to intervene in any ecclesiastical domain. Such assignments included the reformation of cloisters, the visitation of a diocese, and inquisition, but they might also involve the exercise of temporal sovereignty in a papal territory and the mediation of conflicts between the curia and secular rulers.[21] Johannes Klenkok received at least one extraordinary assignment and one other more routine papal mandate.

The more routine mandate came in the summer of 1373, on or before 1 July. Karl IV petitioned the holy see that an interdict against a knight of the diocese of Constance, Johannes Flach of Riesbach, be removed.[22] Flach, together with Johannes of Riethem (a knight from the diocese of Augsburg), had served as a captain of troops of Perugia in the most recent mutiny of a city from the papal states.[23] They had even participated in the attack on Viterbo while Urban V was resident there (in the summer of 1368).[24] For violating the interdict against Perugia and threatening the papal court, they were excommunicated on 22 May 1370, and an interdict was pronounced against a castle, a village, and two towns belonging to Flach in southern Germany.[25] Flach repented, and Gregory XI now lifted the interdict and conceded absolution under the usual conditions (oath, restoration, and some

---

[20]Note 1, p. 78, above. A third German, Walter Murner of Strasbourg, served as procurator of the penitentiary. Meyer, *Pönitentiarie-Formularsammlung*, p. 13 n. 1.

[21]Examples in Majic, "Pönitentiarius," pp. 132-34, 175-76, and Guillemain, *Cour*, p. 338.

[22]*Acta Gregorii XI*, ed. Stoukal, pp. 393-94 no. 689.

[23]Meyer, *Pönitentiarie-Formularsammlung*, pp. 75-77, for Perugia's rebellion.

[24]Meyer, *Pönitentiarie-Formularsammlung*, p. 76; Walter Murner preserved the penance and absolution prescribed for a soldier who had burned, despoiled, and robbed church property, consecrated and secular, during the campaign, ibid., p. 305 no. 349.

[25]Karl Rieder, ed., *Monumenta Vaticana Historiam Episcopatus Constantiensis in Germania Illustrantia. Römische Quellen zur konstanzer Bistumsgeschichte zur Zeit der Päpste in Avignon, 1305-1378* (Innsbruck: Wagner'sche Universitäts Buchhandlung, 1908), p. 513 no. 1625. *Regesta Episcoporum Constantiensium. Regesten zur Geschichte der Bischöfe von Constanz von Bubulcus bis Thomas Berlower, 517-1496*, 5 vols. (Innsbruck: Wagner'sche Universitäts Buchhandlung, 1894-1931), 2:379 no. 6109. The absolution tells us of the interdict against the towns, Rieder, *Monumenta*, p. 558 no. 1762.

stipulated service for the church) with an abiding penance. He must never take up arms against the church of Rome again. For as long as he should live, Flach also must perform a fast on every Wednesday and a fast of bread and water on the vigil and feast of the apostles Peter and Paul. Should there be a church, chapel, or oratory dedicated to one or both of these apostles in the place where he finds himself on that feast, he must reverently offer a candle, simple or elaborate (*cereum seu torticium*), of four pounds of wax. And on the next Easter, he must give 1,200 florins of gold for the construction of a chapel.[26]

An apostolic penitentiary made the absolution. It was Johannes Klenkok.[27] The penance required an annual performance of devotion to the papacy's two principal Roman saints, Peter and Paul, the established guardians of papal authority.[28] The penitentiary, knowing his own tangled interest in society's compliance with papal government, must have liked these conspicuous and permanent requirements.

The extraordinary assignment came 22 June 1372, and it shows that Gregory XI or some cardinal recognized a gifted casuist in this Augustinian theologian. According to a contemporary biographer of king Ludwig I of Hungary, this eastern Angevin initiated a Catholic offensive against Bosnian heretics in the 1340s and established a Franciscan, Peregrin (the new vicar of Bosnia), as Bosnian bishop in 1349.[29] In fact, the Bosnian ruler, Ban Stjepan Kotromanić, who was about to convert to Catholicism from Orthodoxy himself, brought the Franciscans to his realm, where they established a Bosnian vicariat between 1340 and 1342.[30] He

---

[26]Rieder, *Monumenta*, p. 559 no. 1762. Notably lacking are the pilgrimages prescribed to other members of the Perugian League (as well as the Florentine League and the supporters of Bernabó Visconti in Milan). Meyer, *Pönitentiarie-Formularsammlung*, pp. 307-11 no. 354, here pp. 310-11.

[27]*Acta Gregorii XI*, ed. Stoukal, pp. 393-94 no. 689, dated 1 July 1373.

[28]The witness of the martyrs Peter and Paul assured the steadfast authority of the Roman Church. *Sexti*, I.vi.17, CICan 2:957 (Nicholas III); *Extra.*, V.ix.1, CICan 2:1303-04 (Boniface VIII's "Antiquorum habet" of 22 February 1300 establishing the first Roman jubilee and a general absolution for pilgrims to Rome).

[29]According to the archdeacon Ivan. Jaroslav Šidak, "Franjevačka 'Dubia' iz g. 1372/3. kao izvor za provijest Bosne" [The Franciscan "dubia" of 1372/73 as source for the history of Bosnia], idem, *Studije o 'Crkvi bosanskoj' i bogumilstvu* [Studies on the "Bosnian Church" and Bogomilism] (Zagreb: Sveučilišna naklada Liber, 1975), pp. 225-48, German précis on p. 248, here 234. I am grateful to Dr. Mary P. Coote for bringing this article to my attention and for help in fathoming the Croatian. The bishop of Bosnia emigrated out of his diocese in the 1230s and into Djakova, in Slavonia, in the 1250s. John V.A. Fine, Jr., *The Bosnian Church: A New Interpretation*, vol. 10 of *East European Monographs* (Boulder: East European Quarterly, 1975). Peregrin's appointment was a short-lived attempt to return the see to its territory. Ivan's view is repeated by Heribert Holzapfel, who also believed that Peregrin was the first bishop of Bosnia, *Handbuch der Geschichte des Franziskanerordens* (Freiburg im Breisgau: Herder, 1909), pp. 244-45. See also Eubel, 142.

[30]Šidak, "Franjevačka 'Dubia,' " p. 231.

was closely allied with the king of Hungary at the time, and both king and chieftain supported the Franciscan mission as a harmless concession to papal desire: the alternative was a crusade by Croatian princes, which they had just averted.[31]

The papacy had long been interested in the extermination of heresy in south Slavic lands. John XXII first sent a Franciscan there to conduct an inquisition fifteen years earlier, and popes sent waves of letters to rulers calling for the support of inquisitors and suppression by violence.[32] As a result, regional leaders discovered the accusation of heresy as a method to gain papal support. When Kotromanić died in 1353, Ludwig I of Hungary tried to gain direct control over Bosnia. What he failed to accomplish through warfare (in 1363), he also attempted by subversion, accusing Kotromanić's young successor, Ban Tvrtko, of flagrantly supporting heretics. Although this assured Hungary of papal sympathy, it did not accomplish Ludwig's ambitions. But suddenly, in 1366, Tvrtko faced an insurrection apparently led by his own brother, and he fled to the Hungarian court and swore his fealty. Ludwig supported Tvrtko's restoration. Tvrtko's brother went into exile, where he began a literary campaign with Avignon alleging his brother's heresies. But the papacy had learned the limitations of religious war east of the Adriatic. To the benefit of the Hungarian peace (accomplished twenty years later than Ivan the archdeacon claimed), the papacy merely encouraged new support of Franciscan missions.[33]

In spite of these revolutions and reinforced by Tvrtko's Hungarian turn, the Franciscans accomplished a queerly successful and problematic mission in the Balkans, hardly able to keep up with the converts and confronting new problems in their rare monopoly of spiritual jurisdiction.[34] The people were "schismatics" and "heretics." The "schismatics" must refer to the Orthodox, probably Serbian Orthodox. The "heretics" may refer to Bogomils, although nothing suggests their adherence to dualistic beliefs. Or they may have been members of the shadowy "Bosanska crkva." This "Bosnian Church" apparently arose after the emigration of the Catholic bishop from his diocese in the 1230s. It

---

[31]Fine, *Church*, pp. 179-82.

[32]Šidak, "Franjevačka 'Dubia,' " pp. 227-28. Fine, *Church*, pp. 169-80.

[33]Fine, *Church*, pp. 188-91. Thus the missions were closely related to Hungary's southern expansion. Šidak, "Franjevačka 'Dubia,' " pp. 235-37.

[34]For the absence of Catholic bishops, consider BF 6:479-82 no. 1202, and compare ibid., n. 2, questions 8, 9, and 14 (bishops of neighboring dioceses were sending priests, who tried to impede the Franciscans in the performance of all the sacraments).

may be that the ambiguity of their allegiance reflects their genuine ambivalence toward the Roman and Byzantine churches.[35]
They were certainly independent and, like other Europeans, reluctant to abandon their traditional rites and laws. The vicar of
the Bosnian Franciscans sent a nuncio, Berengar of Aragon, a
Franciscan "professor," to Avignon with a list of 23 problems encountered by Franciscan missionaries and with orders to get
more friars. He apparently went first to the Franciscan minister
general, who in turn sent Bartholomew of Auvergne as his vicar
to Gregory XI with the petition.[36] Gregory ordered the Franciscan
minister general to put all available friars to preach in Bosnia,
and the minister general prescribed liberal terms of recruitment
in a letter to all provincials, custodies, guardians, and their vic-
ars, dated 22 June 1372.

He made Franciscan transfers to the east easy: lay brothers
could be licensed to assist the friars already there; any friar seeking license to go to Bosnia could not be denied (all regulations,
even apostolic ones, notwithstanding); and any friar making the
August pilgrimage to Sta. Maria della Porziuncula, on the testimony of two other Franciscan friars, could be licensed by the cus-
todial minister of the custody of Assisi or by the minister
provincial of the province of St. Francis to join the mission.[37] Gregory also appointed a commission to solve the 23 problems: two
bishops (one of them a Franciscan) from nearby sees with good
ties to the curia, another bishop apparently resident in Avignon
at the time, the master of the sacred palace, the *magister regens* of
the Avignon Dominicans, and from the apostolic penitentiary,
Johannes Klenkok.[38] Klenkok must have been occupied with the

---

[35]Fine, *Church*, pp. 192-97. Šidak believes the people in question were all orthodox and,
in fact, not Bosnian but residents of the area of Vidin, in the northeast corner of Bulgaria,
where Franciscans claimed fantastic success and which also belonged to the Bosnian
vicariat. "Franjevačka 'Dubia,' " pp. 235-37, 240. For options in the identity of the schismatic priests, ibid., p. 245 n. 94.

[36]Berengar of Aragon is named as nuncio of the vicar of Bosnia in the letter of the minister general, BF 6:478 no. 1201, and Bartholomew of Auvergne is named as the vicar of the
minister general and the Franciscans of Bosnia in the papal letter, BF 6:479-82 no. 1202.

[37]BF 6:478-79 no. 1201. The minister general also ordered Berengar, on pain of excommunication, not to presume to receive more than sixty friars "inter litteratos et laicos."

[38]Gauffredus, bishop of Quimper; Françoise, bishop of Cavaillon; Walter, bishop of
Glasgow; Guillaume (Romain), master of the apostolic palace; Klenkok, "poenitentiarius
noster"; and Isnard of Castellano, *magister regens* of the Dominican convent in Avignon,
the last two also identified as professors and doctors of sacred theology. Gregory noted
that they were chosen because they were all masters of sacred theology, erudite in the law,
and zealous in charity for the salvation of souls, and that they would consult other masters of theology and *doctores decretorum* at the Roman curia and ultimately present their
answers by apostolic authority according to sacred scripture and the canons. BF 6:479-82
no. 1202. The diocese of Quimper provided the papacy with a number of curialists;
Gauffredus was appointed bishop by Innocent VI in 1357. Guillemain, *Cour*, p. 463. Eubel,

requisite consultations over the course of the year or until as late as November 1373, although the problems do not appear particularly difficult or the answers profound.[39]

But the problems are interesting nonetheless. Missionary friars had trouble creating Catholic communities.[40] Converts stuck with their old priests; "schismatics" attended Catholic services; rural folk argued their personal opinions of the Faith; even enemies of Ludwig of Hungary sought Franciscan absolutions. The curiously mixed circumstances raised embarrassing questions about the legitimacy of Orthodox sacraments and the sufficiency of confessing the Orthodox creeds (both of which the Catholics had to concede) and the moral obligations of Catholic converts in their inevitable social relations with "infidels."[41] Matters were complicated by the incompatibility of Roman canon law and Bosnian marital custom. Men took wives with a convenient proviso, "if you are a good woman to me," and they were loath to give it up.[42] Bosnians were also loath to abandon sexual intercourse during menstruation (which was required by canon

---

p. 211. The see of Cavaillon provided the papacy with at least one cardinal (during the reign of Urban V); Françoise, a Franciscan, was made bishop by Urban V in 1366. Guillemain, op. cit., p. 209. Eubel, p. 179. Walter was also promoted by Urban V in 1367; he had been a canon of Glasgow. Eubel, p. 264. Guillaume Romain was a Breton and master of the sacred palace from 1362 to 1374. Guillemain, op. cit., pp. 384 n. 182, 385 n. 185.

[39]The commission's answer is dated by the year alone, 1373, and published in BF 6:480-82 n. 2. A papal rescript of 5 November 1373 empowers the commission (consisting of the same members with one difference: Guillaume Romain was now apostolic auditor and no longer master of the palace) to extend their apostolic declaration on the doubts of the preachers of the word of the cross which answered the supplications of Bartholomew of Auvergne, vicar of the Franciscan minister general and the Franciscans of Bosnia, to the parts of Corsica, Russia, and ultramarine areas. This shows that the commission still existed but had completed its work, which may suggest that it only recently had issued its declaration. Mollat, ed., *Lettres Grégoire XI*, p. 316 no. 2273.

[40]BF6:480-82 n. 2, questions 3, 21, for converts staying in Orthodox communion.

[41]Ibid., questions 2, 3, 13, 15, 16, 18, 19. This problem was exacerbated by the Franciscans' lack of numbers. So, for example, Orthodox priests offered to help the Franciscans baptize, using the Latin rite, for a fee, which the commission allowed, so long as the arrangement created no "perversion of the will" (i.e. of the baptizand, whose will might be perverted by colluding with the Orthodox priest to make a little money; this would create an impediment to baptism). Ibid., question 1. To do so, however, openly demonstrated that the sacramental power of Greek bishops, who ordained these priests, was effective (consider question 2). Consider also question 8, which notes the lack of priests and defined parishes, and asks if the friars might "supplement" their insufficient number in the performance of the sacraments (which the commission granted). The supplementary performers or dispensers of the sacraments could refer to Orthodox priests (which would perhaps be redundant) or lay members of the order or other laity (who were permitted to assist friars by the minister general in his letter of 22 June 1372; ibid., pp. 478-79 no. 1201). Such accommodations were suggested first by Stjepan Kotromanić in 1347. Fine, *Church*, p. 186.

[42]BF 6:480-82, question 4, for the condition, and questions 11 and 12, for the reluctance of converts to adhere to Catholic marital law. It raised several problems regarding the validity of marriages so contracted (which the commission easily concluded were not mar-

law).[43] Latin Christians—German merchants—had their mis-
tresses openly, embarrassing Franciscan claims to represent the
better tradition.[44] And the Franciscans could not avoid the con-
ventional conflict of the west: they were too few, so neighboring
bishops moved diocesan clergy into the new lands of the Hungarian king, and the intrusive priests promptly warned friars not
to assume the sacramental roles of parochial clergy.[45]

The papal commission followed the letter of the law and displayed little interest in proselytizing strategies. Questions that
involved sacraments were answered by applying precise defini-
tions of those sacraments. Problems of building a Catholic community were answered by applying norms of an Augustinian
church (disallowing "schismatic" practices, but recognizing the
community as a mixed body of saints and sinners). The pastoral
privilege of the friars was stated in forceful terms.[46] Although
the committee claimed to have done much research, it is difficult to imagine that it took them much time. Their confident
explanations display paltry scholarship—three references to the
Bible, two references to Augustine, and four citations and five
vague allusions to the canon law. The contributions of members

riages according to canon law) and women who converted, abandoned first husbands,
and married Catholic men (which seems a reasonable means of averting the social inse-
curity of a traditional Bosnian marriage). Ibid., questions 4, 5, 20.

[43]Ibid., question 6. The Franciscans wondered if their power as apostolic legates en-
abled them to dispense from the law. The commission noted that a clause of their privilege, "nec non et alia facere, quae ad augmentum divini nominis et ampliationem
catholicae fidei videbitur expedire," applies here: much progeny is good for new converts;
dispense away!

[44]Surprisingly the Franciscans needed to ask if the German merchants, especially the
ones with wives back home, should be censured. The commission said yes. Ibid., question
7. But the commission would not exclude these merchants from hearing mass, if they had
not been formerly condemned by the church. Ibid., question 17.

[45]Ibid., questions 9 and 10. The commission affirmed their right to perform all the sacraments by virtue of their papal mandate. Question 10 asks whether Catholic priests entering the region enjoy the same right. This is the only question for which an answer is not
recorded. The priests may have been of the bishop of Djakova, Bosnian bishop resident in
Slavonia (again since the death of Peregrin in 1356). Franciscans had earlier conflicts with
Djakova over tithes and lost (Fine, *Church*, p. 185). Most recently, in 1369, they had been
granted the right to collect alms throughout the vicariat (Šidak, "Franjevačka 'Dubia,' "
p. 234).

[46]The commission's responses to particular questions are given in the previous notes.
Consider also questions 22 and 23 on the administration of baptism (its relation to con-
fession and the proper formula) and question 14, where the commission affirms the authority of the Franciscans to absolve cases ordinarily reserved to bishops (although a
bishop or his commission should hear them, the friars may occupy the same position according to their apostolic legation, "tamquam episcopi et amplius ex privilegio," and they
may absolve and grant absolution). A similar justification is given in answer to question
19, concerning the absolution of those who bear or make Bosnian arms ("ni talium abso-
lutio sedi apostolicae fuerit reseruata, cum dicit fratres ex privilegio tanta quanta episcopi
et maiori in certis casibus fungantur auctoritate").

of the commission remained anonymous, but we may assume that Klenkok, who had become acquainted with similar conflicts in Saxony, played a useful role.

Penitentiaries had better access to popes, and Johannes probably exploited this to bring to fruition one staunch conviction—the injustice of some Saxon laws. By letter, before coming to Avignon, he appealed to the primitive instincts of papal dominion, to the sense of vigilance conveyed in Gregory XI's name, "which means vigilance," for gathering the church out of her languid fissions and overcoming the negligence of her sleeping pastors and doctors who ignored the law of God and let the *Sachsenspiegel* subvert the unity of the gospel.[47] He could now reinforce his correspondence to the pontiff and to Pierre of Vergne with back-room campaigning. The letters, and whatever else Klenkok may have done, worked. Gregory XI appointed a commission of cardinals, "masters of the sacred page," and doctors of both laws, who recommended the unequivocal condemnation of 14 articles of Saxon law that roughly correspond to Klenkok's final 21 articles.[48] The language of the papal condemnation, the bull "Salvator humani generis" of 8 April 1374, also alluded to Klenkok's self-defense against the Magdeburg *Rat*, which implies that he himself took a leading position on the commission.[49] His was a stunning victory, even if only accomplished in that remote court, whose authority he intended to defend only in his own country.

No individual in Avignon made policy cold, in a rational and disinterested solitude. The workers of the curia came to Avignon through networks of people. Old bonds stayed. Therefore, one could work to advance partisan interests and preserve one's own people, even while participating in an ostensibly neutral ideal—the ideal of a uniform Christian society. Near what was to be the end of Johannes Klenkok's life, he received a list of complaints against Jan Milič Kroměříž from Prague. Klenkok was to be a partisan implanted deep within the apostolic palace.

Jan Milič was a priest of the diocese of Olomouc, who climbed the imperial chancellory of Johannes of Neumarkt from registrar

---

[47]In Klenkok's letter to Gregory XI, Scheidt, *Biblioteca*, p. 64.

[48]"Salvator humani generis," paragraph 2, *Bullarium*, 4:574-75. Homeyer, *Johannes*, pp. 398-99. Bütow, "Lebensgeschichte," pp. 565-66. The composition of the commission and the date of its formation are not known.

[49]The allusion says precisely what Klenkok, in his "Universis Christi fidelibus," lacked the authority to say: "Universis Christi fidelibus per apostolica scripta mandantes, quod ipsis scriptis seu legibus reprobatis de caetero non utantur, et domini terrarum tam ecclesiastici, quam saeculares suos uti subditos non permittant." Paragraph 4, *BR*, 4:575.

to corrector to notary, and he was a comfortably endowed canon and archdeacon of Litomyšl when Neumarkt was her bishop. He heard the preaching of the reformer, Konrad Waldhausen, and interrupted a potentially brilliant career in imperial circles, abandoned his prebends and offices in 1364 to preach as an impoverished and humble priest, and became the flash point of the recent phase of rivalry between friars and secular clergy in Prague. Klenkok had probably learned his name before coming to Avignon.[50] Soon after his conversion, Milič had indulged in some biblical chronography and concluded that the antichrist had appeared between 1365 and 1367. It was his great indiscretion to reveal the enemy's identity in a sermon before the antichrist himself: Karl IV. He promptly landed in jail, was then released, and the indefatigable reformer embarked for Rome to intercept the returning pope Urban V and proclaim the dawning of the apocalypse. He arrived in early April 1367, some weeks before Urban even left Avignon, and, impatient, decided to reveal to the eternal city the dangers lurking in the immediate future, before trying to meet the pope in Avignon or underway. He posted a bill on the door of St. Peter's announcing his sermon. He was arrested again and released more than a year later, perhaps at the instigation of Karl IV—at the arrival of Urban in Rome in October, 1368. He improved his doctrine, easing its anti-establishment intonations; he abandoned individual associations of the antichrist and adapted a typology that identified the archenemy as all

---

[50]The most thorough treatment of Milič's life that I know of is František Loskot, *Milíč z Kroměříže, Otec české Reformace* (Milič of Kroměříž, father of the Czech Reformation), vol. 2 of *Velicí mužové české reformace* (Leading men of the Czech Reformation) (Prague: Nákladem Volné Myšlenky, 1911). A more recent work, in an abridged German translation, is Miloslav Kaňák, *Milíč aus Kremsier. Der Vater der böhmischen Reformation*, trans. Vilém Schneeberger, ed. Gerhard Bassarak (Berlin: Evangelische Verlagsanstalt, 1981). A useful summary of Milič's biography may be found in Paul De Vooght, *L'Hérésie de Jean Huss*, 2 vols. (Louvain: Université de Louvain, 1975), 1:11-24. For the acquisition of his prebends, at the supplication of Johannes of Neumarkt, *Acta Innocentii VI. Pontificis Romani, 1352-1362*, ed. Joannes Fridericus Novák, vol. 2 of *Mon. Vat. Res Gestas Boh. Illust.* (Prague: Gregerian, 1907), pp. 471-72 no. 1174, 1175. For his surrender of the prebends to a chaplain of Karl IV, approved by Urban V on 1 December 1364, *Mon. Vat. Res Gestas Boh. Illust.*, 3:248-50 no. 418. The previous protonotary of Karl IV, Nicolaus of Kroměříž (1357 to 1364) came from Milič's home town. Jan Očko of Vlašim, bishop of Olomouc (1351-1364) and archbishop of Prague (1364 to 1380), had been Karl's notary when the emperor was only margrave of Moravia. Notaries of the archiepiscopal chancellory could also enjoy good chances of promotion. St. Jan Nepomuc was public notary (1372), notary of the archiepiscopal chancellory (1373), and protonotary of the general vicariate (1376), before becoming archdeacon of Prague (1390) and dying his famous death (1393). Antonius Podlaha, *Series Praepositorum, Decanorum, Archidiaconorum Aliorumque Praelatorum et Canonicorum S. Metropolitanae Ecclesiae Pragensis* (Prague: Metropolitanum Capitulum, 1912), pp. 33, 39, 58, no. 295, 334, 457.

who undermine the spiritual well-being of the church.[51] He found a sympathizer in Anglic Grimoard, brother of Urban V and cardinal, who granted him an audience in his house, and he finally left Rome with an exoneration by Urban V.[52]

Neither this nor any other accomplishment would mollify his opponents in Prague, and Milič maintained his virulent criticisms of "hypocritical" clergy and friars, and he preached to the outcasts. He converted the women of a celebrated house of prostitution—known, in (clerical) Latin and people's Czech, as "Venice"—destroyed the building and erected "Jerusalem" in its place, with a chapel to Mary Magdalene, in the midst of Babylonian Prague.[53] His opponents denounced him before the archbishop. An inquisitor assembled evidence that Milič publicly denied the rights of the mendicant orders to hear confessions, obviously trying to pin the error of Jean of Pouilly on him, and someone, probably the Augustinian friars of St. Thomas' cloister in Prague, sent a list of articles to Johannes Klenkok with a request that he present them to the pope.[54] He did, and the pope

---

[51]Matthew of Janow would later describe Milič's preaching as an unreserved accusation that high prelates, archbishops, bishops, pope, and cardinals are all antichrist and that Prague is Babylon. "De praedicatoribus qui revelant antichristum et de multitudine ipsorum successiva," K. Höfler, ed., *Geschichtsschreiber*, pp. 40-46, here 42. For details of the return of Urban V and Gregory XI to Rome, Michel Hayez, "Avignon sans les papes (1367-1370, 1376-1379)," in *Genèse*, pp. 143-57.

[52]Milič then presented a less apocalyptic view of the dangers to the church and of the coming of the antichrist in a letter to Urban V, stressing Urban's position between God and the people and his mission to redeem an erring Jerusalem. Edited by Ferdinand Menčik, "Milič a dva jeho spisy z reho 1367" [Milič and two of his writings from the year 1367] *Věstnik kralouska česke společnosti naukové, třída filosoficko-historicko-jazykozpytná* (Prague: Královské české společnosti naukové, 1891), pp. 309-36, here 318-25, and also found, as Milič's *Libellus de Antichristo*, in Matthias de Janov, *Regulae Veteris et Novi Testamenti*, ed. Vlastimil Kybal, 4 vols. (Innsbruck: Libraria Universitatis Wagnerianae, 1908-1913), 3:368-81. His earlier chronography may be found in Menčik, op. cit., pp. 328-36.

[53]Matthias de Janov, "De praedicatoribus," p. 43.

[54]*Vita venerabilis presbyteri Milicii, praelati ecclesiae Pragensis*, ed. Josef Truhlář, *Fontes Rerum Bohemicarum*, vol. 1, *Vitae Sanctorum et Aliorum quorundam pietate insignium*, ed. František Palacký (Prague: Nákladem Musea Království Českého, 1873), p. 424. The author of the life counted himself among Milič's traveling companions to Avignon in 1374 (p. 426). Testimony against Milič may be found in Menčik, "Milič," pp. 317-18. Cf. Bütow, "Lebensgeschichte," p. 569, who noted that a pastor of Prague sent the articles, which conclusion is derived from the claim of the life of Milič: that Klenkok said the articles were sent him by a *plebanus* of Prague. *Vita*, pp. 426-27. In fact, a priest of St. Štěpána, from whose parish Milič had acquired some territory and the right of patronage for his Jerusalem (but also encroaching upon the parishes of St. Filipa and St. Jakuba), worked with the friars to formulate the heresy charge in twelve articles, which surely the friars then forwarded to Avignon. Consider Loskot, *Milíč*, pp. 95-96; Kaňák, *Milíč*, p. 34. The priests of St. Stepána, St. Filipa, and St. Jakuba had ostensibly consented to the construction of the new parish out of their domains. Wácslaw Wladiwoj Tomek, *Základy starého místopisu Pražského* [Foundations of the old topography of Prague], series 5, vol. 15 of *Abhandlungen der königlichen Böhmischen Gesellschaft der Wissenschaften* (Prague: Köngl. böhm. Gesel. d. Wissensch., 1866), p. 98.

reacted, on 13 January 1374, by sending letters to the archbishops of Prague and Gnesen and to the bishops of Litomyšl, Wrocław, Olomouc, and Cracow ordering that they proceed against Milič, who was, the letter alleged, preaching illegally in Gnesen and converting people of both sexes to his sect; the prelates were not to be remiss in trying him and, if he was found guilty of the accusations, in censuring him.[55] A second letter to Karl IV, dated 10 February 1374, sought the emperor's support of the mandate to the archbishops and bishops.[56] Milič was summoned before the archbishop of Prague, where he allegedly laughed off ("hilariter") his enemies in court with a dismissal of their unspiritual furor, with confidence in the suasive effect of the truth of the matter, and with hope in God.[57] The archbishop's reaction is unknown, but Milič was summoned before the inquisitor—a Dominican named Albert. But seeing the hysteria of the court aligned against him, Milič appealed to the apostolic see, before a public notary, before the inquisitor, and then publicly in the cathedral of St. Giles and in the church of St. Gallus Major.[58]

Milič had learned a great deal since his last trip abroad, now scrupulously displaying his sanctity on the way to Avignon, without any hint of the earlier extremes. He collected money from supporters; he traveled with four companions, liberally dispensing alms along the way, saying the divine office, reciting psalms, and keeping vigils. They went during Lent. When the pilgrims arrived in Avignon, his generosity became copious, and no mention was made of the Apocalypse. The subsequent trial, according to the single account (made by his supporters) became a travesty,[59]

---

[55]*Acta Gregorii XI*, pp. 444-45 no. 783 (see also the note, which claims that the bull was published in Prague only on 19 July 1374). Bütow believed the letter was dated 10 January 1374. "Lebensgeschichte," p. 569.

[56]*Acta*, pp. 449-50 no. 789. Huber, *Regesten*, p. 520.

[57]*Vita . . . Milicii*, p. 425.

[58]*Vita*, p. 425. For the inquisitor, Koudelka, *Geschichte*, 25:89. The right of appeal is assured in *Decretum*, C. ii, q. 6.

[59]The account of the journey to Avignon is found in *Vita*, pp. 425-26. It took place during Lent. Ibid., p. 426. "Talem vero virtutem et gratiam deus contulerat sibi, quod et inimici videntes ejus personam sibi pacifice loquebantur, in nullo eum accusabant; et istud manifeste apparet in adventu ejus in curiam Romanam, licet prius nimium criminose accusatus fuisset, postmodum eo veniente omnes sibi benefavebant, et ejus major adversarius, magister videlicet Klonkoth, cujus mentio superius facta est, cum fuisset per dominum cardinalem Albanensem vocatus et quid de Militio sentiret interrogatus, dicebat: ego nihil mali invenio in homine isto, sed solum id est: cum fuissem litteratorie per quendam plebanum Pragensem monitus et rogatus de articulis talibus, eosdem domino apostolico porrexi." *Vita*, pp. 426-27. Trapp believed Milič chose Klenkok as his judge in Avignon, without adducing any evidence. "Notes," p. 362. De Vooght called attention to their pilgrim's habit, *L'Hérésie*, pp. 17-18.

even the enemies, seeing his person, spoke peacefully to him, accused him of nothing. And it became apparent at his arrival to the Roman curia that although he had been previously accused of criminal excess, later as he came, everyone offered him good favour, and his great adversary, namely master Klonkoth . . . —when he had been called by the lord cardinal of Albano and asked what he felt about Milič—said, "I find nothing evil in this man, it's just that since I had been admonished and asked in a letter by a certain pastor of Prague about these articles, I forwarded them to the apostolic lord."

The lord cardinal of Albano was Anglic Grimoard. No mention is made of an examination of Milič before the meeting between Grimoard and Klenkok, but such would seem likely. After his exoneration, Milič remained in the city, but nothing of his activity is known, until 15 May, when Grimoard asked Milič to preach, presumably in his chapel, the sermon for the feast of the Holy Spirit. The cardinal was sufficiently impressed to ask Milič to his table, placing him third from his side, "so much indeed was the grace of preaching given to [Milič] by the Lord, that he went from preaching before whores to preaching before cardinals and from the table of publicans to the table of cardinals and bishops."[60]

Klenkok may have been less innocent of discrediting Milič than he might have liked Anglic Grimoard to believe: it would not be the first time that a scrupulously sincere aggression backed him into a corner and forced him to mild words.[61] Klenkok, if he had found the opportunity, may have informed the friars of Prague of the Avignon proceedings. Although Milič seemed a victor, enough to confirm his status as the Elias of the Apocalypse among his followers in the tumultuous Bohemian years to come, neither he nor his fellows yet participated in a community with any real strength outside of their cliques of disgruntled citizens in Prague.[62] The reason for which Milič remained in Avignon must have been an outbreak of the plague from 15 April to 2 July, during which he might have been prudently isolated.[63] We know

---

[60]Ibid., p. 427: "Tanto vero praedicationis gratia fuit sibi a domino collata, ut a praedicatione meretricum iverit ad praedicationem cardinalium et a mensa publicanorum ad mensam cardinalium et episcoporum; et talis reverentia fuit sibi exhibita non desideranti post praedicationem, quam fecerat coram domini cardinali Albanensi in die Sancti Spiritus, ut eodem die idem cardinalis in tabula eum tertium a latere suo collocauit."

[61]Consider the rather sensitive appeals to social welfare and justice in his defense against the Magdeburg *Rat*. Page 54, above.

[62]For Milič as Elijah, Matthias de Janov, "De praedicatoribus," p. 45. Idem, *Tractatus de Antichristo*, in idem, *Regulae*, 3:355-57, applying the figure to both Milič and Konrad Waldhausen.

[63]Guillemain, *Cour*, p. 214.

nothing certain of Klenkok's activity after what must have been his embarrassment, but he would probably have done the same. Both men succumbed to the disease, Klenkok first, on 15 June, then Milič, on 29 June, the feast of Saints Peter and Paul.[64] Later, Matthew of Janow, apparently unaware of Grimoard's flattering treatment, lamented that Milič died as one of the disciples whom Christ predicted would be "rejected from the synagogue," as an exile in Avignon.[65] His enemies continued to denounce him to the archbishop and emperor after his death, and "Jerusalem" was soon closed and converted to a college of Cistercian students of the University of Prague.[66]

By whatever means, perhaps encouraged by unknown collusions with leaders of the Order of Augustinian Hermits and of the church during the last months of Klenkok's life, the campaign against the *Sachsenspiegel* also continued after Klenkok's death. Gregory XI, who originally issued the bull of condemnation to five German archbishops, addressed it to Karl IV, 15 October 1374, and at least one Augustinian friar, a Gothart in Wrocław, tried to persuade his city council to acknowledge the superiority of papal law by abandoning the reproved articles in 1375 (to no known effect; the bull was published by the bishop of the city only in 1397).[67] Klenkok would remain reputed among his

---

[64]Klenkok's day of death is so given by Joseph Pamphilus, *Chronica*, p. 52, with an incorrect year; the day, which was more important for performing *suffragia* for dead friars, is likely to be correct. Bütow, "Lebensgeschichte," p. 570. Trapp, "Notes," p. 362. The *Vita . . . Milicii* gives the day of Milič's death as the feast of St. Peter, which can only refer to the feast of Saints Peter and Paul. *Vita*, p. 427. The literature has neglected to note that both their deaths coincided with an outbreak of the plague. In his last days, Klenkok may well have ominously remembered that the swellings, so he believed, were once inflicted by an angel upon an opponent of apostles, Herod Agrippa, who killed the apostle James and jailed the apostle Peter (*Postilla super Actus apostolorum*, Eichstätt 204, f. 169vb). Avoidance of the disease would have been on his mind most of his adult life; such a preoccupation probably inspired a very novel interpretation of the prohibition against eating strangled animals (Ac 15.20): Klenkok believed that it refers to animals that died of the plague (*Postilla super Actus apostolorum*, ibid., f. 173va). The fate of Klenkok's personal effects is not known. Damasus Trapp speculated that the books passed to Giovanni Romani, an Augustinian friar and papal librarian, who gave them to the papal library. There is, however, no trace of any work of Klenkok in the well-studied library documents of the papal library from that time. Trapp, "Notes," p. 362. F. Ehrle, *Historia Bibliothecae Romanorum Pontificum tum Bonifatianae tum Avenionensis* (Rome: Typus Vaticani, 1890), pp. 451-560. When an Augustinian friar died outside of his home province, the books would normally go to the convent in which he died, although they were also known to pass to another friar. K.W. Humphreys, *The Book Provisions of the Mediaeval Friars, 1215-1400*, vol. 1 of *Studies in the History of Libraries and Librarianship* (Amsterdam: Erasmus Booksellers, 1964), p. 69. Such provisions, however, pertain most properly to friars living in convents. As was mentioned earlier, penitentiaries usually rented quarters in the city.

[65]"De praedicatoribus," p. 44.

[66]*Vita*, p. 427. R. R. Betts, *Essays in Czech History* (London: The Athlone Press, 1969), pp. 21-22.

[67]Huber, *Regesten*, p. 520. Bütow, "Lebensgeschichte," p. 567 n. 99.

students and known for his campaign against the Saxon law, but beyond the fifteenth century, remembered only among more antiquarian chroniclers of his order.[68]

His accomplishment was to put sophisticated ideas to work on very practical problems, informing the religious and professional activities of friars and priests. The aspirations associated with those ideas are seen in his own offices and campaigns. Johannes Klenkok undertook the campaign against the *Sachsenspiegel* as a regional leader of his order and as a teacher in his order's school, and he pursued it, not as a political enterprise (which it was), but as a disputation with heresy. These activities voice both his commitment to a mendicant order and its place within ecclesiastical society, and it is by no means unusual that he should end this sincere and troubled life as a functionary of the papal court advocating a mendicant concern in which he had no personal interest. There are gaping incongruities in the last events: that Milič should be prosecuted and exonerated in Avignon, but "Jerusalem" should be closed down in Prague; or that Saxon laws should be condemned at the papal court, when they experienced no real opposition at home. Johannes Klenkok's life ends in the disparities of Christian society, in the divergence between a distant court's influence and effective religious authority in central Europe.

---

[68]Pages 47-50, 62-63 f., above. For Augustinian historians, T. de Herrera, *Alphabetum Augustinianum*, 2 vols. (Matriti: n.p., 1644), 1:449 and 2:34-35. Klenkok's role in the condemnation of articles of the *Sachsenspiegel* appears to have been forgotten after the fifteenth century and rediscovered by Christian Ludwig Scheidt, who published the *Decadicon*. Homeyer, *Johannes*, pp. 380-81.

BIBLIOGRAPHY

1. UNPUBLISHED SOURCES

Acta pauca capitulorum quorundam prouincialium prouincie Thuringie et Saxonie. Munich, Bayerische Staatsbibliothek, Clm 8491, ff. 165r-166r.

Anonymous. *Expositio in Summulam iuris canonici de Heinrich de Merseburg edita*. Stadtbibliothek Mainz, Hs. II. 330, ff. 1r-59v.

Herbord de Spangenberg. *Disputatio cum Johanne Klenkok de Decadicon suo*. Wolfenbüttel, Codex Guelferbetanus 314 Nov., ff. 7v-16v; Cod. Guelf. 203 Extrav., ff. 49r-60v (Herbord's refutation). Cod. Guelf. 314 Nov., ff. 17r-21v (Klenkok's response), ff. 22r-31r (Herbord's answer to Klenkok's response).

Johannes Klenkok. *Exposicio litteralis in quattuor libris Sentenciarum*. Erfurt, Wissenschaftliche Allgemeinbibliothek, Amplon. F. 117, ff. 1-166; Amplon. Q. 118, ff. 86r-107v, 119r-135v (books I, II); Klosterneuburg, Stiftsbibliothek, Ms. 304, ff. 68r-195r; Siena, Biblioteca Comunale, G.V.16., ff. 1r-105v (books I, III, IV, and the *redactio lectoris* of book II).

———— . *Postilla super Actus Apostolorum*, Eichstätt, Bayerische Staatsbibliothek, Ms. 204, ff. 117ra-192rb.

———— . *Questiones super II. Sententiarum*. Eichstätt, Bayerische Staatsbibliothek, Ms. 471, ff. 157v-186r. Incorrectly attributed to Facinus de Ast.

———— . *Questiones super totam materiam canonice Johannis*. Oxford, Bodleian, Hamilton Ms. 33, ff. 247ra-258v.

———— . *Sermones magistrales*. Erfurt, Allgemeinbibliothek Wissenschaftliche, Amplon. Q. 118, ff. 108ra-117rb.

Meinhardus Sublector. *Glossa super poeniteas cum reportatis lectis bonis lecta per Meinhardum sublectorem in Erfordia*. Stadtbibliothek Mainz, Hs. I. 166, ff. 90-98.

2. PUBLISHED SOURCES AND COLLECTIONS

Acta capitulorum generalium ordinis praedicatorum. Edited by Benedictus Maria Reichert. 3 vols. Rome: Typographia polyglotta s. c. de propaganda fidei, 1898-1900.

Aegidius Romanus. *De ecclesiastica potestate*. Edited by Richard Scholz. Aalen: Scientia Verlag, 1961; reprint of Weimar: Hermann Böhlaus Nachfolger, 1929.

Analecta Augustiniana. 1(1901)ff. Early volumes contain transcriptions of the extant medieval acts of general chapters and some provincial chapters of the Order of Augustinian Hermits.

Biblia sacra cum glossis, interlineari et ordinaria, Nicolai Lyrani postilla et mo-ralitatibus, Burgensis additionibus et Thoringi replicis. Lyon: Anthoine Vincent, 1545.

Bliss, W. H., ed. *Calendar of Entries in the Papal Registers relating to Great Britain and Ireland.* 3 vols. *Petitions to the Pope,* vol. 1: *1342-1419.* London: Her Majesty's Stationery Office, 1896.

Bremisches Urkundenbuch. Edited by D. R. Ehmck, W. von Bippen. Bremen: C. E. Müller, 1873-1902.

Bullarium Diplomaticum et Privilegiorum Sanctorum Romanorum Pontificum. Vol. 4. Turin: S. Franco, H. Fory, and H. Dalmazzo, 1859.

Bullarium Franciscanum. Edited by J. H. Sbaralea and Conrad Eubel. 7 vols. Rome, 1759-1904.

Caspar, Erich, ed. *Das Register Gregors VII.* 2 vols. Vol. 2. fascicle 1-2 of *Epistolae Selectae in Usum Scholarum ex MGH separatim editae.* Berlin: Weidmann, 1955.

Chartularium Universitatis Parisiensis. Edited by H. Denifle and E. Chatelain. 4 vols. Paris, 1889-97.

Corpus Christianorum Series Latina. 176 vols. Turnholt: Brepols, 1954. +

Corpus Iuris Canonici. 2 vols. Edited by Emil Friedberg. Leipzig: Bernhardt Tauchnitz, 1879, 1891.

Corpus Iuris Civilis. 3 vols. Edited by Theodor Mommsen. Berlin: Weidmann, 1877, 1880, 1883.

Corpus Scriptorum Ecclesiasticorum. 89 vols. +. Vienna: Hoelder-Pichler-Tempsky, 1866-1986+.

Collectio judiciorum de novis erroribus. 3 vols. Edited by C. du Plessis d'Argentré. Paris: Andrea Cailleau, 1728.

Fredericq, P. *Corpus Documentorum Inquisitionis Haereticae Pravitatis Neerlandicae.* 5 vols. Ghent: J. Vvylstaken en Gravenhage Martinus Nijhoff, 1885-1902.

Gerardi Magni epistolae. Edited by Willelmus Mulder. Vol. 3 of *Tekstuitgaven van Ons Geestelijk Erf.* Antwerp: Uitgever Neerlandia, 1933.

Gregorius Ariminensis. *Lectura super primum et secundum Sententiarum.* Edited by D. Trapp and V. Marcolino. 6 vols., vols. 6-12 of *Spätmittelalter und Reformation, Texte und Untersuchungen.* Berlin: Walter de Gruyter, 1981-1987.

Gregorius de Arimino. *Registrum generalatus, 1357-1358.* Edited by A. de Meijer. Rome: Institutum Historicum Augustinianum, 1976.

Historia archiepiscoporum Bremensium. Edited by Johann Martin Lappenberg. *Geschichtsquellen des Erzstifts und der Stadt Bremen.* Aalen: Scientia Verlag, 1967 reprint of the Bremen edition of 1841.

Höfler, K., ed. *Geschichtsschreiber der hussitischen Bewegung in Böhmen.* Section 1, vol. 6/2 of *Fontes Rerum Bohemicarum.* Vienna: Kaiserliche königliche Hof- und Staatsdruckerei, 1865.

Huber, Alphons, ed. *Die Regesten des Kaiserreichs unter Kaiser Karl IV, 1346-1378.* Vol. 8 of *Regesta Imperii.* Johann Friederich Böhmer, general editor. Innsbruck: Wagnersche Universitätsbuchhandlung, 1877.

Jana Milíče z Kroměříže. Tři řeči synodní [Jan Milič of Kroměříže. Three Synodal Sermons]. Edited by Vilém Herold, Milan Mráz. Prague: Academia, 1974.

Jean de Ripa [Giovanni of Ripa]. *Determinationes.* Edited by A. Combes. Vol. 4 of *Textes philosophiques du moyen âge.* Paris: J. Vrin, 1957.

———. *Lectura super primum Sententiarum.* Edited by A. Combes. 2 vols., vols. 8, 16 of *Textes philosophiques du moyen âge.* Paris: J. Vrin, 1961, 1970.

———. *Quaestio de gradu supremo.* Edited by A. Combes. Vol. 12 of *Textes phil. du moyen âge.* Paris: J. Vrin, 1964.

Johanes de Geylnhusen. *Collectarius perpetuarum formarum Johannes de Geylnhusen.* Edited by Hans Kaiser. Innsbrück: Wagnersche Universitätsbuchhandlung, 1900.

Johannes de Hildesheim. *Epistole.* Edited by Otto Hendricks. "A Register of Letters and Papers of John of Hildesheim, O.Carm (d. 1375)." *Carmelus* 4(1957):116-235.

Johannes Klenkok. *Decadicon.* Edited by Christian Ludwig Scheidt. In part I of *Bibliotheca historica Goettingensis.* Göttingen and Hannover: Polwiz und Barmeier, 1758.

———. *Universis Christi fidelibus.* Edited by Gustav Homeyer in *Johannes Klenkok wider den Sachsenspiegel* (see below), pp. 432a-432c.

Johannes Noviforensis. *Cancellaria Johannis Noviforensis.* Edited by F. Tadra in *Archiv für österreichische Geschichte* 68(1886).

Jordanus de Saxonia. *Liber vitasfratrum.* Edited by R. Arbesmann, W. Hümpfner. American series vol. 1 of *Cassiciacum.* New York: Cosmopolitan Science and Art Service Co., 1943.

Lehmann, Paul, ed. *Mittelalterliche Bibliothekskataloge Deutschlands und der Schweiz.* Vol. 2. Munich: C.H. Beck, 1928.

Libri cancelarii et procuratorum. Edited by Henry Anstey. Vol. 1 of *Munimenta Academica or Documents Illustrative of Academic Life and Studies at Oxford.* 2 vols., vol. 50/1-2 of *Rerum Britanicarum Medii Aevi Scriptores or Chronicles and Memorials of Great Britain and Ireland during the Middle Ages.* London: Longmans, Green, Reader, and Dyer, 1868.

Lübeck. 3 vols., vols. 19, 26, 28 of *Die Chroniken der deutschen Städte.* Göttingen: Vandenhoeck und Ruprecht, 1967 reprint of the first ed., Leipzig: Solomon Hirzel, 1884.

Magdeburger Recht. Edited by Friedrich Ebel. Vol. 2: *Die Rechtsmitteilungen und Rechtssprüche für Breslau.* Part 1: *Die Quellen von 1261 bis 1452.* Vol. 89/II/1 of *Mitteldeutsche Forschungen.* Cologne: Böhlau, 1989.

Matthias de Janov. *Regulae Veteris et Novi Testamenti.* Edited by Vlastimil Kybal. 4 vols. Innsbruck: Libraria Universitatis Wagnerianae, 1908-1913.

Mirot, L. and Jassemin, H., eds. *Lettres secrètes et curiales du pape Grégoire XI (1370-1378) relatives à la France.* Paris: E. de Boccard, 1935.

Mollat, G., ed. *Lettres secrètes et curiales du pape Grégoire XI (1370-1378) intéressant les pays autres que la France.* Paris: Éditions E. de Boccard, 1962-1965.

Monumenta Vaticana Res Gestas Bohemicas Illustrantia. Vol. 2: Johann Neumarkt, *Acta Innocentii VI. Pontificis Romani, 1352-1362.* Edited by Joannes Fridericus Novák. Prague: Gregerian, 1907. Vol. 3: *Acta Urbani V, 1362-1370.* Edited by Fredericus Jenšovský. Prague: Středočeská Tiskárna, 1944. Vol. 4: *Acta Gregorii XI.* Part 1, *1370-1372.* Edited by Carolic Stoukal. Prague: Gregerian, 1949.

Nicolai de Bibera Carmen satiricum. Edited by Theobald Fischer. Vol. 1 of *Geschichtsquellen der Provinz Sachsen und angrenzender Gebiete.* Halle: Waisenhaus, 1870.

Patrologia Cursus Completus Series Latina. 221 vols., 5 supplementary vols. Paris: Garnier Frères, 1879-1974.

Raymundus von Wiener-Neustadt. *Summa brevis levis et utilis.* Edited by Alexander Gal. *Die Summa legum brevis levis et utilis des sogennanten Doctor Raymundus von Wiener-Neustadt.* Weimar: Hermann Böhlaus Nachfolger, 1926.

Regesta Episcoporum Constantiensium. Regesten zur Geschichte der Bischöfe von Constanz von Bubulcus bis Thomas Berlower, 517-1496. 5 vols. Innsbruck: Wagner'sche Universitäts Buchhandlung, 1894-1931.

Rieder, Karl, ed. *Monumenta Vaticana Historiam Episcopatus Constantiensis in Germania Illustrantia. Römische Quellen zur konstanzer Bistumsgeschichte zur Zeit der Päpste in Avignon, 1305-1378.* Innsbruck: Wagner'sche Universitäts Buchhandlung, 1908.

Ruf, Paul. *Mittelalterliche Bibliothekskataloge Deutschlands und der Schweiz.* Vol. 3/1: *Bistum Augsburg.* Munich: C.H. Beck, 1932. Vol. 3/3: *Bistum Bamberg.* Munich: C.H. Beck, 1939.

Sachsenspiegel. Edited by Karl August Eckhardt. 2 vols. Göttingen: Musterschmidt Verlag, 1955-1956.

Schmidt, Gustav, ed. *Päbstliche Urkunden und Regesten.* 2 vols., vols. 21-22 of *Geschichtsquellen der Provinz Sachsen.* Halle: Otto Hendel, 1886, 1889.

Scriptores Rerum Germanicarum praecipue Saxonicarum, Edited by Johannes Burchard Menken. Leipzig: Johann Christian Martin, 1730.

Tullius Cicero. *De lege.* Edited by Georg Heinrich Moser. Frankfurt am Main: Broenner, 1824.

——— . *Paradoxa Stoicorum.* Edited by Renato Badali. Milan: Arnoldo Mondadori, 1968.

Urkunden und Regesten zur Geschichte der Augustinerklöster Würzburg und Münnerstadt. Edited by Adolar Zumkeller. 2 vols. Würzburg: Schöningh, 1966, 1967.

Urkundenbuch der Erfurter Stifter und Klöster. Edited by A. Overmann. 3 vols. Magdeburg, 1926-1934.

Urkundenbuch der Stadt Erfurt. 2 parts. Edited by Carl Beyer. Vols. 23, 24 of *Geschichtsquellen der Provinz Sachsen und angrenzender Gebiete.* Halle: Otto Hendel, 1889, 1897.

Urkundenbuch der Stadt Grimma. Edited by L. Schmidt. Part 2, vol. 15 of *Codex Diplomaticus Saxoniae Regiae.* Leipzig: Giesecke und Devrient, 1895.

Urkundenbuch der Stadt Magdeburg. Edited by Gustav Hertel. Vol. 26 of *Geschichtsquellen der Provinz Sachsen u. angr. Geb.* Halle: Otto Hendel, 1892; reprinted Aalen: Scientia Verlag, 1975.

Urkundenbuch des Hochstifts Halberstadt und seiner Bischöfe. Edited by Gustav Schmidt. 4 vols. Osnabrück: Otto Zeller, 1965 reprint of the 1889 edition.

Urkundenbuch des Klosters Berge bei Magdeburg. Edited by H. Holstein. Vol. 9 of *Geschichtsquellen der Provinz Sachsen u. angr. Geb.* Halle: O. Hendel, 1879.

Urkundenbuch des Klosters Unser Lieben Frau zu Magdeburg. Edited by Gustav Hertel. Vol. 10 of *Geschichtsquellen der Provinz Sachsen u. angr. Geb.* Halle: Otto Hendel, 1879.

Vita venerabilis presbyteri Milicii, praelati ecclesiae Pragensis. Edited by Josef Truhlář, in *Vitae Sanctorum et Aliorum quorundam pietate insignium.* František Palacký, general ed. Vol. 1 of *Fontes Rerum Bohemicarum.* Prague: Nákladem Musea Království Českého, 1873.

3. SECONDARY LITERATURE

Adams, Marilyn McCord. *William Ockham.* Vol. 26/1-2 of *Publications in Medieval Studies.* Notre Dame, Indiana: University of Notre Dame Press, 1987.

Adinolfi, Marco. "Due strane postille di Nicola de Lyre." *Rivista Biblica* 6(1958):255-62.

Aidnik, Erwin-Erhard. "Die 'articuli reprobati' des Sachsenspiegels in altlivländischen Rechtsbüchern." *Rigasche Zeitschrift für Rechtswissenschaft* 1(1926-1927):222-47.

Altaner, Berthold. "Aus den Akten des Rottweiler Provinzialkapitels der Dominikaner vom Jahre 1396." *Zeitschrift für Kirchengeschichte* 48(1929):1-15.

Arbesmann, Rudolph. *Der Augustinerorden und der Beginn der humanistischen Bewegung.* Vol. 19 of *Cassiciacum.* Würzburg: Augustinus-Verlag, 1965.

Arnold, Benjamin. *German Knighthood, 1050-1300.* Oxford: Clarendon Press, 1985.

———. *Princes and Territories in Medieval Germany.* Cambridge: Cambridge University Press, 1991.

Arnold, Klaus. *Kind und Gesellschaft im Mittelalter und Renaissance. Beiträge und Texte zur Geschichte der Kindheit.* Series B, vol. 2 of *Sammlung Zebra.* Paderborn: Schöningh, and Munich: Lurz, 1980.

Arts libéraux et philosophie au moyen âge. Actes du quatrième congrès international de philosophie médiévale, Université de Montréal, 27 août-2 septembre 1967. Montréal: Institut d'Études Médiévales, 1969.

Barraclough, Geoffrey. "Praxis Beneficiorum. A Contribution to the History of Practical Legal Literature in the Later Middle Ages." ZRG,KA 58(1938):95-134.

Berg, Dieter. *Armut und Wissenschaft. Beiträge zur Geschichte des Studienwesens der Bettelorden im 13. Jahrhundert.* Vol. 15 of *Bochumer historische Studien.* Düsseldorf: Schwann, 1977.

Betts, R. R. *Essays in Czech History.* London: The Athlone Press, 1969.

Böhlau, Hans. "Zur Lebensgeschichte des Augustinermönches Johannes Klenkok, Bekämpfers des Sachsenspiegels." *Historische Vierteljahrschrift* 29(1934):541-75.

Böhlau, Hugo. "Aus der Praxis des Magdeburger Schöffenstuhls während des 14. und 15. Jahrhunderts." *Zeitschrift für Rechtsgeschichte* 9(1870):1-50.

Böhner, Philotheus. Gilson, Etienne. *Christliche Philosophie von Ihren Anfängen bis Nikolaus von Cues.* 3rd ed. Paderborn: Ferdinand Schöningh, 1954.

Borchert, Ernst. *Die quaestiones speculativae et canonicae des Johannes Baconthorpe über den Sakramentalen Charakter.* New series vol. 9 of *Veröffentlichungen des Grabmann-Instituts.* Munich: Schöningh, 1974.

Bosl, Karl. *Europa im Aufbruch.* Munich: C.H. Beck, 1980.

Boyle, Leonard E. "The *Summa confessorum* of John of Freiburg and the Popularization of the Moral Teaching of St. Thomas and of Some of his Contemporaries." *St. Thomas Aquinas, 1274-1974. Commemorative Studies.* 2 vols., 2:245-68. Edited by A. A. Maurer, et al. Toronto: Pontifical Institute of Mediaeval Studies, 1974. Reprinted in idem, *Pastoral Care, Clerical Education, and Canon Law,* no. 3. London: Variorum, 1981.

Brieskorn, Norbert. *Die Summa confessorum des Johannes von Erfurt.* Series 2, vol. 245 of *Europäische Hochschulschriften.* Frankfurt am Main: Peter D. Lang, 1980.

Brünig, Kurt, ed. *Niedersachsen und Bremen.* Vol. 2 of *Handbuch der historischen Stätten Deutschlands.* Stuttgart: Alfred Kröner, 1986.

Bünger, Fritz. "Ein Dominikaner Provinzialkapitel in Luckau (1400)." *Zeitschrift für Kirchengeschichte* 34(1913):74-88.

Bütow, Hans. "Zur Lebensgeschichte des Augustinermönches Johannes Klenkok, Bekämpfers des Sachsenspiegels." *Historische Vierteljahrschrift* 29(1934):541-75.

——— . "Johannes Merkelin, Augustinerlesemeister zu Friedeberg/Neumarkt, Leben und Schriften." *Jahrbuch für Brandenburgische Kirchengeschichte* 29(1934):3-35.

Coing, Helmut. *Europäisches Privatrecht.* Vol. 1: *Älteres Gemeines Recht (1500 bis 1800).* Munich: C.H. Beck, 1985.

——— . "Kanonisches Recht und Ius Commune." *Proceedings of the Sixth International Congress of Medieval Canon Law.* Series C: subsidia, vol. l7 of *Monumenta Iuris Canonici.* Vatican City: Biblioteca Apostolica Vaticana, 1985, pp. 507-18.

———. *Römisches Recht in Deutschland*. Vol. 6 of *Ius Romanum medii aevi*. Milan: Collegio Antiqui Iuris Studiis Provendis, 1964.

Combes, A. "La metaphysique de Jean de Ripa." In *Die Metaphysik im Mittelalter*, pp. 543-57. Edited by P. Wilpert. Vol. 2 of *Miscellanea Mediaevalia*. Berlin: Walter de Gruyter, 1963.

———. "Presentation de Jean de Ripa." *Archives d'histoire doctrinale et littéraire du moyen âge* 23(1956):145-242.

Courtenay, William J. *Adam Wodeham: An Introduction to His Life and Writings*. Vol. 21 of *Studies in Medieval and Reformation Thought*. Leiden: E. J. Brill, 1978.

———. "Augustinianism at Oxford in the Fourteenth Century." *Augustiniana* 30(1980):60-70.

———. "The Bible in the Fourteenth Century: Some Observations." *Church History* 54(1985):176-87.

———. *Covenant and Causality in Medieval Thought*. London: Variorum, 1984.

———. "The Effect of the Black Death on English Higher Education." *Speculum* 55(1980):696-714.

———. "The Franciscan *Studia* in Southern Germany in the Fourteenth Century." *Gesellschaftsgeschichte: Festschrift für Karl Bosl zum 80. Geburtstag*. 2 vols., 2: 81-90. Edited by F. Seibt. Munich: R. Oldenburg, 1988.

———. "Friedrich von Regensburg and Fribourg Cordeliers 26." In *Die Philosophie im 14. und 15. Jahrhundert. In Memoriam Konstanty Michalski (1879-1947)*, pp. 603-13. Vol. 10 of *Bochumer Studien zur Philosophie*. Amsterdam: B. R. Grüner, 1988.

———. "Nominalism and Late Medieval Religion." In *The Pursuit of Holiness in Late Medieval and Renaissance Religion*, pp. 26-59. Vol. 10 of *Studies in Medieval and Reformation Thought*. Leiden: E.J. Brill, 1974.

———. *Schools and Scholars in Fourteenth-Century England*. Princeton: Princeton University Press, 1988.

De Geer, B. J. L. "Klenkok's Decadicon." *Nieuwe Bijdragen voor Rechtsgeleerdheid en Wetgeuing* 18(1882):367-409.

de Rijk, Lambert Marie. *Die mittelalterlichen Traktate De modo opponendi et respondendi. Einleitung und Ausgabe der einschlägigen Texte*. New series vol. 17 of BGPTM. Münster im Westfalen: Aschendorff, 1980.

De Vooght, Paul. *L'Hérésie de Jan Huss*. 2 vols. Louvain: Université de Louvain, 1975.

Dictionnaire de droit canonique. S.v. "Henri de Mersebourg," by R. Naz; "Sous-diaconat," by R. Naz, 7:1074-78.

Dictionnaire de théologie catholique. S.v. "Benedict XII.," by X. Le Bachelet; "Eymeric, Nicolas," by E. Mangenot; "Pierre Aureol," by Am. Teetaert.

Doelle, Ferdinand. "Das Partikularstudium der sächsischen Provinz im Mittelalter." *Franziskanische Studien* 14(1927):244-51.

———. "Die Rechtsstudien der deutschen Franziskaner im Mittelalter und ihre Bedeutung für die Rechtsentwicklung der Gegenwart."

Geisteswelt des Mittelalters, ed. A. Lang, 2:1037-64.

Douais, C. *Essai sur l'organisation des études dans l'ordre des frères prêcheurs au treizième et au quatorzième siècles*. Paris: Alphonse Picard, 1884.

Eckermann, Willigis. "Eine unveröffentlichte historische Quelle zur Litteraturgeschichte des westfälischen Augustiner des Spätmittelalters." *AA* 34(1971):185-235.

―――. *Gottschalk Hollen O.E.S.A. (+1481). Leben, Werke und Sakramentenlehre*. Vol. 22 of *Cassiciacum*. Würzburg: Augustinus-Verlag, 1967.

―――. *Wort und Wirklichkeit. Das Sprachverständnis in der Theologie Gregors von Rimini und sein Weiterwirken in der Augustinerschule*. Vol. 33 of *Cassiciacum*. Würzburg: Augustinus-Verlag, 1978.

―――. "Zwei neuentdeckte theologische Principien Hugolins von Orvieto." In *Schwerpunkte und Wirkungen des Sentenzenkommentars Hugolins von Orvieto O.E.S.A.*, pp. 43-83.

Ehrle, F. *Historia Bibliothecae Romanorum Pontificum tum Bonifatianae tum Avenionensis*. Rome: Typus Vaticani, 1890.

―――. *Der Sentenzenkommentar Peters von Candia des Pisaner Papstes Alexanders V*. Beiheft 9 of *Franziskanische Studien*. Münster: Aschendorff, 1925.

Elm, Kaspar. "Mendikantenstudium, Laienbildung und Klerikerschulung im spätmittelalterlichen Westfalen." *Studien zum städtischen Bildungswesen des späten Mittelalters und der frühen Neuzeit*, pp. 586-617. Edited by B. Moeller et al. Göttingen: Vandenhoeck und Ruprecht, 1983.

―――. "Termineien und Hospize der westfälischen Augustiner-Eremiten-Klöster Osnabrück, Herford und Lippstadt." *Jahrbuch für Westfälische Kirchengeschichte* 70(1977):11-49.

Elm, Kaspar, ed. *Stellung und Wirksamkeit der Bettelorden in der städtischen Gesellschaft*. Vol. 2 of *Ordensstudien*, vol. 3 of *Berliner historischer Studien*. Berlin: Dunker und Humbolt, 1981.

Emden, A. B. *A Biographical Register of the University of Oxford to 1500*. 3 vols. Oxford: Oxford University Press, 1957-1959.

Erbstösser, Martin. *Sozialreligiöse Strömmungen im späten Mittelalter*. Vol. 16 of *Forschungen zur mittelalterlichen Geschichte*. Berlin: Akademie Verlag, 1970.

Eubel, Conrad. *Hierarchia Catholica Medii Aevi*. Vol. 1: *Ab Anno 1198 usque ad Annum 1431*. Munich: Libraria Regensbergiana, 1898.

Feine, Hans Erich. *Kirchliche Rechtsgeschichte*. 2 vols. Weimar: Hermann Böhlaus Nachfolger, 1950.

Fine, John V. A. Jr. *The Bosnian Church: A New Interpretation*. Vol. 10 of *East European Monographs*. Boulder: East European Quarterly, 1975.

Finke, Heinrich. "Zur Geschichte der deutschen Dominikaner im 13. und 14. Jahrhundert." *Römische Quartalschrift* 8(1894):367-92.

Flade, Paul. "Römische Inquisition in Mitteldeutschland." *Beiträge zur sächsische Kirchengeschichte* n.v.(1896):58-96.

————. *Das römische Inquisitionsverfahren in Deutschland bis zu den Hexen-prozessen.* Vol. 9/1 of *Studien zur Geschichte der Theologie und der Kirche.* Leipzig: Dietrich, 1902.

Frank, Isnard. *Die Bettelordensstudia im Gefüge des spätmittelalterlichen Universitätswesens.* Vol. 83 of *Institut für Europäische Geschichte Mainz, Vorträge.* Stuttgart: Franz Steiner Verlag, 1988.

————. "Die Spannung zwischen Ordensleben und wissenschaftlicher Arbeit im frühen Dominikanerorden." *Archiv für Kulturgeschichte* 49(1967):164-207.

Fried, Johannes, ed. *Schulen und Studium im sozialen Wandel des hohen und späten Mittelalters.* Vol. 30 of *Vorträge und Forschungen.* Sigmaringen: Jan Thorbecke, 1986.

Friedensburg, W. "Ein Inventar der Habe Erfurtischer Geistlichen aus dem Jahre 1375." *Anzeiger für Kunde der Deutschen Vorzeit* 29(1882):322-26.

Friemal, Salesius. *Die theologische Prinzipienlehre des Augustinus Favaroni von Rom O.E.S.A. (+1443).* Vol. 12 of *Cassiciacum.* Würzburg: Augustinus-Verlag, 1950.

Aus der Geisteswelt des Mittelalters. Edited by Albert Lang, et al. 3 vols. Supplement vol. 3 of BGPTM. Münster: Aschendorf, 1935.

Genèse et Début du Grand Schisme d'Occident. Avignon 25-28 septembre 1978. No. 586 of *Colloques internationaux du Centre National de la Recherche Scientifique.* Paris: Centre National de la Recherche Scientifique, 1980.

Glorieux, P. "Jean de Falisca. La formation d'un maître en théologie au quatorzième siècle." *Archives d'histoire doctrinale et littéraire du moyen âge* 33(1966):23-104.

Göller, Emil. *Die päpstliche Pönitentiarie von ihrem Ursprung bis zu ihrer Umgestaltung unter Pius V.* 2 vols. Rome: Loscher and Company, 1907.

Graesse, Johann Georg Theodor. Benedict, Friedrich. Plechl, Helmut. *Orbis Latinus.* 3 vols. Braunschweig: Klinkhardt und Biermann, 1972.

Grimm, J. Grimm, W. *Deutsches Wörterbuch.* 16 vols. Leipzig: S. Hirzel, 1873.

Grotefend, Hermann. *Zeitrechnung des deutschen Mittelalters und der Neuzeit.* 2 vols. Hannover: Hahn'sche Buchhandlung, 1891; reprinted Aalen: Scientia Verlag, 1970.

Grundmann, Herbert. *Vom Ursprung der Universität im Mittelalter.* 2nd ed. Darmstadt: Wissenschaftliche Buchgesellschaft, 1960.

Gudian, Gunter. "Zur Charakterisierung des deutschen mittelalterlichen Schöffenrechts." *Europäisches Rechtsdenken in Geschichte und Gegenwart. Festschrift für Helmut Coing zum 70. Geburtstag.* 2 vols., 1:113-27. Edited by Norbert Horn. Munich: C. H. Beck, 1982.

Guillemain, Bernard. *La cour pontificale d'Avignon (1309-1376).* Paris: Éditions E. de Boccard, 1962.

Gutiérrez, David. *Die Augustiner-Eremiten im Spätmittelalter.* 2 vols.

Trans. Beda Kriener. Würzburg: Augustinus-Verlag, 1982, 1985.

Guyot, Bertrand-Georges. "Quelques aspects de la typologie des commentaires sur le *Credo* et le *Décalogue.*" In *Les genres littéraires dans les sources théologiques et philosophiques médiévales. Définition, critique et exploitation.* Louvain-la-Neuve: Institut d'Études Médiévales de l'Université Catholique de Louvain, 1982.

Gwynn, Aubrey. *The English Austin Friars in the Time of Wyclif.* London: Oxford University Press, 1940.

Hackett, M. B. "The Spiritual Life of the English Austin Friars in the Fourteenth Century." In *Sanctus Augustinus Spiritualis Magister.* 2 vols., 2:421-92. Rome: Analecta Augustiniana, 1959.

Handbuch zur deutschen Rechtsgeschichte. S.v. "Buch, Johann von," by H. Schlosser.

Hayez, Michel. "Avignon sans les papes (1367-1370, 1376-1379)." In *Genèse et Début du Grand Schisme d'Occident,* pp. 143-57.

Herzig, Arno. "Die Beziehung der Minoriten zum Bürgertum im Mittelalter. Zur Kirchenpolitik der Städte im Zeitalter des Feudalismus." *Die alte Stadt* 6(1979):21-53.

Herrera, T. de. *Alphabetum Augustinianum.* 2 vols. Madrid: n.p., 1644.

Heynck, Valens. "Studien zu Johannes von Erfurt." *Franziskanische Studien* 40(1958):329-60.

Hinnebusch, William. *The History of the Dominican Order.* 2 vols. New York: Alba House, 1966, 1973.

Höhn, A. *Chronologia provinciae Rheno-Suevicae Ordinis Fratrum Eremitarum Sancti Patris Augustini.* Würzburg: n.p., 1744.

Holzapfel, Heribert. *Handbuch der Geschichte des Franziskanerordens.* Freiburg im Breisgau: Herder, 1909.

Homeyer, Gustav. *Johannes Klenkok wider den Sachsenspiegel.* Berlin: Königliche Akademie der Wissenschaften, 1855.

Horn, Norbert. "Die legistische Literatur der Kommentatoren und der Ausbreitung des gelehrten Rechts." *Handbuch der Quellen und Literatur der neueren Europäischen Privatrechtsgeschichte.* 3 vols. Edited by Helmut Coing. Munich: C. H. Beck, 1973-1988. Vol. 1: *Mittelalter (1100-1500),* pp. 261-364.

Hourlier, Jacques. *L'Age classique (1140-1378). Les religieux.* Vol. 10 of *Histoire du droit et des institutions de l'Èglise en occident.* Paris: Éditions du Cerf, 1974.

Humphreys, K.W. *The Book Provisions of the Mediaeval Friars, 1215-1400.* Vol. 1 of *Studies in the History of Libraries and Librarianship.* Amsterdam: Erasmus Booksellers, 1964.

Janetschek, Clemens d'Elpidio. *Das Augustiner-Eremitenstift S. Thomas in Brünn.* Brno: Päpstliche Benedictiner-Buchdruckerei, 1898.

Kadlec, Jaroslav."Das Augustiner-Generalstudium bei Sankt Thomas zu Prag in vorhussitischen Zeit." *Augustiniana* 17(1967):389-401.

——— . *Das Augustinerkloster Sankt Thomas in Prag vom Gründungsjahr 1285 bis zu den Hussitenkriegen, mit Edition seines Urkundenbuches.* Vol.

36 of *Cassiciacum*. Würzburg: Augustinus-Verlag, 1985.

────── . "Das Augustiner-Generalstudium bei Sankt Thomas zu Prag in vorhussitischen Zeit." *Augustiniana* 17(1967):389-401.

────── . *Leben und Schriften des Prager Magisters Adalbert Rankonis de Ericinio*. New series vol. 4 of BGPTM. Münster: Aschendorff, 1971.

Kaeppeli, Thomas. "Kapitelsakten der Dominikanerprovinz Teutonia (1349, 1407)." *Archivum Fratrum Praedicatorum* 22(1952):186-95, 26(1956):314-19.

Kalb, Herbert. "Bemerkungen zum Verhältnis von Theologie und Kanonistik am Beispiel Rufins und Stephans von Tournai." ZRG, KA 72(1986)338-48.

Kałuza, Zenon. "Le problème du 'Deum non esse' chez Étienne de Chaumont, Nicolas Aston et Thomas Bradwardine." *Mediaevalia Philosophica Polonorum* 24(1979):3-19.

────── . *Thomas de Cracovie. Contribution à l'histoire du collège de la Sorbonne*. Wrocław: Ossolineum, 1978.

Kaňák, Miloslav. *Milíč aus Kremsier. Der Vater der böhmischen Reformation*. Vilém Schneeberger, trans. Gerhard Bassarak, ed. Berlin: Evangelische Verlagsanstalt, 1981.

Kejř, Jiří. "Das Hussitentum und das kanonische Recht." In *Proceedings of the Third International Congress of Medieval Canon Law*, pp. 191-204. Series C: subsidia, vol. 4 of *Monumenta Iuris Canonici*. Vatican City: Biblioteca Apostolica Vaticana, 1971.

Kiesow, Gottfried, et al. *Bremen. Niedersachsen*. In *Handbuch der deutschen Kunstdenkmäler*, Georg Dehio, general ed. Darmstadt: Wissenschaftliche Buchgesellschaft, 1977.

Kisch, Guido. "Biblische Einflüsse in der Reimvorrede des Sachsenspiegels." *Publications of the Modern Language Association of America* 54(1939):20-36; reprinted in *Forschungen*, pp. 36-52.

────── . *Forschungen zur Rechts- und Sozialgeschichte des Mittelalters*. Vol. 3 of idem, *Ausgewählte Schriften*. Sigmaringen: Jan Thorbecke, 1980.

────── . "Magdeburg Jury Court Decisions as Sources of Jewry-Law. A Study in Source History." *Historia Judaica* 5(1943):27-34; reprinted in *Ausgewählte Schriften*, 3:122-29.

────── . *Sachsenspiegel and Bible. Researches in the Source History of the Sachsenspiegel and the Influence of the Bible on Mediaeval German Law*. Vol. 5 of *Publications in Mediaeval Studies*. Notre Dame, Indiana: University of Notre Dame, 1941, reprinted 1960.

Klapper, J. *Johann von Neumarkt, Bischof und Hofkanzler. Religiöse Frührenaissance in Böhmen zur Zeit Karls IV*. Vol. 17, *Erfurter Theologische Studien*. Leipzig: St. Benno-Verlag, 1964.

Kłoczowski, Jerzy. "Panorama geografico, cronologico e statistico sulla distribuzione degli 'studia' degli ordini mendicanti: Europa centro-orientale." In *Le scuole*, pp. 127-49.

Knowles, David. "The Censured Opinions of Uthred of Boldon." *Proceedings of the British Academy* 37(1951):305-42.

Koschaker, Paul. *Europa und das römische Recht*. Munich and Berlin: C. H. Beck, 1953.

Koudelka, Vladimir. "Zur Geschichte der böhmischen Dominikaner-provinz im Mittelalter." *Archivum Fratrum Praedicatorum* 25(1955):75-99, 27(1957):39-119.

Kugler, Hartmut. *Die Vorstellung der Stadt in der Literatur des deutschen Mittelalters*. Munich and Zürich: Artemis Verlag, 1986.

Kullmann, Hans Josef. "Klenkok und die 'articuli reprobati' des Sachsenspiegels." Ph.D. dissertation, Frankfurt am Main, Johann Wolfgang Goethe Universität, 1959.

Kunzelmann, Adalbero. *Geschichte der deutschen Augustiner-Eremiten*. 4 vols. Vol. 26 of *Cassiciacum*. Würzburg: Augustinus-Verlag, 1969-1979.

Kurtscheid, Bertrand. "Die Tabula utriusque iuris des Johannes von Erfurt." *Franziskanische Studien*, 1(1914):269-90.

Landmann, F. *Das Predigtwesen in Westfalen in der letzten Zeit des Mittelalters. Ein Beitrag zur Kirchen- und Kulturgeschichte*. Vol. 1 of *Vorreformationsgeschichtliche Forschungen*. Münster: Aschendorff, 1900.

Lang, Albert. *Heinrich Totting von Oyta. Ein Beitrag zur Entstehungsgeschichte der ersten deutschen Universitäten und zur Problemgeschichte der Spätscholastik*. Münster: Aschendorff, 1937.

──── . "Johann Müntzinger, ein schwäbischer Theologe und Schulmeister am Ende des 14. Jahrhunderts." *Geisteswelt des Mittelalters*, 2:1200-30.

Lasch, Agathe. Borchling, Conrad. *Mittelniederdeutsches Handwörterbuch*. 3 vols. + Neumünster: Kark Nachholtz, 1956+.

Le Goff, J. *Les intellectuels au moyen âge*. Paris: Seuil, 1957, 1985.

Lehmann, Paul. *Mitteilungen aus Handschriften. Sitzungsberichte der Bayerischen Akademie der Wissenschaften, philosophische-philologische Klasse, 1929*. Munich: Bayerische Akademie der Wissenschaften, 1929.

Lerner, Robert E. *The Heresy of the Free Spirit*. Berkeley: University of California Press, 1972.

Lexikon des Mittelalters. S.v. "Albert von Sachsen," by E. Neuenschwander.

Lexikon für Theologie und Kirche. S.v. "Nikolaus von Gorran," by G. Gieraths.

Lickteig, F. B. *The German Carmelites at the Medieval Universities*. Rome: Institutum Carmelitanum, 1981.

Little, A. G. *The Grey Friars in Oxford*. Vol. 20 of *Oxford Historical Society*. Oxford, 1892.

Loskot, František. *Milíč z Kroměříže, Otec české reformace* [Milíc of Kroměříže, father of the Czech Reformation]. Vol. 2 of *Velicí mužové české reformace* [Leading men of the Czech Reformation]. Prague: Nákladem Volné Myšlenky, 1911.

McDonnel, E.W. *The Beguines and Beghards in Medieval Culture*. New Brunswick: Rutgers University Press, 1954.

Majic, Timotheus. "Die apostolische Pönitentiarie im 14. Jahrhundert."

Römische Quartalschrift für christliche Altertumskunde und Kirchengeschichte 501,2(1955):129-77.

Marcolino, Venício. "Der Augustinertheologe an der Universität." *Gregor von Rimini. Werk und Wirkung bis zur Reformation*. Berlin and New York: Walter de Gruyter, 1981.

Meier, Ludger. *Die Barfüsser Schule zu Erfurt*. Vol. 38/2 of BGPTM. Münster: Aschendorff, 1958.

Menčik, Ferdinand. "Milič a dva jeho spisy z reho 1367" [Milič and two of his writings from the year 1367]. In *Věstnik kralouska česke společnosti naukové, třída filosoficko-historicko-jazykozpytná*. Prague: Královské české společnosti naukové, 1891.

Meyer, Matthäus. *Die Pönitentiarie-Formularsammlung des Walter Murner von Strassburg. Beitrag zur Geschichte und Diplomatik der päpstlichen Pönitentiarie im 14. Jahrhundert*. Vol. 25 of *Spicilegium Friburgense*. Freiburg: Universitätsverlag Freiburg Schweiz, 1979.

Mitteis, Heinrich and Liberich, Heinz. *Deutsche Rechtsgeschichte. Ein Studienbuch*. 18th expanded ed. Munich: C.H. Beck, 1988.

Mor, Carlo Guido. "Das Rittertum." Translated from Italian by Ilse Kraski. In *Das Rittertum im Mittelalter*, pp. 247-65.

Moran, Jo Ann Hoeppner. *The Growth of English Schooling, 1340-1548*. Princeton: Princeton University Press, 1985.

Moraw, Peter. *Von offener Verfassung zu gestalteter Verdichtung: das Reich im späten Mittelalter, 1250 bis 1490*. Vol. 3 of *Propyläen Geschichte Deutschlands*. Berlin: Propyläen Verlag, 1985.

Müller, Theodor. *Das Amt Thedinghausen. Seine Geschichte und seine Entwicklung*. Thedinghausen: Gutenberg-Werkstätte, 1928.

Murdoch, John. "From Social into Intellectual Factors: An Aspect of the Unitary Character of Late Medieval Learning." *The Cultural Context of Medieval Learning*, pp. 271-348. Edited by J. E. Murdoch, Edith Dudley Sylla. Vol. 26 of *Boston Studies in the Philosophy of Science*. Boston: D. Reidel Company, 1975.

———. "Mathesis in philosophiam scholasticam introducta. The Rise and Development of the Application of Mathematics in Fourteenth Century Philosophy and Theology." In *Arts libéraux et philosophie au moyen âge*, pp. 215-65.

Murray, A. "Archbishop and Mendicants in Thirteenth-Century Pisa." In *Stellung und Wirksamkeit*, pp. 19-75.

Naendrup-Reimann, Johanna. "Territorien und Kirche im 14. Jahrhundert." *Der deutsche Territorialstaat im 14. Jahrhundert*. Edited by H. Patze. Vol. 13 of *Vorträge und Forschungen*. Sigmaringen: Jan Thorbecke, 1970, pp. 116-74.

Nelson, Benjamin N. *The Idea of Usury. From Tribal Brotherhood to Universal Otherhood*. Princeton: Princeton University Press, 1949.

Neumann, Augustin. *Prameny k dějinám duchovenstva v době předhusitské a Husově* [Sources of church history in the Prehussite and Hussite periods]. Olomouc: Nákladen Matice Cyrilometoděsjské, 1926.

Nowak, Elisabeth. "Die Verbreitung und Anwendung des Sachsen-spiegels nach den überlieferten Handschriften." Ph.D. dissertation, Universität Hamburg, 1965.

Oberman, Heiko Augustinus. *Contra vanam curiositatem*. Vol. 113 of *Theologische Studien*. Zürich: Theologischer Verlag, 1974.

Ocker, Christopher. "Augustinianism in Fourteenth-Century Theology." *Augustinian Studies* 18(1987):81-106.

———. "The Fusion of Exegesis and Papal Ideology in Fourteenth-Century Theology." In *Biblical Hermeneutics in Historical Perspective*, pp. 131-51. Edited by M. Burrows, P. Rorem. Grand Rapids: Eerdmans, 1991.

Page, William, ed. *The Victoria History of the County of Oxford*. Vol. 2. London: Archibald Constable, 1907.

Pantin, W. A. *The English Church in the Fourteenth Century*. Cambridge: Cambridge University Press, 1955.

Paqué, R. *Das Pariser Nominalistenstatut. Zur Entstehung des Realitäts-begriffs der neuzeitlichen Naturwissenschaft*. Vol. 14 of *Quellen und Studien zur Geschichte der Philosophie*. Berlin: Walter de Gruyter, 1970.

Patschovsky, Alexander. *Quellen zur böhmischen Inquisition im 14. Jahrhundert*. Vol. 11 of *Monumenta Germaniae Historica, Quellen zur Geistesgeschichte des Mittelalters*. Weimar: Hermann Böhlaus Nachfolger, 1979.

Peters, Günter. "Norddeutsches Beginen- und Begardenwesen im Mittelalter." *Niedersächsiches Jahrbuch für Landesgeschichte* 41/42 (1969/70):50-133.

Pfeil, Sigurd Graf von. "Karl der Grosse in der deutschen Sage." Pages 326-36, *Das Nachleben*. Edited by W. Braunfels, Percy Ernst Schramm. Vol. 4 of *Karl der Grosse. Lebenswerk und Nachleben*. Düsseldorf: L. Schwann, 1967.

Pinborg, Jan. *Die Entwicklung der Sprachtheorie im Mittelalter*. Vol. 42/2 of BGPTM. Münster: Aschendorf, 1967.

———. "The Fourteenth-Century Schools of Erfurt, Repertorium Erfordiense." *Cahiers de l'Institut du moyen âge grec et latin* 1(1982): 171-92.

———. "Neues zum Erfurter Schulleben des 14. Jahrhunderts nach Handschriften der Jagiellonischen Bibliothek zu Krakow." *Bulletin de philosophie médiévale* 15(1973):146-51.

Plöchl, Willibald. *Geschichte des Kirchenrechts*. 4 vols. Munich: Herold, 1953-1966.

Podlaha, Antonius. *Series Praepositorum, Decanorum, Archidiaconorum Aliorumque Praelatorum et Canonicorum S. Metropolitanae Ecclesiae Pragensis*. Prague: Metropolitanum Capitulum, 1912.

Pötschke, Dieter. Schroll, Heike. "Fragment einer Glosse zu 'Sachsen-spiegel'-Landrecht aufgefunden." *Archivmitteilungen* 38(1988):122-27.

———. "Rolande als Problem der Stadtgeschichtsforschung." *Jahrbuch für die Geschichte Mittel- und Ostdeutschlands* 37(1988):4-45.

Post, R. R. *The Modern Devotion. Confrontation with Reformation and Hu-*

manism. Vol. 3 of *Studies in Medieval and Reformation Thought.* Leiden: E. J. Brill, 1968.

Powitz, G. *Die Handschriften des Dominikanerklosters und des Leonhardstifts in Frankfurt am Main.* Vol. 2/1 of *Kataloge der Stadt- und Universitätsbibliothek Frankfurt am Main.* Frankfurt/Main: Vittorio Klostermann, 1968.

Probleme der Edition mittel- und neulateinischer Texte. Edited by Ludwig Hödl and Dieter Wuttke. Boppard: Harald Boldt, 1978.

Quetif, J. and Echard, J. *Scriptores Ordinis Praedicatorum.* 4 vols. Paris, 1719-23; reprinted New York: Burt Franklin, 1959.

Rabe, Horst. "Stadt und Stadtherrschaft im 14. Jahrhundert, die schwäbische Reichsstädte." Pages 302-24, *Stadt und Stadtherr im 14. Jahrhundert, Entwicklungen und Funktionen.* Edited by Wilhelm Rausch. Vol. 2 of *Beiträge zur Geschichte der Städte Mitteleuropas.* Linz/Donau: Österreichischer Arbeitskreis für Stadtgeschichtsforschung, 1972.

Rashdall, H. Powicke, F. M. Emden, A. B. *The Universities of Europe.* 3 vols. Revised edition. Oxford: Oxford University Press, 1936.

Reichert, B.M. "Akten der Provinzialkapitel der Dominkanerordensprovinz Teutonia aus den Jahren 1398, 1400, 1401, 1402." *Römische Quartalschrift* 11(1897):287-331.

———. "Zur Geschichte der deutschen Dominikaner am Ausgange des 14. Jahrhunderts." *Römische Quartalschrift* 14(1900):79-101, 15(1901): 124-52.

Die Religion in der Geschichte und Gegenwart. S.v. "Thomas von Strassburg," by R. Schwarz, 6:864-65.

Richter, K. "Konrad Waldhauser." *Karl IV. und sein Kreis,* pp. 159-74. Edited by F. Seibt. Vol. 3 of *Lebensbilder zur Geschichte der böhmischen Länder.* Munich: Oldenbourg, 1978.

Das Rittertum im Mittelalter. Edited by Arno Borst. Vol. 349 of *Wege der Forschung.* Darmstadt: Wissenschaftliche Buchgesellschaft, 1976.

Rössler, Emil Franz. *Das altprager Stadtrecht aus dem 14. Jahrhunderte, nach dem vorhandenen Handschriften zum ersten Mal.* Vol. 1 of *Deutsche Rechtsdenkmäler aus Böhmen und Mähren.* Prague: J. G. Calve, 1845.

Roth, Franz. "Deutsche Generalkapitel." *Cor Unum* 12/1(1954):18-22.

———. "A History of the English Austin Friars." *Augustiniana* 8(1958):22-47, 465-96; 11(1961):533-63; 12(1962):93-122, 391-442; 13 (1963):515-51; 14(1964):163-215, 670-710; 15(1965):175-236, 567-628; 16 (1966):204-63, 446-519; 17(1967):84-166.

Ruh, Kurt. "Votum für eine überlieferungskritische Editionspraxis." In *Probleme der Edition mittel- und neulateinischer Texte,* pp. 35-40.

Samaran, Charles. Marichal, Robert. *Catalogue des manuscrits en écriture latine portant des indications de date, de lieu ou de copiste.* 7 vols. Paris: Centre National de la Recherche Scientifique, 1959-1984.

Schimmelpfennig, Bernhard. "Die Funktion des Papstpalastes und der kurialen Gesellschaft im päpstlichen Zeremoniell vor und während des Grossen Schismas." In *Genèse et Début,* pp. 317-28.

Schmidt, Hans-Joachim. *Bettelorden in Trier. Wirksamkeit und Umfeld im hohen und späten Mittelalter.* Trier: Trierer historische Forschungen, 1986.

Schnapper, Bernard. "Rentes chez les théologiens et les canonistes." In *Études d'histoire du droit canonique dédiées à Gabriel Le Bras.* 2 vols., 2:965-95. Paris: Sirey, 1965.

Schneyer, Johannes Baptist. *Repertorium der lateinischen Sermones des Mittelalters.* 9 vols. Münster: Aschendorff, 1969-1980.

Schubart-Fikentscher, Gertrud. *Die Verbreitung der deutschen Stadtrechte in Osteuropa.* Vol. 4/3 of *Forschungen zum deutschen Recht.* Weimar: Hermann Böhlaus Nachfolger, 1942.

Schulte, Johann Friedrich von. *Die Geschichte der Quellen und Literatur des canonischen Rechts.* 3 vols. Graz: Akademische Druck- und Verlagsanstalt, 1956; reprint of Stuttgart: Ferdinand Enke, 1875.

Schum, Wilhelm. *Beschreibendes Verzeichnis der Amplonianischen Handschriftensammlung zu Erfurt.* Erfurt, 1887.

Le scuole degli ordini mendicanti (secoli xiii-xiv). Vol. 17 of *Convegni del Centro di Studi sulla spiritualità medievale.* Rimini: Maggioli Editore, 1978.

Schwerpunkte und Wirkungen des Sentenzenkommentars Hugolins von Orvieto O.E.S.A. Edited by Willigis Eckermann. Vol. 42 of *Cassiciacum.* Würzburg: Augustinus-Verlag, 1990.

Schwinges, Rainer Christoph. *Deutsche Universitätsbesucher im 14. und 15. Jahrhundert. Studien zur Sozialgeschichte des Alten Reiches.* Vol. 123 of *Veröffentlichungen des Instituts für Europäische Geschichte Mainz, Abteilung Universalgeschichte.* Wiesbaden: Franz Steiner, 1986.

Seckel, Emil. *Beiträge zur Geschichte beider Rechte im Mittelalter.* Vol. 1 *Zur Geschichte der populären Literatur des römisch-kanonischen Rechts.* Tübingen: J. C. B. Mohr, 1898; reprinted Hildesheim: Georg Olms, 1967.

Seiffert, Arno. "Studium als soziales System." In *Schulen und Studium*, pp. 601-19. Ed. J. Fried.

Sello, Georg. *Die territoriale Entwicklung des Herzogtums Oldenburg.* Osnabrück: H. Th. Wenner, 1975 reprint of the edition of Göttingen, 1917.

Šidak, Jaroslav. "Franjevačka 'Dubia' iz g. 1372/3. kao izvor za provijest Bosne" [The Franciscan "dubia" of 1372/73 as source for the history of Bosnia]. Pages 225-48, idem, *Studije o 'Crkvi bosanskoj' i bogumilstvu* [Studies on the "Bosnian Church" and Bogomilism]. Zagreb: Sveučilišna naklada Liber, 1975.

Siegel, Heinrich. *Die deutschen Rechtsbücher und die Kaiser Karls Sage.* Vol. 140, Abhandlung 9 of *Sitzungsberichte der philosophisch- historischen Classe der kaiserlichen Akademie der Wissenschaften.* Vienna: Carl Gerold's Sohn, 1899.

Smalley, Beryl. "Jean de Hesdin O. Hosp. S. Ioh." *Recherches de théologie ancienne et médiévale* 28(1961):285-330. Reprinted idem, *Studies in Medieval Thought and Learning*, pp. 345-92.

————. "John Baconthorpe's Postill on St. Matthew." *Medieval and Renaissance Studies* 4(1958):91-115, reprinted in *Studies in Medieval Thought and Learning*, pp. 289-343.

————. *Studies in Medieval Thought and Learning*. London: The Hambleton Press, 1981.

Sonntag, Franz Peter. *Das Kollegiatstift St. Marien zu Erfurt von 1117-1400*. Leipzig: St. Benno Verlag, 1962.

Steffenhage, Emil. *Catalogus codicum manuscriptorum bibliothecae Regiae et Universitatis Regimontanae*. 2 vols. Königsberg: Schubert Seidel, 1861, 1867, 1872.

————. *Die Entwicklung der Landrechtsglosse des Sachsenspiegels*. Vol. 12 of *Johann von Buch und die kanonische Glosse*. Vol. 195/1 of *Abhandlungen der Akademie der Wissenschaften in Wien, philosophisch-historische Klasse*. Vienna and Leipzig: Hödler-Pichler-Tempsky, 1923.

————. *Die Landrechtsglosse des Sachsenspiegels nach der Amsterdamer Handschrift*. Part 1: *Einleitung und Glossenprolog*. Vol. 65 of *Denkschriften*, 1. Abhandlung, *Akademie der Wissenschaften in Wien, philosophisch-historische Klasse*. Vienna and Leipzig: Hölder-Pichler-Tempsky, 1925.

Stegmüller, Fridericus. *Repertorium Biblicum Medii Aevi*. 11 vols. Madrid: Consejo Superior de Investigaciones Científicas, 1940-1980.

Strauss, Gerald. *Law, Resistance, and the State. The Opposition to Roman Law in Reformation Germany*. Princeton: Princeton University Press, 1986.

Stroick, Clemens. *Heinrich von Friemar. Leben, Werke, philosophisch-theologische Stellung in der Scholastik*. Vol. 68 of *Freiburger theologische Studien*. Freiburg: Herder, 1954.

Teewen, N. de Meijer, A. "Documents pour servir à l'histoire médiévale de la province augustinienne de Cologne." *Augustiniana* 9(1959):202-20, 339-56, 431-77; 10(1960):115-77, 297-327, 424-61; 11(1961):181-224, 383-413, 602-44.

Theologische Realencyklopedie. S.v. "Augustiner-Eremiten," by Adolar Zumkeller; "Augustinus Favaroni," by Willigis Eckermann; "Grote, Gerhard (1340-1384)," by A. G. Weiler.

Tillmann, Curt. *Lexikon der deutschen Burgen und Schlösser*. 4 vols. Stuttgart: Anton Hiersemann, 1958-1961.

Timm, Albrecht. "Das Magdeburger Recht an der Brücke von West und Ost." *Hamburger Mittel- und Ostdeutsche Forschungen* 2(1960):71-96.

Tomek, Wácslaw Wladiwoj. *Základy starého místopisu Pražského* [Foundations of the old topography of Prague]. Series 5, vol. 15 of *Abhandlungen der königlichen Böhmischen Gesellschaft der Wissenschaften*. Prague: Königliche böhmische Gesellschaft der Wissenschaften, 1866.

Trapp, Damasus. "Angelus de Dobelin, Doctor Parisiensis, and His Lectura." *Augustinianum* 3(1963):389-413.

————. "Augustinian Theology of the Fourteenth Century." *Augustiniana* 6(1956):146-274.

————. "Hiltalingen's Augustinian Quotations." *Augustiniana* 4(1954): 412-49.

————. "Notes on John Klenkok (+1374)." *Augustinianum* 4(1964): 358-404.

Tříška, Josef. "K počátkům české školské vzdělanosti a humanismu" [On the beginnings of Czech school culture and humanism]. *Acta Universitatis Carolinae—Historia Universitatis Carolinae Pragensis* 7/1(1966):49-61.

Ullmann, Walter. "John Baconthorpe as Canonist." *Church and Government in the Middle Ages: Essays Presented to C. R. Cheney on His Seventieth Birthday*, pp. 223-46. Cambridge: Cambridge University Press, 1976. Reprinted in idem, *Scholarship in the Middle Ages*, no. 10. London: Variorum, 1978.

Uth, G. "Die Augustiner in Polen vor der Gründung der selbständigen polnischen Ordensprovinz (1547)." AA 33(1970)263-308.

Verger, Jacques. "*Studia* et universités." In *Le scuole*, pp. 175-203.

Vinke, Johannes. "Volkstum und apostolische Pönitentiarie im 14. Jahrhundert." ZRG, KA 27(1938):414-44.

Walsh, Katherine. "Archbishop Richard FitzRalph and the Friars at the Papal Court in Avignon, 1357-1360." *Traditio* 31(1975):223-45.

————. "The 'De vita evangelica' of Geoffrey Hardeby, O.E.S.A. (c. 1320-1385). A Study in Mendicant Controversies of the Fourteenth Century." AA 33(1970):151-261, 34(1971):5-83.

————. *A Fourteenth-Century Scholar and Primate: Richard FitzRalph in Oxford, Avignon, and Armagh*. Oxford: Basil Blackwell, 1981.

Wander, Karl Friedrich Wilhelm. *Deutsches Sprichwörter-Lexikon*. 5 vols. Leipzig: F.A. Brockhaus, 1867-1880.

Wattenbach, Wilhelm. "Johannes Klenkok." *Anzeiger für Kunde der deutschen Vorzeit* new series 30(1883):80.

————. "Über das Handbuch eines Inquisitors in der Kirchenbibliothek St. Nicolai in Greifswald." Vol. 4 of *Abhandlungen der königlichen Akademie der Wissenschaften zu Berlin, philosophisch-historische Abhandlungen*. Berlin: Königliche Akademie der Wissenschaften, 1889.

Wentz, Gottfried. Schwineköper, Berent. *Das Erzbistum Magdeburg*. Vol. 1 of *Die Bistümer der Kirchenprovinz Magdeburg*, in *Germania Sacra*. New York: Walter de Gruyter, 1972.

Werbeck, Wilfrid. *Jacobus Perez von Valencia. Untersuchungen zu seinem Psalmenkommentar*. Vol. 28 of *Beiträge zur historischen Theologie*. Tübingen: J.C.B. Mohr, 1959.

Wilks, Michael. *The Problem of Sovereignty in the Later Middle Ages. The Papal Monarchy with Augustinus Triumphus and the Publicists*. Cambridge: The University Press, 1963.

Winter, Johanna Maria van. "Die mittelalterliche Ritterschaft als 'classe sociale.' " Translated from Dutch by Heinz Wolters. In *Das Rittertum im Mittelalter*, pp. 370-91.

Workman, Herbert B. *John Wyclif. A Study of the English Medieval Church*. Oxford: Clarendon, 1922; reprinted Hamden, Connecticut: Archon Books, 1966.

Wriedt, Klaus. "Bürgertum und Studium in Norddeutschland während des Spätmittelalters." In *Schulen und Studium*, pp. 487-525. Ed. J. Fried.

Xiberta, B. *De Scriptoribus Scholasticis Saeculi XVI. ex Ordine Carmelitanorum.* Louvain: Revue d'histoire ecclésiastique, 1931.

Ypma, Eclecko. *La formation des professeurs des Èremites de Saint-Augustin de 1256 à 1354.* Paris: Centre d'Ètudes des Augustins, 1956.

————. "Notice sur le 'studium' de Paris au cours de la deuxième moitié de quatorzième siècle." *Augustiniana* 17(1967):14-36.

Zacke, A. *Ueber das Todten-Buch des Dominikaner-Klosters und die Prediger-Kirche zu Erfurt.* Erfurt: Carl Villaret, 1861.

Ziekow, Jan. *Recht und Rechtsgang. Studien zu Problemen mittelalterlichen Rechts anhand von Magdeburger Schöppensprüchen des 15. Jahrhunderts.* Pfaffenweiler: Centaurus, 1986.

Zumkeller, Adolar. "Der Augustinertheologe Johannes Hiltalingen von Basel (+ 1392) über Urstand, Erbsünde, Gnade und Verdienst." AA 43(1980):59-162.

————. *Erbsünde, Gnade, Rechtfertigung und Verdienst nach der Lehre der Erfurter Augustinertheologen des Spätmittelalters.* Vol. 35 of *Cassiciacum.* Würzburg: Augustinus-Verlag, 1984.

————. "Johannes Klenkok O.S.A. (+ 1374) im Kampf gegen den 'Pelagianismus' seiner Zeit. Seine Lehre über Gnade, Rechtfertigung und Verdienst." *Recherches Augustiniennes* 13(1974):231-333.

————. "Leben und Werke Hugolin von Orvieto." In *Schwerpunkte und Wirkungen des Sentenzenkommentars Hugolins von Orvieto O.E.S.A.,* pp. 3-42.

————. *Manuskripte von Werken der Autoren des Augustiner-Eremitenordens in mitteleuropäischen Bibliotheken.* Vol. 20 of *Cassiciacum.* Würzburg: Augustinus-Verlag, 1966.

————. *Schrifttum und Lehre des Hermann von Schildesche O.E.S.A. (+ 1357).* Vol. 15 of *Cassiciacum.* Würzburg: Augustinus-Verlag, 1959.

INDEX